SHIPS, SHIPS & MAGGIEMOU

BY MAGGIE THORPE

SHIPS,SHOES & MAGGIEMOU

SHIPS,SHOES & MAGGIEMOU

BOOK FRONT AND BACK COVERS WERE

DESIGNED BY THE AUTHOR,

MAGGIE THORPE

ORGINAL PHOTOS OF HER OWN SHOES.

3

To my late mother Renée
who taught me the values in life.

Contents

WHO THE 'ECK IS MAGGIEMOU?

I grew up in the Northern industrial town Bradford in
Yorkshire, England, in the depressed years after WW11.
One of three girls to parents who worked hard and had little
money.

My mother worked evening shifts in the dark satanic mills that
dominated Bradford. My father worked away from home as an
insulation engineer. Mother was a weaver and that
was the job she had learnt from leaving school at 14 years old.
She always had high expectations of her three daughters,
keeping us all well fed and well dressed in the clothes she would
make for us. We were never going to have to work "in t' mill" as
she had done.

I was the middle girl in the family. I was slow to learn to talk
from birth and had learning difficulties. I could not speak
correctly and so never spoke (I have made up for it since over
the years!). Reading and writing was something I never
mastered 'till after the age of 11. I was dyslexic but no one
spotted it so nothing was done to help me.

Fortunately for my mother my two other sisters had more brains
than me but less common sense - they went to Grammar school

and passed exams. I did neither and I was a bit of a rebel, probably due to the frustration of not being able to speak.

I left school at 15 without an qualifications, but over the years I had proved to be artistic. Good at things done with my hands - sewing, embroidery, flower arranging and anything to do with make-up and hair. I had my first manicure set by the time I was 7 and kept it for years.

I loved playing with hair as a child but we were never allowed long hair - only short bobs with fringes (bangs) that stuck out like a sore finger on my forehead. Every Friday we three girls lined up to have our hair combed over a sheet of newspaper with a fine tooth comb. Mother was looking for nits which were common in those days! After the nit inspection we had it washed in Derbac soap which I can still smell to this day.

Not sure if this was where my interest in hairdressing came from, but after leaving school I went to work as an apprentice hairdresser in an up-market salon in Bradford.

I say up-market it was probably the only "posh " shop around at the time. It was owned by a Swiss couple - Heidi and Anton. Heidi was very strict and made me get my eyebrows trimmed on my first day at work. When I told my mother that night she freaked out.

Heidi told mother I had to wear make-up each day because

I was working in a job making people glamorous and I had to look the part. That was great news for me as I loved all things to do with glamour! I loved clothes, not that I had any only what mother had made, or the hand me downs from my elder sister. That would change and a clothes / shoe addiction would affect me for the rest of my life! Working in the salon I soon found out what real glamour was when all the wealthy mill owners' wives came to have their hair done by Heidi.

They turned up wearing beautiful clothes, dripping in gold, and reeking of Estee' Lauder Youth Dew. I earned seven shillings and sixpence each week and if I shampooed a certain client's hair I would get a tip!! Two shilling and sixpence. I was rich! I was good at saving and soon saved my tips to buy clothes like the "posh" ladies who came to the salon wore.

I soon discovered they went on holidays on something called a "cruise". What was a cruise, I wondered? Pub landladies were also ones who went on cruises and over time I learnt all about what a cruise was. I was told they employed hairdressers. So bearing this in mind I continued my five year apprenticeship with Heidi and Anton and became a good hairdresser. When Vidal Sassoon opened a salon in Leeds I went to work for him. I was one of two ladies at Sassoon's who became the first female managers in the company.

11

Working in London, Manchester and Leeds for Sassoon's I became more interested in the world of fashion and makeup, and where my clients went for holidays on cruises and private yachts. I have to say I started going overseas when I was "sweet" 16 with old school friends. Spain was the place and Majorca the destination. My first trip overseas cost £64. It was on a flight operated by Dan Air (some nicknamed it Dan Dare!) but we made it there and back and without having to take the brace position. Over the years I travelled a lot but I had never been on a cruise. So it was while at Vidal Sassoon's I was offered a job in the United States. It was to work as a hairdresser on a cruise ship.

I was hesitant about it at first as it meant a change of job. But I was 33 years old and ready for a change in life so decided to go for it. I was interviewed in Southampton at a company called Ocean Trading on West Quay Road and I was offered a job on Holland America Line's flagship - the SS Rotterdam. "Where was she going"? I asked. "Around the World" I was told. "Oh! does she go to Hong Kong"? "Yes", came the reply.

I'd always wanted to go to Hong Kong so that was it - "sold" to the lady with the red shoes, me. I was told go and buy the biggest suitcase I could find and rent out my home. "Buy a Globetrotter", said one of the people after the interview.

Not knowing what a Globetrotter was - and thinking it was the British TV roving reporter Alan Whicker - I headed back to London to buy such a suitcase.

I went straight to Selfridges and bought a Globetrotter - it was the ugliest suitcase I had ever seen, and the most expensive! It was huge and was the size of two ordinary suitcases. Completely square in shape with leather corners. It held everything including the kitchen sink! It turned out to be my best buy ever. I ended up with three Globetrotters when I realised world cruising was addictive because you need a lot of things, and you buy a lot of things.

It was 1980 when I first set foot on the SS Rotterdam. She was a true old style liner and known as the "Grande Dame". And nothing like the floating blocks of flats that are cruise ships today. She was magnificent and I was awestruck when I first saw her in port in New York where I had travelled to join the ship.

I had never seen a liner before or a small cruise ship for that matter. I didn't know how you got on it and I must have looked lost as I stood looking up at the huge bow of the ship. I was rescued and taken onboard. My first sighting of the inside of this magnificent liner and I was overwhelmed, but the feeling soon dispersed as I was shown to my living quarters below deck in a crew area known as "the harem" all shop girls lived here. I had to share a cabin with three other girls. Two bunk beds either side of the room and a small hand washbasin.

No toilet or shower. We had to walk down a corridor and use shared shower facilities. There was no natural light and we had not even got a port hole. We had a small cupboard in the cabin for our clothes. Goodness knows how I got all my lovely dresses in and all my shoes that I had taken after stocking up at Russell & Bromley shoe shop in Leeds. I soon discovered I would have the cabin to myself as three other girls had all got boyfriends on board (officers as they had the bigger and better cabins) and slept in their cabins.

I settled in although I had left my nice apartment in Central London to live in such an awful room I soon began to love my time at sea especially as we were going around the world on a truly beautiful world class liner. Queen Mary 2 is the only liner at sea today. Some of her features were taken from the Rotterdam by Queen Mary 2's designer Stephen Payne like the grand staircase and her wrap round walking deck. The SS Rotterdam is now a floating Hotel and conference centre in Rotterdam Harbour in the Netherlands. So her memory lives on and I was privileged to have sailed on her. I still remember my working days at sea with great fondness. The crew had fun and I learnt a lot from my world cruise passengers.

The old style of cruising from the early 1980s hardly exists nowadays. Then there was a flamboyant style of dressing and the glamorous formal balls with ladies in flowing gowns and men in white tie suits or tuxedos and white silk scarves.

Those doing the world would have large trunks and some had a second cabin just to store them. Then lots of cruisers were moneyed people who didn't appear to bat an eyelid at the costs involved. They had it (money), flaunted it and spent it - some of it on hairdressing with me thankfully. Many clients had their hair done daily and always gave me a tip.I made over US$3000 on my first world cruise in tips alone. Nowadays people moan about tipping even though they know about it in advance. Most passengers did a world cruise every year; they'd be in their 70s and often they never left the ship when it was in port. They went for company - they met other regular cruisers and played bridge and did jig saws most of the day. But for the ladies, and I am sure for some of the men, it was the dressing up that they most enjoyed.They'd dress up to the nines and try and outdo each other in a friendly yet deadly serious way. Some went to spend the remainder of their life cruising; some passed away on a world voyage.

As time went by I knew I had to return to the real world of hairdressing. And I did but what I hadn't realised was just how addictive cruising can be and, yes, I started getting withdrawal symptoms. Only one thing for it - return not below decks but above...as a passenger. And 33 years later I am still cruising.

I've cruised as a solo passenger (a good way to meet people), I introduced my late dear mum to cruising after my father passed away at an early age. I have cruised with friends and my former husband. I've loved almost every minute of being on the High Seas and I still do. I love to dress up and more often than not I probably have more clothes and shoes, than any other woman on board but it is not to show off, it is just the way I am. Mother taught us how ladies should dress and it stood me in good stead. I love to create a new hair up style - hairdo each night and I can go all around the world and not repeat the style . Easy as I am still a working State Registered Senior Hairdresser   with the UK Hairdressing Council. I have worked 51 years and still love my job. Fortunately for me as I am older I get four months leave to do the World Cruise each year and so my two loves, well three, the third being my husband are all still with me.

I am lucky I am fit and healthy (working has kept me looking years younger than I am) and you need to be to do a world cruise. Do it while you can! In the past ten years, since my husband retired, we have done several world cruises and world cruise segments.

Hairdressers do it standing up!
Well in these shoes we're a cut above the rest!

CARRY ON CRUISING....

In 2012 we decided to do a full world cruise on Queen Mary 2 she was going to circumnavigate Australia - somewhere MR MM (shorthand for my husband) had not been but had wanted to see. So no contest. We booked. We knew the ship because we'd sailed on her from Singapore to Southampton. And we like Cunard's style of cruising.

In fact MR MM first proper cruise (he'd sailed on the grey funnel line but those voyages didn't count!) was on the QE 2 to the Land of the Midnight Sun. That was magical, the scenery stunning and the sights outstanding.

We were particularly taken with the Arctic Cathedral in Tromso. That was the year Cunard agreed to sell QE2 to the Arabs. That same year (2008) we were on Queen Victoria's maiden world cruise although we only did segments of that cruise. We were also on the maiden world cruise on the new Queen Elizabeth in 2011.

Although my interest in cruising stretched back 40 years, something "new" had appeared over the horizon in the past decade - cruise forums. I enrolled on the one run by an award

winning travel company in the UK called Victoria Travel -
www.cruise.co.uk

I began posting answers to questions but had never written a blog - something I could never have done before computers were invented because of my dyslexia. I began writing on the cruise forum and while spell checker is my best mate I still make mistakes.

Who would have thought a dyslexic hairdresser would sail the world let alone write about it! So on our next cruise I decided to write a blog. My username is Maggiemou on the forum. I refer to my husband as MR MM, sometimes MR Movie Maker other times as my butler as he does everything for me including bringing breakfast to the cabin. Well, I am a working woman remember! So now you know.

HOW DO YOU PREPARE FOR A WORLD CRUISE?

For many people taking a voyage around the world would be unthinkable. They have questions, questions, questions. Would it cost a small fortune? The thought of being away from home and leaving family, friends, cats and dogs and the budgie behind fills them with dread. They wonder if they will be bored being at sea for four months; would they be fed up after a few weeks seeing the same people?

ANSWERS, ANSWERS, ANSWERS

It all depends on the individual. You can spend a lot or a little (relatively speaking depending on the style of cabin you choose). We are lucky we have no family ties and no pets. Most people who do world cruises in my experience have family but with email and Skype it is easy to keep in touch from long distances and across oceans.

Some regular world cruisers we know take family on board. Not for the whole world cruise just a segment or two. Not many families with young child do world cruises but there are exceptions. On the 2012 world cruise on Queen Mary 2 there were twin girls aged six on for the full 108 days and they loved it.

They were American and they were educated on board by their parents. On the 2014 world cruise on Queen Elizabeth a young man aged 13 was on for the whole 118 days. He, too, was being educated at sea.

Most ships are large enough to have space and freedom. It never feels like being in Piccadilly Circus at rush hour! Cruising is largely hassle-free. No long lines at airports, few if any delays, and at Southampton at the terminals used by Cunard embarkation has always been reasonably swift when we've sailed.

Cruising is a wonderful way to travel; to see new places, and to visit old favorites and being well looked after and entertained for four months. There are, naturally, exceptions! Given modern communications it's not unusual to find some passengers working while on the High Seas. The wonders of the internet!

As for the fear of being bored. If you want to be you can be you have that choice. But on sea days there is usually an action-packed programme that has things of interest to suit certainly to relax. Travelling on land sightseeing is tiring. You need to relax and unwind and as most ports are not next to each other sea days give passengers that opportunity because you can cherry-pick what lectures, classes or films you want to see. Or do nothing but that doesn't mean you'll be bored.

Our biggest challenge is getting from the hotel (we always stay at The Premier Inn on Harbour Parade in Southampton) to the ship. We generally have between 15 and 19 pieces of luggage so getting the taxi order right is very important. It has to be big enough to get that lot in and the two of us. Only once did it fail but the taxi company quickly rectified it and sent a people carrier.

How do you pick a world cruise? Some, like us, do it first by ports of call by their favourite cruise line. Ours is Cunard. We like the style, the formal evenings, the dress code and the efficient crew. If you read on you'll see we did a world cruise with P&O. It was not successful for us for a variety of reasons which are all explained.

We know some repeat world cruisers who just pick the ship, never bother about the countries or ports of call for they rarely leave the ship. You'd be surprised how many passengers there are like that at sea. After deciding which ship the next thing is to pick your cabin. Do you want an inside? (usually cheaper than the other options but often with more space), a cabin with a balcony? A cabin with a port hole/small window (they call these ocean views) or go the whole hog and have a suite?

Such choice! We pick a cabin midships if they are available because in rough seas there is less movement. And ours must be close to a laundrette because you still have to wash and these places can get really busy. You wouldn't store your dirty knickers at home for four months without washing them would you? Mind you on one world cruise we knew of a lady who took over 100 pairs with her so she didn't have to wash them until she got home!

There is a laundry service offered on all cruise lines that I know but it can be costly. At the time of booking you indicate what size of table for dinner you require (this does not apply to Grills passengers travelling in suites on Cunard.) We ask for one that seats eight to 10 people. That way you hopefully have a good mix of individuals and the conversation shouldn't dry up after a few days.

But it can and does happen. It's happened to us. We just asked to be moved tables. Cruise lines make an error in my judgment when they stick those doing the full voyage on the same table. Unless you're extremely lucky conversation most certainly WILL dry up after a few weeks. We like it when we share a table with passengers who are only doing a segment or two. And we do prefer to be seated with people of different nationalities rather than just Brits.

But as there are around 2,000 passengers coming and going the tables should have a regular turn over...unless all world cruisers are stuffed together by the maitre d "for ease".

At the time of booking you should be asked what configuration of bed you want? Twin or King size are the options. Most importantly don't forget to get health insurance for your voyage. Some household policies have medical cover but you must check that this covers cruises. It is unlikely in our experience.

You should make sure it covers for all the days of the cruise. We buy insurance that will cover us for the full reimbursement if we have to cancel the cruise for any reason. You have to ask for it because a lot of insurance companies will just offer you cover for, say, £5,000 for cancellation when it could be three times that amount you've paid. It's difficult to give prices because it depends on any health issues people may have. We haven't any.

For our 118-day cruise on Queen Elizabeth it was under £1,000 with the extra cover. Being away from home for such a long time can lead to problems with household insurance.

We arrange for someone to check the property regularly. It all sounds a lot of work but it's fun, believe me! With all that done there's still much research to do. Cruise lines send their detailed itineraries out months before you set off giving plenty of time to investigate not only the ship's tours but ones on the internet you can do independently which can work out a lot less expensive. But beware, if you are on an independent tour and late back to the ship you could find it has sailed - it doesn't wait except for official ship's tours to return.

Visas are another issue. America and Australia use the ESTA system which is straight forward and you're informed quickly if your application (done on the internet) has been successful (or not!). At the time of writing the Australian visa is free; there is a small charge for the American ESTA. The problem countries for us have always been China and India.

In fact on the 2014 world cruise to get them cost us almost £1,000. We used Cunard's official agents in the end. You MUST have an Indian Visa and a Chinese visa or you can be barred from even getting on the ship in Southampton.

Visas for other countries you visit are usually organised by the ship and charged to your onboard account. Not usually a lot - about £20 or thereabouts. Internet Cruise Forums can be a good source for information and making contact with fellow cruisers. Join a roll call and discuss your forthcoming cruise with others going on the same voyage - cruise critic.com and cruise.co.uk are two I have found useful.

Arrange your money before hand. We only take American dollars which are accepted in most countries around the world, and some Euros. We take three credit cards and before we set off we phone all three companies to tell them we are travelling and give them our itinerary that's to ensure they don't put a block on a transaction say in Vietnam, or China, even America. Their records tell them where we are.

What I take on a world cruise: Warm clothes for certain sections of the cruise especially if you're setting off from Northern Europe - a warm jacket/duvet coat with a hood as it can be cold on deck in places like New York in the middle of January.

A pair of thick tights, a raincoat, a thermal vest because it is bitter cold on deck in certain parts of the world such as South America going around The Horn. A scarf and a warm hat and gloves; day wear such as trousers and tops for colder climes when inside the ship, an umbrella for use in rain and in sun, a pair of boots. Casual day clothes for warmer climes and beach wear, sun hat, sun screen and sun glasses.

Now for my favourite bit - the evening wear!

I take approx 100 or more different outfits for evenings - I love to dress up. This is enough to see me through a whole world cruise. I have long dresses for formal nights, cocktail dresses and dresses for semi formal occasions. I DO NOT do casual ever at night time for dinner.

There are often theme dress nights on a world cruise such as Night of the Raj when in India. Chinese nights in China and so on. I always have the appropriate dress code with me. I love dressing up in the theme of things it is such good fun. Many people buy their outfits for these evening when we are in the country of origin.

I take 12 different coloured pashminas because it is often cold in the main dining room; black silk evening trousers and glitzy tops which are good for elegant casual nights.

I take around 40 pairs of shoes, plus 30 bags mainly evening bags. The shoes consist mainly of evening shoes but I also take Zumba/trainers for exercise dance classes, walking shoes, beach shoes, smart day shoes for around the ship. A pair of UGG boots. A day bag, beach bag, and a PAC SAFE security bag (check these out on Amazon) for sightseeing that crosses over your body for safety.

I take my workout clothes - I go to the gym almost every day. On top of this I take all things to do with hair - I can create a new style every night. I take fascinators, hair decorations and cocktail hats, flowers, clips and hair pins. I have two shoeboxes full of hair decorations. I wear a hat if there is a Royal Ascot Ball.

I also have my party silly dressing up stuff like wigs and costume jewellery that I wear at sailaways. I like to have a bit of fun!

I take an IKEA fold up under bed storage box for all my evening bags plus eight folding IKEA shoe boxes to store some of my shoes. Now I can hear you sighing - but this is how I am! If I couldn't take enough dresses, shoes, bags etc for a world cruise I wouldn't go.

The rest of the things I take are cosmetics, make-up, toiletries, perfume, leg waxing products, hair colour and hair products, medications and a first aid kit.

Hair brushes, heated rollers, straighteners, hair pieces, eyebrow tweezers, nail clippers and emery boards. Two torches in case of power failure and yes we needed them on QM2 in 2012 when she lost power several times.

A mini screw driver, a bottle opener and a champagne bottle stopper! The Yorkshire flag (being a Yorkshire gal) which I fly around the World. Scissors including my hairdressing scissors and clippers so I can do MR MM's hair (I have been known to cut friends hair, too, on our world voyages); a sewing box, birthday cards, thank you cards, some gift wrapping, small gifts in case of an emergency invitation, a tube of glue, some Sellotape/duck tape.

I also take a few clothes pegs for use in the cabin for my smalls, or holding my sun bed towel in place; soap powder, silk wash for my smalls, Comfort fabric softener and tumble dryer sheets, an ironing cloth. Cunard supply soap powder free but we use our own. Stain remover for the odd mark on clothes is vital.

Shoe cleaning products, a jewellery cleaning cloth, dark coloured towels for my hair as I have vivid hair colour and it stains the white ones supplied by the ship. Three bottles of spray bathroom cleaner with bleach to clean the shower, a box of rubber gloves for doing hair colour, mosquito wipes or spray. Bathroom air freshener.

I also take Anti VIRAL wipes and I clean all surfaces in the cabin as soon as I arrive. I use these as well whilst on tours for hand wipes. Dental kit in case you break a tooth; glasses and a spare pair. Herbal tea (enough for the whole cruise).

Actimel probiotic drink and Probiotic tablets. I buy Actimel or the equivalent in the shops around the globe when I run out. Mobile phone and charger, MP3 player /chargers, Laptop/charger, Ipad, a small printer on which I print off photos taken on my camera to give to people I have met. Binoculars, two cameras and a camcorder. Chargers and spare batteries. A four way adaptor for three pin plugs (a must as there are never enough sockets).

Coat hangers. I take my long dresses and other dresses on board on a coat hanger so I don't have to re-hang them. I remove the bulky ship's wooden ones and hand them to the steward. You get more in the wardrobe this way. Credit cards, plenty of single US dollar bills for tipping/bus fares shore side.

A laminated copy of passports, insurance documents and spreadsheet of dress codes. I plan ahead what I'll be wearing for all the different events. We usually go onboard with around 19 pieces of luggage and get off with 19 if possible - 14 are suit cases and the rest are holdall type bags and small cases - same amount of luggage each year. We photograph them so we can remember what we have with us four months down the line. I also have a separate vanity case for my jewellery.

I take some costume jewellery but mainly the real thing as it nice to be able to have your good things with you. I can hear some of you shouting WOW! But this is what this girl needs to survive four months at sea. If you sail from Southampton all the way round of course you can take as many bags as needed.

My husband likes his very colourful ties and bow ties. He always takes a tuxedo, plus a morning suit and top hat for the Ascot Ball and a white tie outfit along with shirts, jackets, shoe, socks, hankies, underpants and deodorant.

If you are wondering what we do with 19 pieces of luggage once we have unpacked, the cases are taken away by the cabin steward for storage.

We do not travel in a large suite, just a regular cabin so we have to be organised. And yes, I really do pack all that but hey, if you are going to be away for so long a girl needs her favourite things with her!

The packing and planning's all done….now for sailaway.

Read on and follow me on a 2013 South American and Pacific Adventure aboard P&O's Arcadia and then in 2014 I join Cunard's Queen Elizabeth for her 118-day world cruise...oh and I'd climbed Sydney Harbour Bridge in the meantime!

Off WE GO AGAIN

Having been lucky enough to see a great deal of the world the one place we had never been was South America. On Queen Mary 2's world cruise we sailed down the North Atlantic and across the Indian Ocean to reach Australia and we returned to Europe on the northern route - China, Hong Kong, Japan, Vietnam, Singapore, India and through the Suez and in to the Med to get back to Southampton.

Queen Mary 2 is too big to get through the Panama Canal (there's an ongoing debate about whether or not she will fit in the Panama Canal bypass that is under construction) and one year did go round the Horn. It wasn't apparently that much of a success so we were told there were no plans for a repeat South American voyage around The Horn on the Mary. We double-checked and found that to be the case.

That meant we had to find a cruise ship that was going to do South America and the Pacific on a world cruise. In 2012 we booked a world voyage on a different cruise line as the itinerary was just what we wanted. We would leave Southampton, call in Brazil, Uruguay, Argentina, The Falklands sail around The Horn and up the Pacific coast to Chile before heading to exotic South Pacific Islands and on to Australia. This cruise was billed as A South American and Pacific Adventure on board P&O's adult ship, Arcadia. P&O, like Cunard, is part of the Carnival Corporation which has its headquarters in Miami, Florida, and has the flamboyant Micky Arison at the helm.

We spent eighteen months preparing for the cruise. As departure time drew closer I got a gut feeling about how this might be the wrong decision. Just little things kept cropping up on cruise forums that left me with a nagging doubt. Our final payment was made in the October before the deadline. We were now fully paid up and would be off. How wrong we were.

In late December, a few days before Christmas, we found out all of our ports in Argentina had been cancelled! I was devastated. Visiting South America was the main reason we'd booked. I found out of these port cancellations via the internet cruise forums. P&O had not notified us. We arrived in Southampton a few days early to give us time to take our cruising gear out of store, get dry cleaning done and do some last minute shopping. We joined Arcadia on 5th January, 2013, to go on our South American and Pacific Adventure.

What lay in store for us I could never have imagined in a million years. The day of embarkation we left our hotel with a whole minivan of luggage for our 99-day voyage. We were quickly onboard after checking in but had to wait two hours for our cabin to be made ready. Not a problem, we went for lunch in the Belvedere Restaurant and explored the ship - our home for the next three months.

When we get to our cabin on any cruise the first thing I do is go and inspect the facilities - ie the bathroom and loo - the loo was filthy and the floor dirty. It didn't look as though it had been touched after the previous passengers left, presumably in Southampton. No one from the ship was in sight so I got our cleaning materials I always take with us and started cleaning. MR MM went ballistic. "We haven't paid all this money for a cruise for you to start cleaning our cabin," he blasted.

Our cabin steward then appeared. I pointed out the state of the bathroom. He said he had just joined in Southampton and would attend to cleaning the place up. I keep my shoes and evening bags under the bed in storage boxes I take on board. When I looked under the bed it was thick of dust - can't have been hoovered in months!

The steward said he would attend to the dust. Then I discovered there were no slippers or dressing gowns provided. I requested them only to be told they were only supplied to passengers in suites. We were travelling steerage as MR MM calls it.

I protested but politely. A deck supervisor came to the cabin. I again asked for slippers and dressing gowns. He, too, refused with the same lame excuse. I pointed out that everyone, even in steerage on Cunard, get dressing gowns and slippers.

He left, could see we were very unhappy and we still hadn't left port! About five minutes later slippers and dressing gowns arrived.

I later met a lady who told me she had complained, too, and pointed out to the housekeeping that being on Arcadia was no different to staying in a four star hotel where slipper and dressing gowns were always provided. You spend a small fortune on a 99-day cruise and P&O don't provide you with simple things like slippers and dressing gowns - it makes no sense.

Other silly things reared their head as the cruise progressed. For instance, I like green tea after dinner (I rarely drink coffee). It was served as a tea bag in a cup and warm water poured over meaning you're left with a soggy tea bag on your saucer.

I asked for it to be served in a teapot - sometimes it was, sometimes it wasn't. If you want green tea bags in your cabin you had to take tea bags from the Belvedere Restaurant.

The stewards aren't allowed to put them in the cabin. Daft if you ask me but nobody did. P&O put a kettle in the cabin for tea making.

I prefer not to have one as they take up too much precious space. And we are not caravanning!

Don't get me wrong - whether cruising or staying in an hotel I expect to have the same standards as I'm used to at home - or better - certainly nothing less. Not a lot to ask of a cruise company that used to be one of the most respected brands around the world. How the mighty have fallen!

As in all our previous voyages we opt for second sitting. It was like that on Arcadia. We asked for and got a table for eight - usually that guarantees a good mix - and with that number you don't as a rule run out of conversation at least during a segment. However, this eight didn't work out. On day six of the cruise we were "evicted." Shock, horror! We were four couples, all English - well one couple lived in Wales but didn't have that much of a twang - all doing the full 99 days.

It's often not easy to gel right away. We had small talk most nights. It's a pity more attention isn't paid by cruise lines - Cunard are no different - to seating those doing a full voyage. We generally ask the maitre d to be moved at the end of each segment so we meet different people from other nationalities. I hadn't realised that P&O attracts largely British passengers.

Montevideo was the end of our first leg and that's when we planned to leave but others around the table had different ideas. I'd noticed on the first formal night only one lady dressed in a long dress or a cocktail type dress. The other two wore ordinary day dresses. The other nights they were in casual trousers and tops.

Now I've always dressed for dinner at sea or on land as does MR MM. He wears a jacket and tie no matter whether one is required or not. On day six (an informal night) I arrived dressed up as did MR MM. One woman at our table(a non dresser type) could not wait for me to sit down and she went into rage about how we had to leave THEIR table, "We do not want you on our table! It will be a lot happier place when you've gone." So I asked who are the "WE" - tell me. Her anger was aimed at me. One guy stood up and left the table in disgust, leaving his wife on her own. Another guy butted in as the woman had dragged his wife in for support. He said "do not bring my wife into this." And so on it went. The woman's husband then joined in and started saying to me "you come swanning in here each night thinking you are oh so beautiful'. He said this twice. I laughed and said "don't be ridiculous. Beautiful I have never been, attractive yes"!

37

He was as mad as Hell and he repeated it so I laughed again saying how silly and told him he was very rude.

He then said and all you can do is laugh. So I said "I laugh as I am a happy person and not a sad sod like you appear to be". He went berserk!! Shouting at me. His wife started at me again so I turned to her and said "I have worked for 50 years with ladies and I cruised for over 33 years and I have never met a bitch before!" I thought she was going to blow a gasket; her eyes filled with anger she hurled some other nasty, abusive comments at me. Things quietened down for a few minutes (may be seconds) and the pair of them left the table.

He had a bottle of wine in front of him which he'd not finished and within seconds he returned, grabbed it and stormed off adding "I don't know about your husband having a medal, he deserves a bigger one being married to you!" then stormed off again clutching the half bottle of plonk. The meal carried on in a subdued atmosphere. We were now five in number.

MR MM was gob-smacked. He told the man whose pint-sized wife had instigated the confrontation that on all our cruises we had never encountered problems with any of our other table companions, or such rudeness.

The right thing to do in the circumstances as it could have led to a fight as the guy was so heated. So dear husband carried on chatting politely to the guy next to him and did not involve himself. He knew I could stand up for myself.

However, I have to say it was very upsetting and took a few days to get over. I guess the woman was just a jealous person. She was about my age but looked years older. One thing that could have got her hackles up was each evening the waiters all fussed around me and said things like "madam your dress is lovely". Which probably angered the woman because I had a different outfit for all 99 days.

We left that table that evening. MR MM went to see the Maitre 'd, told him what had happened and we were reseated for the rest of the cruise with people who were fun and who were not full of their own self unimportance, as MR MM put it.

Day seven at sea was my birthday. I invited passengers we'd met on previous Cunard cruises who were on Arcadia for the "South American experience". We dined in the Ocean Grill, an alternative venue that levies a modest cover charge. The meal was the best we had all cruise.

SOUTH AMERICA. BRAZIL URUGUAY

After five days at sea we arrived in Recife, Brazil - very noisy, smelly, very untidy but full of atmosphere. We wandered off the ship and headed in the direction of the town following the crowds from the ship. There were lots of shoe shops and you'd have thought Maggieshoemou would be in her element. No! I looked but they were not my type of shoes. However, having said that I did buy a pair. Oh, how could I resist a pair of red plastic/rubber type shoes that looked 1960s style made by the famous company in Brazil called "Melissa" - they were eco friendly shoes suitable for vegans! I knew this make. They've been around over 20 years and nowadays Vivienne Westwood and other designers add their names and touches to Melissa shoes.

I knew they'd go with the 1960 style dress I'd had made for a 60s theme night on board Arcadia but there was just one snag the only pair they had in the shop were on the feet of a model in the window. You've heard that song about a doggie in the window, well the shoes waiting for me were in a window! They weren't for sale said the shop assistant but I managed to persuade him to let me have them. We (no I) spotted lots of Black & White two tone shoes for men. Now these were good leather shoes made for Tango dancing. I wanted MR MM to buy a pair for black & white ball night. He is not as impulsive as me and showed strong will power and said "no I don't need them". When did "need" ever come into it where shoes are concerned?

I doubt they would have improved his Tango - he has two left feet and no sense of direction on the dance floor. Walking back to the ship we noticed men washing down the dirty streets with a power jet spewing out disinfectant. Gives you an idea of what was on the streets!

We ventured into a fruit market. We love these places and they are often colourful, smelly and have fabulous looking fruit all laid out on the ground or a trestle table. Another eye opener.

I spotted a shop that had Spanish looking white blouses and they were reduced. I needed such a white top because I was learning to tap dance on board ship and the tappers were due to perform on stage further into the cruise.

I didn't have a white top in my extensive collection of clothes as virginal white I am not! I bought it as you do and a final thing I took away from Recife was a colourful long wig.

It was off the wall but I thought it would come in handy at sailaways - and it did.

I met a man in Recife
Danced salsa and sang in the street
Give me your hand we dance through 'till dawn
In these shoes, I think they may give me a corn!

Salvador da Bahia (City of the Holy Saviour on the Bay of all Saints"):

Salvador is known as Brazil's capital of happiness due to its countless popular outdoor parties, including its street carnival. It claims to have the largest carnival in the world but I expect Rio would have something to say about that.

It's 33 years since I was last here on a world cruise, it hadn't changed that much. The locals were out in full force and the streets were jam packed - it was a bank holiday; there was a procession to a church 7k away from downtown.

One passenger went ashore alone and when she returned described it as "Hell on earth". We took a ship's tour and were pleased we had done. We enjoyed the atmosphere, the dancing, the bands, the firecrackers. We visited the Cathedral and had a look round Jesus Square. Our rendezvous point was outside the upmarket jewellery company of H Stern. When I worked at sea as a hairdresser on Holland America's SS Rotterdam, one of my regular clients was MRS STERN.

I remember she was a lovely, elegant lady who was a regular passenger on the Rotterdam.

A word of warning for future visitors to this part of the world - leave ALL valuables on the ship, even things that don't look expensive. Three passengers reckoned they'd been attacked from behind and had their necklaces ripped off.

RIO and JC Shrouded in cloud:

Rio, one of the great cities not only of South America but the world. For most travellers and wannabe tourists it's usually high on their "to visit" list. I'd been before but MR MM hadn't.

Three things above all else you must see in Rio are the statue of Jesus Christ, and Sugar Loaf Mountain and (for the men) the statuesque near naked bodies of the beauties sprawled out on the golden sand of Copacabana Beach. On the sail-in Sugar Loaf was hardly visible because of cloud, and the statue of JC was shrouded in cloud all day and into the night. We didn't see HIM at all. There was better luck for MR MM with the third Rio must see sight - the girls were plentiful!

We enquired in one of the hotels on Copacabana about heading up to the statue of JC. A taxi driver said he could only take us so far then we would have to walk. The wait could be up to three hours he said. We didn't bother.

Around 2,000 passengers from Arcadia had, I believe, booked with the ship to go up to the statue. They got close to JC but saw nothing of the beach or the city below.

We wandered along the beach, MR MM took some photos of girls in thongs (talk about an Englishman abroad!) but he walked on the beach fully clothed and claimed he had not noticed the girls' bare bums. Ya, he would tell me anything. Anyway we eventually arrived at the fort that is such a feature of the Rio water's edge at the end of Copacabana Beach.

We looked around the Fort and then decided we needed lunch. We found a nice shore side restaurant and waited for a table and had a lite bite and some liquid refreshments. We took a taxi to the Cathedral (a wonderful but very different type of structure) and then had a wander around that part of the city. We took another taxi ride to see more of the sights of Rio before heading back to the ship.

The sailaway from Rio was late in the evening. MR MM was feeling tired and had a headache. He decided to miss dinner. I went on my own to the dining room and seeing as we were in Rio I dresses for the occasion. I wore a samba style off the shoulder dress with ruffles down one side of the skirt. I then piled all the flowers from my hair collection into my hair.

I looked like Carmen Miranda! I do all this dressing up for the laugh as I do like to laugh at myself.

As I walked through the restaurant people were looking and started clapping. By the time I reached the table everyone around stood up and applauded. I thought it was so funny but nice. Some lady came over and said I'd made her night by dressing up. I often wonder why others don't make the effort. It is just about getting into the mood and the feel of the country and I really like the fun it gives me and many others.

After dinner I checked out the back deck and we were still in port and JC was just about visible like a white light on the top of Corcovado. Too far away to make a big impression. Ah! well I think I'd made a bit of one in the dining room that's for sure.

The man in Brazil looked like he could kill
Eyes burning like fire and a look of desire
I take you to Corcovado Mountain to see JC
We run up the hill and climb hundreds of stairs
It is the best view in Rio they say.
WHAT! In these shoes? No way Jose

Montevideo: An Australian relative by marriage brought a gift when she visited about three years ago - leather coasters from Montevideo. It said so on the box.

They were something different. At the time I had no idea we would be visiting Uruguay and its capital. What a fabulous port of call it was - very friendly people who absolutely loved the British.

They hadn't forgotten, they told us, how Britain helped their country gain independence. Makes a change normally many countries just what to slag us off. That was good to hear. Montevideo was an overnighter (because P&O had cancelled Buenos Aires the Argentinean capital). Montevideo is the second largest metropolitan area after Great Sao Paulo.

Passengers who were due to board in Buenos Aires were still flown there and then transferred by ferry to Montevideo - a journey of several hours. On our first day we went on a ship's tour - Highlights and Steam Train. We were picked up by coach went for a drive around the city and then went on a restored Steam train. The train ride (just one way we returned by coach for some unexplained reason) took about 40 minutes. It gave us a chance to see the development along the railway line and then the countryside outside the city. The restorers looked to have done a very good job. The coaches, too, had been restored. Journey's end on this train was a town called PENAROL. It had seen more prosperous days. It had been an industrial town built by the British over 100 years ago. There was a small museum with information on the history of the town but for most passengers - and all the carriages were full - the steam engine was the star of the show. The smoke and the whistle blowing and the chuff - chuff sound of a bygone era.

But we were not given much time to linger before our coaches whisked us back on the scenic route into Montevideo. We hugged the coast, passed parks and residential areas. There were the odd stops for photographs. We had some free time and came across some floats that were being prepared for the Montevideo Carnival - not of Rio proportions but lots of floats never-the-less.

What was surprising was the scantily-dressed young women in the parade, and the half naked men. Certainly different to the Lord Mayor's Show in London! This part of the world we knew was famous for Tango. So we'd booked a ship's outing to tango/folklore with dinner and drinks and transport included in the price.

Many of the lady passengers, myself included, got dolled up and dressed for the occasion in black and red. Passengers entering into the spirit of the evening looked a good sign but it was anything but. Nine coach loads had booked this tour that's how popular it was. We were on bus 8. We left by numbers. Our transport didn't leave the ship until 9pm. It was like the stacking system at Heathrow Airport as we waited for out slot.

At the venue, called El Milongon, we couldn't get off our bus right away. We had to wait until bus 7's passengers had alighted. There was a queue to get inside the building and when we did all the ground floor tables had been taken and people were already eating their first course. We looked around and saw there were seats on a balcony but some on our coach refused to climb the stairs and waited for seats to become vacant at ground level.

They missed out. I'd researched Tango places on the internet and discovered most were two tier. We had front row seats looking down directly on to centre stage with unobstructed views - we couldn't have been better placed to watch the show. We had the best seats in the house! Waiters appeared within minutes with bottles of wine and jugs of water. I sat next to a nice couple and MR MM had a charming disabled lady from OZ next to him whom he'd helped climb the stairs.

Starters arrived soon after we were seated and the music began but no more food appeared. We looked down and saw most of those on the ground floor had finished their starter, main and sweet but on our level we'd just had the starter. Not to worry we weren't starving. The show went on, and on, and on, and still no food. People on the ground level began to leave the table then a rumour spread like wildfire on the upper deck that they had run out of meat - we were due to have steak - something of a "sensation" in Uruguay. It never arrived but the show still went on. And a good show it proved.

The wine continued to flow. It was midnight when the ice cream arrived. Word got round that the coaches were leaving. But we were on a P&O official tour so we knew they wouldn't leave without us. MR MM, the disabled lady from Oz and I and a few others around us didn't rush. We finished the ices then made our way to the coach. We were among the last to leave but no queues to get on the last buses back to the ship. Of course there were the moaners who complained but no one was starving and missing out on a meal was no big deal, at least that's what we thought.

We'd loved the show, the dancers were just brilliant and the drink had flowed which pleased MR MM.

It looked as though the management were just overwhelmed with 450 people arriving in one go. We left happy thinking what an experience. That morning (we got back to the ship around 1am) when we got up there was a letter in our box saying "sorry for the mess last night" and a full refund (£75 per person) would be given to all on the tour. It was a generous gesture by the ship.

In fact MR MM went to see the excursions people, thanked them for their generosity of a full refund but said it was too much - the cost of the entertainment should not be deducted because that was brilliant. And there had been no shortage of wine served!

But the excursion people said it was easier to give a full refund. MR MM said he hoped just because things had not worked out it didn't mean the venue would be abandoned on future cruises. He was assured P&O agents would speak with the management to get things right!

Would you believe even after getting all their money back some were still complaining two days later? One of the excursions staff told me about half the passengers were happy to have seen the show and weren't that fussed at missing some of the meal but others were irate and swearing at him and carrying on they felt they had to refund everyone. MR MM put his observations made to the excursions staff in writing.

Montevideo is an easy place to navigate. It's laid out in a grid system similar to cities like New York. There was a care free carnival atmosphere about the place; lots of cafe type bars and restaurants and musicians played their instruments on street corners.

A short walk from the harbour we found a cluster of restaurants most offering free wi-fi. We picked El Peregrino. First we just had a drink and logged on then we met a couple we knew and we decided to stay and eat.

The steaks were just fabulous. Just after we'd finished (and licked the plates - just kidding!) a funny thing happened.

Usually you get waiters or waitresses coming up to your table to take your orders (they'd already been because we'd finished our meal) what we hadn't expected was a man in a white coat (the sort doctors wear) carrying a blood pressure monitor. He asked if any of us wanted our blood pressure tested. We were a bit dubious and said "no thank you". He wandered off to another restaurant. We watched him and thought we should really give him a chance to take ours.

So on his way back we called him across. He took our blood pressure and he signalled the reading using his fingers. All ours were good. MR MM offered the man a large glass of red wine telling him it was good for his cholesterol - he picked up the glass said "cheers" and downed it in one. It was all very funny. He then wanted a "consultation fee" (a tip) so we gave him US$20. He went away happy. I guess this maybe a new take on begging. At least he didn't just stick his hand out expecting money, he did something to "earn" his donation. We never found out if he was a beggar or someone who was a medic raising money for charity, or for himself!

We didn't really care.

It was something we'd not seen before and probably never would again unless we returned to Montevideo. We had a great two days in Montevideo and it really was a good port of call.

I then met a man in Montevideo.
He rode a wild stallion in a rodeo show
He said We can ride naked and buck up and down
I said "In these shoes?" I doubt you'd survive!

Two days out from Montevideo heading towards The Falkland Islands the seas started to get rough, very rough, and the temperatures dropped but that's what we'd expected as we headed towards Antarctica. Winter clothes were out of their cases. Tap dancing classes resumed - a new course and different participants because some of the first group had disembarked in Montevideo. Remiss of me I never got to tell you about the show we tappers did the day before Montevideo (must have had a "senior moment").

PLENTY OF TALENT ON BOARD. The day before we arrived in Montevideo there had been a passenger talent show in the Palladium Theatre. I was part of the tap dancing team - about 40 of us and all but three were women. Yes, I can now say I danced at The Palladium! We all wore black trousers and white tops so looked the part. The routine had taken us 14 hours of practice. There was some very good talent on show, too - comics told "new to us jokes"; a clever lady who was a member of the Magic Circle amongst them. Our team of tappers were first on. We danced to I'm Putting on my Top Hat (I was still singing it in my sleep four days later). It was quite nerve racking when we went on stage for a practice run - we seemed to lose the plot. Our instructor was not impressed.

But it was all right on the night (or the afternoon to be precise). Our routine was timed to last two and a half minutes and one of the ladies said it seemed much longer to her - she hoped we'd get through it. To which I replied: "Well at least it's half a minute less than having sex!" That cracked her up and we couldn't stop laughing.

For the passenger talent show the theatre was packed - standing room only. One memorable act was the magician called Majik Ann from Lancashire. She had the audience spell-bound and was so good she was asked by the ship to put on other performances. She obliged.

SHIP'S COCKTAIL PARTIES: These can be exciting, or dire. On Arcadia in our opinion they were dreadful. They were held around the Neptune Pool midships. It just felt like you were in the municipal swimming baths. It was a real scrum to get a drink. In fact when we arrived (late by choice) we failed to get served before they rang the bell, a bit like they used to do in pubs in England to call "time".

Not that we needed the cheap booze. There was no atmosphere, just passengers pushing and shoving to get near any booze. Some had glasses lined up on the edge of the swimming pool, I'd noticed. We never heard the Captain's speech properly because people carried on talking. Most disrespectful if you ask me.

We never went to another one all cruise.BTW we'd joined a new table for dinner - got some nice Australians who were all aged around 50 and fun people.

THE FALKLAND ISLANDS

There was excitement tinged with sadness as Arcadia approached at around 5am local time. Would we or wouldn't we get ashore? There were very strong winds as we approached the entrance to Port Stanley outer harbour gusting at between 40 and 50 knots. We could see through our binoculars penguins all lined up waving to us!

This was a tender port so sea conditions had to be right so passengers could be transferred safely from ship to shore and back. Ominously there was a red sky and that saying came immediately to mind - "red sky at night sailors' delight, red sky at morning sailors' take warning!" How appropriate for what happened to Arcadia's attempts to land passengers ashore in The Falklands.

We'd booked a tour to Volunteer Point to see the largest colony of King penguins on the islands, with Patrick Watts, MBE, an experienced local guide. We'd been excited for months about this tour which we thought would be one of the main highlights of the 99-day voyage. Two attempts were made at getting into the outer harbour entrance - the first at 6am and the other at 9am - both were aborted.

In between those attempts Arcadia sailed around in circles in deep water. The most frustrating thing for passengers, especially those who'd brought wreaths, was the lack of information from the bridge. We were all kept in the dark for hours on end when it looked very unlikely because of the high winds and rough seas we were ever going to make it to our anchorage. We didn't! Later in conversations with Falkland Islanders MR MM was told Arcadia's captain had been asked to hang around until 11am because the winds were forecast to drop substantially (which they did apparently).

Ironically if P&O hadn't cancelled the Argentinean ports and we'd kept to the ship's schedule we would have been in The Falklands not on Jan 26, 2013, but on Jan 27. And yes, that day there were clear skies and calm seas! But before Arcadia could head away from The Falklands the medi-vac of an ill passenger had to take place. It took two attempts for the launch to get close enough in for the passenger to be transferred. I felt sorry for the passenger but I also felt sorry for the islanders who had missed out on some revenue from 2,000 passengers who most certainly would have all gone ashore even if to just wander around Port Stanley.

*Tap dancing commenced and tappers now numbered 60. Christine Noble, the ship's cruise director was still the teacher. She's a former dancer herself and an excellent teacher who had the patience of JOB! She needed to have dealing with "us oldies". MR MM had made a DVD of our tap performance in the Passenger Talent Show and somebody put it up on You Tube. Will we be famous or infamous?

*Celebrations around the ship for Australia Day and Burns Night.

*The Tom O' Connor show was top notch.

*Our new dinner companions are excellent company - not an ounce of bitterness or bitchiness. They get off in Valparaiso and we have been asked to join a table with a truly international flavour - an Irish Lady, a Frenchman, two Australians and two English and two Yorkshire folk (us).

*Spanish lady, who is actually Irish and from Dublin, went to the ship's cinema and witnessed a dispute over seats. It's small, holds probably about 30, and there's often apparently a scrum for seats if there's a popular film being shown. One guy turned to a lady and told her to get her big fat a..e off the seat because it was "reserved" for his wife. She stuck to her guns and stayed put. Things got heated and tempers frayed. Staff had to calm the situation. Some very rude people onboard.

*Ever been invited to a coffee morning on board a ship - or on land for that matter - where they served biscuits not on a plate but wrapped in a paper napkin? Nor had we until we went to the world cruise coffee morning on Arcadia.

Oh, and the coffee was clap cold and it wasn't brought to your table you had to stand in line. No style! A lot different to what we have experienced on Cunard but there again what a difference a cruise line makes even when they're owned by the same company!

AROUND THE HORN

Before the days of reality television and when radio was popular with the masses there was a BBC programme called Round the Horne - a parody a week, several catchphrases and memorable characters like Kenneth Horne, Betty Marsden, Bill Pertwee and Kenneth Williams.

It was compulsive listening for many. The name was a pun for the nautical phrase sailing around the Horn and that's what we did - and one of the chief reasons for booking this cruise. It was never going to be sunshine, more cloud ladened skies, strong winds and heavy seas. It lived up to its reputation.

We approached around four in the afternoon. Earlier in the day MR MM had sussed out a suitable spot to stand and stare and take video footage. We arrived in our hideaway a good hour before the stated time to be sure of our corner which was out of the howling wind as much as was possible being high up on deck 11.

It was colder than cold, windy and there were heavy passing showers. It was a grey afternoon. I was well prepared in my duvet coat and hood so was tucked up like a bug in a rug!

I didn't feel any of the cold. I'd got a Yorkshire Flag to wave as we passed around The Horn. We past several rock formations and worked out that we had "turned the corner" so must have gone round. We stayed on deck till 5-45p.m. when we eventually went into the South Atlantic again after sailing around the Horn and passing the island either side . The sea was very rough where the South Atlantic met the South Pacific and wind speeds of 45 knots were recorded across the decks. It was great. I loved the rough sea. It was amazing how the weather changed in such a short time.

MAGGIE HITS THE DECK IN BEAGLE CHANNEL

Not Maggiemou but "MR Maggiemou" here...Maggie is indisposed and unable to communicate without great difficulty....in fact she is in a clinic in Punta Arenas. That's how MR MM announced my horrific accident to members of cruise forums who were following our voyage.

Our sail around The Horn and transit of The Beagle Channel had begun so well - more or less clear skies and the glaciers were something to behold. I told MR MM the scenery was a cross between Alaska and Norway - he's never been to Alaska and has no desire to go. It was a sea day and every sea day since we left Southampton I had attended the ship's tap dancing class. On Jan 28, 2013, my tap dancing days ended around 14-30 that was when I took a tumble and smashed my right wrist in several places.

The class had started at 14-00hrs as normal. We were on class three of our new routine and learning new steps. There was at one point a list in the ship's movement. Christine Noble, our instructor and cruise director, demonstrated a step.

We all had a laugh as she moved sideways. like a penguin. The next minute the whole room of tappers all swayed left and then right.

We all laughed again and business was back to normal. We carried on walking our new steps when suddenly I felt myself slide forward. I was falling and I remember my arms flying up and my body falling backwards. I landed on my back. I was in complete shock. I couldn't speak, I managed to turn onto my front but my hand was very badly smashed up with bones jutting out.

Panic! The ladies and Christine tried to assist me. Three ladies helped to get me to the medical centre; 999 had been dialed. One lady asked me if I was married; where would my husband be? What's his name? I could not remember his name. I was in total shock and horrific pain in my hand, arm and shoulder.

The elevator arrived and I managed to get in with help of the ladies. I laid on the floor and they lifted my legs up high to stop me passing out. When we got to deck one the medical team were there with a wheelchair and took me into the medical centre.

I was injected with morphine. Dr Tanya Watson, the ship's doctor, explained they had to put me out while they treated me.

I was told I had smashed my wrist to "smithereens". I didn't know at the time (I was out cold) but Dr Watson and her team had manipulated by wrist back in to something like the shape it should be and then applied a cast. When I did come round I was told I would need surgery as I had five fractures in my wrist. I was still groggy from the morphine when a ship's officer in uniform started to question me about what had happened. I later found out he was the security officer. I remember the security guy speaking to me. Asking what had happened?

I said I was not sure but I'd slipped and I said the ship may have moved, to which he replied STERNLY: "there is no movement today". I remember thinking "oh! yes there was" as we had laughed about it earlier in the tap lesson.

I thought it very odd that someone should be asking me questions when I was still under the influence of the anaesthetic. MR MM had arrived by now and was shocked at seeing me in such pain and distress. The next thing this security bloke said to MR MM. You HAVE to fill in this form now. Why? He said: "Because I need to send to Southampton (presumably to P&O HQ). But MR MM hadn't been at the tap class, and didn't know what had happened because I couldn't tell him, and why the urgency? There was not one word of commiseration or compassion from this officer to my plight.

I really thought he acted more like a prison guard than an alleged caring member of the ship's company. MR MM filled in the form as best he could and under protest believing it was certainly unethical, and possibly illegal, to interview someone who was still under the influence of medication administered by a doctor.

MR MM did fear that if he had flatly refused to fill in the form thrust at him by the security bloke it could rebound on my treatment (quite amazing the sort of wild and misguided thoughts that run through your mind at times of great stress). The next day we were due to dock in Punta Arenas, Chile, and I was told I would be medi-vaced because the ship didn't have the facilities to carry out the surgery I needed. We were told to pack our bags as though we weren't returning to the ship - but how do you pack and then transport 14 pieces of luggage ashore?

We decided to just "pack the essentials" (two suitcases and two cabin bags) in the hope, nay expectation, we would rejoin Arcadia. But I did insist we were given our passports because if we had to stay in Chile and then fly say to Australia the photocopy passport would not do.

I was assured by someone from reception (why no purser's office on Arcadia? Oh, and Why an "Executive" notice above the mug shots of the captain and senior officers...must be run by a committeeeee? Heaven help us!) that our passports would be handed over just before we boarded our tender.

Yet when we arrived by the pontoon one with some stripes on his shoulder said that would not happen. I said we are not leaving without our passports they were our property and the ship had no business keeping them against our will. After about five minutes someone from reception arrived with them.

We were off! On shore standing by the tenders as passengers disembarked was that same brusk security officer who'd tried to question me the night before in the ship's medical centre.

He looked at both of us, didn't say a word, and then looked the other way. Such compassion! We were picked up by a chauffeur-driven extended white van and whisked to the Clinica Magallanes (one of the top in South America, allegedly). It was about seven minutes by road.

They treat people from all around the continent including The Falklands, and had received a medi-vaced young man from the Spanish Antarctic survey suffering kidney failure a few nights before I arrived. Once at the clinica a young man called Philip acted as interpreter. Staff swung straight into action but NOT before we showed them we had the means to pay - a credit card with at least a £10,000 limit. Yes, £10,000! Luckily I had just such a card but never thought in a million years I'd need to use it almost to its upper limit. We needed someone like Philip because the first, second and third language was Spanish. Within 10 minutes I, and three other Arcadia passengers, were side-by-side in the emergency admissions section - just a curtain separated the beds.

You could hear all that was being discussed. I was in great pain but actually burst into tears when I heard one of the passengers describe his condition. He seemed to be knocking on Heaven's Door. He did survive though.

I was assessed and assured the orthopaedic surgeon, who was operating in another hospital in the city, would be with me within the hour…and he was. He was Dr Nelson Norambuena. He spoke perfect English and his no-nonsense matter-of-fact manner was just the tonic I needed.

After examining the damaged wrist and examining the X-rays taken on Arcadia by its medical staff, Dr Nelson said fixing the damage would not be a problem largely because of the work the ship's doctors had done immediately after the fall in trying to put the wrist back into its near normal position before putting on the plaster bandage.

Dr Nelson said he would operate sometime between 1pm and 3pm which was less than 24 hours after my fall. I eventually went into the theatre at 2-45pm and the op took 30 minutes but I was kept in the recovery room for almost two hours. I'd had a titanium bridge screwed in to my arm and wrist to hold it together so the bones would heal.

It was going to be a part of me for at least eight weeks. It looked gruesome - something out of a psycho movie. I'd only just been wheeled back to my private room when the bedside phone rang. I picked up the receiver even though I was groggy and light headed because MR MM had gone to check into an hotel downtown. On the other end of the line was Don O'Neil who said he was calling from Los Angeles; that he worked for Princess Cruises & P&O and had personal charge of medi-vacs from the cruise lines. He had a terrific bedside manner over the phone if that isn't double-Dutch.

I explained to Don I had just left the recovery room. He said he would call later to see if there was anything either of us needed. And as good as his word Don did call back several times a day and on at least two occasions around 6am local time in Los Angeles.

Don's cheerful voice was enough to lift the deepest gloom; he was deeply concerned not only about my welfare but of the two other couples who had to leave Arcadia in Punta Arenas because of medical issues.

I have already mentioned that Spanish was the first, second and third language in Punta Arenas. A third good man now identified himself. He was John Rees Jones, MBE. With a name like that you would be correct in thinking he had links with the Valleys. He had, his grandparents emigrated to Chile and while John spoke with a soft Welsh brogue he was born and raised in Chile although he had relatives on the Gower Peninsular and visited them regularly.

John had been a medical journalist but had a career change after a major heart scare and became the International Director at the Clinica.

He was the clinica's "MR Can do, Will do". John received his MBE from the Prince of Wales for services to the British community in Chile. He fielded a myriad of questions from both patients and their partners but he handled them with such grace and most importantly he did get and give answers.

I was in the clinica for four days and during that time there was non-stop cleaning in the public areas and in the private rooms...cleanliness, cleanliness, cleanliness. The food I was served was all right. It didn't have the look or taste of the school dinners I remember. The staff were first rate and even though there was a language barrier sign language kicked in and sorted out basic issues.

At 9pm on the night of my op MR MM was about to leave to go to his hotel when he spotted Dr Norman on his way to perform his last op of the day. "How goes it?", chirped MR MM. "I'm pleased with the way Maggie's wrist is already responding to treatment," gushed the Doc, "She will be fine, rest assured. What the ship's people did was brilliant and it helped me enormously. Maggie will be out of here in a couple of days and she will be fit to return to the ship." Wow! Next day when MR MM visited he told me of the conversation the evening before with Dr Norman. It was just what I wanted to hear. But given the reputation of Dr Norman as a no-nonsense speaker I would have expected another answer if one had been called for.

That was the good news but it was followed by some not so good news. Another call from P&O's Man Friday - Don O'Neil in Los Angeles. Don enquired about the medical insurance we had for the voyage and asked if anyone from the insurance company had been in touch. No one had so Don, who had the details of our insurance to hand, phoned them in what's known as a conference call - three of us on the line.

Don, who made and P&O paid for the call to Ireland where Staysure/Mapfre had its "assistance team" spoke first before calling MR MM. A man answered on behalf of the insurance Staysure's underwriters at the time -Mapfre - and claimed he had tried to contact MR MM at the hotel but was told no one of our name was listed (funny how P & O's man called the same hotel several times a day and managed to speak to MR MM).

When MR MM explained to the insurance man at Mapfre that I was going to be discharged the next day and had been cleared by Dr Norman to return to the ship, the man from the insurance company dropped a bombshell. "Our medical panel will decide if she is medically fit to return to the ship or whether she will be repatriated home", he told MR MM curtly.

How long will that decision take to make? he enquired, "Probably soon after we've received the medical reports from the hospital," said the insurance man. There was no compassion in his voice and MR MM had the distinct feeling he was "being considered a nuisance"!

MR MM had no idea how to make contact with Ireland (we'd left the insurance details on the ship). He asked and the insurance chap only then provided a fax number and an email address.

Anyway MR MM got the clinic to fax the medical report. Then silence from Mapfre. Until, that is, Don O'Neil was back on the phone asking what progress had been made? When MR MM told him none, he immediately got back on the phone to Mapfre in Ireland. This time a chap called Richard answered.

When MR MM asked if they had received the medical report, and by this time the clinica bill which had been paid in full on my credit card and also had been faxed, he went away, came back and said he could find no record of any such fax or email.

So MR MM asked John Rees Jones, MBE, if he would refax the details. He did, and also emailed them. Again they were allegedly "not received" although the clinica's fax showed they had been transmitted to the number given. MR MM was suspicious. He left me in the clinica and went to a travel agent next to the hotel he was in and enquired about flights to Puerto Montt with a view to us picking up the ship in that port.

It wasn't long after he returned to the hospital that Don was on the line from Los Angeles "Any progress with the insurance"? he asked MR MM. "What do you think? was MR MM's retort. Again Don phoned Mapfre in Ireland and this time was put through to a lady who identified herself as Krystal Lane. Notice she identified herself. Krystal turned out to be our heroine. I forgot to mention when the insurer's Richard was on the phone to MR MM he hadn't realised it was a conference call and seemed somewhat miffed that Don was listening in. The tone of this Richard's voice spoke legions when he realised!

Back to Krystal. She pulled up the case number (given to her by Don O'Neil in LA) and MR MM immediately got the feeling

71

this lady was going to sort out our predicament. He was not wrong! Krystal proved to be a trouper. She investigated and told MR MM the medical panel had approved my fitness to return to the ship and that she would sort out plane tickets from Punta Arenas to Santiago, taxis at both ends and the insurance company would pick up the hotel bill in Punta Arenas and in Valparaiso.

Krystal took our passport details and booked and paid for our flight. And she put everything in emails. I really can't praise this young lady's care, compassion and attention to detail enough. I just hoped those at Mapfre in Ireland realise what they have got in Krystal - a gem of an employee who cared about people she would never meet but who were in difficult circumstances somewhere in the world.

At last we felt someone in Mapfre had grasped the nettle. Before Krystal appeared on the scene we were clueless as to what was going to happen next. Getting information was, in my opinion, akin to pulling hens' teeth - not that I have any experience of such a procedure you understand! Our realistic window of opportunity to rejoin Arcadia in Chile ended if the liner left Valparaiso and we were not on board. But with a flight booked to Santiago (the nearest airport to Valparaiso apparently) we were to be on our way in a couple of days.

PPPPICK UP A PENGUIN IN OTWAY BAY.

One of the sights we had hoped to see in The Falklands, King penguins, had been dashed because we had been weathered out and it had looked as though the chance of seeing them in Chile would also be thwarted after my accident. But we had to wait three days for our flight to Santiago which gave us a window of opportunity to go to Otway Bay to see its penguin colony. We had travelled 10,000 miles to see them - this was our last chance. There was a tour company next to the hotel which advertised daily trips to OTWAY BAY PENGUIN COLONY one hour's drive away. We were asked to meet outside the hotel at 10am the next morning. We had not excuse to be late!

Only the two of us had booked (Chilean peso 64 for us both) so instead of going in a minivan we had a private chauffeur-driven car. Not being sure of the weather I wore my Burberry Mac because it went over the arm and I'd found a shawl and a scarf and I had the new penguin hat I'd bought off a market stall opposite our hotel.

73

We arrived at the colony just as a minivan full of German tourists did. My unusual hat got them talking and laughing and they asked to take pictures. Why not!

Everyone with a camera in that group took a photograph - and all because of that hat. We had to walk about one mile to reach the colony but the footpaths were well marked and fenced - it was forbidden to cross over them because that was where the penguins lived....in underground bunkers.

When were arrived at the ocean side and saw all the penguins at play - WOW! What a fantastic sight! Hundreds and hundreds of penguins in their natural environment. Amazing! We had the whole viewing area to ourselves and were able to stand on the viewing platform with full view of the sea and the hundreds of penguins in front of us. What a sight. We watched them for ages.

We saw hundreds more on dry land. It was funny watching them waddle through the trenches to get to the sea. They all seemed to arrive at the same time which was midday so it must have been their time for bathing We were so lucky to see it all. That made my cruise, that and going to the fjords and around The Horn!

Despite the contraption on my right arm, and the discomfort I was in, I was a happy bunny or penguin with a broken wrist but at least I had seen hundreds of penguins. The extended stay in Punta Arenas gave us the chance after I'd been discharged from the clinica to seek out some decent food. With the odd exception the last meal I'd enjoyed was in the Grand Cafe in Southampton.

We went to the restaurant in Hotel Cabo de Hornos. I had a nice fresh hake fish and crab starter but I had no appetite. I thought that would happen so we left after one course and went to our room.

Next day I took a short walk around Punta Arenas. In the square opposite the hotel traders had stalls selling all manner of crafts. It was sunny but very windy and bitterly cold - this was summer in Chile, can't imagine what winter must be like, but hey, we were almost in Antarctica! In the rush to get to hospital I'd left my duvet coat on the ship but had taken my Burberry Mac, a jacket and some jumpers but they turned out to be useless because I couldn't get my right arm in the sleeve because of the titanium bridge. I'd left my warm hat behind too that's why I'd bought my penguin hat which had caused a bit of a sensation at the Otway Bay Penguin Colony. It cost me peso 3. Woolen items were very good and very inexpensive.

But we were still after a good meal. I did get a better appetite so we ventured out for a meal. In the afternoon we'd walked a very short distance and found a well-known coffee house that I'd read about on Trip Advisor -Tapiz Café Almacen - popped in for coffee, a really good Americano, and shared a huge slice of chocolate cake. It was a lovely quirky place with lots of interesting memorabilia.

Then we discovered loads of restaurants on O'Harris Street. We looked at the menus and decided La Luna looked good and that's where we ended up.

We got there just before a party of overseas tourists arrived. This must have been the busiest place in Punta Arenas. MR MM had a steak and I opted for fish. It was very good but my appetite wasn't! La Luna is worth a visit if you're ever in Punta Arenas, Chile...and look up at the ceiling for an unusual sight!

We left Punta Arenas with fond memories despite all that's happened to keep us. The town/city had a certain charm; I loved the street architecture; the memorials; the statues. And we'd got to see penguins in Otway Bay - hundreds and hundreds of them.

We felt safe there day and night, the people were friendly, even charming and it was so clean but there did appear to be a lot of stray dogs although they didn't bother us. The moral of this story - avoid getting injured/ill on board liners but if you do then hope you are close to a port with facilities (like we were) and with the medical skills necessary (which we had available to us in Dr Norman at the Clinica Magallanes). And hope that there will be a

Don O'Neil and a John Rees Jones, MBE, in the wings offering their own special brand of support, and that a Krystal Lane comes riding to the rescue.

Nothing, though, was straight forward come departure day from Punta Arenas! We woke up to rain (crying because we were leaving perhaps?). But this turned out to be an early omen that getting away was going to be anything but a smooth ride. Around 10am I got a call in the room saying transport had arrived to take me to the clinica.

But I said I had been signed out and no longer needed to visit the facility. "But your name is Thorpe isn't it?" I went to reception to try and sort it out and on the way down in the lift met the couple from Arcadia who still had daily appointments. The transport was for them so how had someone managed to get our name involved?

That was Mystery No 1.

Mapfre, our insurance company's assistance people, had told me by phone and in an email, they had arranged to pick up the hotel bill in Punta Arenas (room only); had booked and paid for transport to the airport; had booked and paid for airline tickets to Santiago; had booked and paid for transport from Santiago to Valparaiso and also booked a hotel for two nights while we waited for the ship to arrive.

Wrong on three counts! Only the airline tickets had been booked and that was made from Ireland after I'd given our passport details to Mapfre's helpful Krystal Lane. Our transport to Punta Arenas Airport was due to arrive at 1pm. At 2pm still no sign so I got the hotel to phone a cab. One arrived after about 10 minutes. The driver took one look at our luggage (two suitcases and two cabin-size bags) and said in Spanish to the hotel receptionist we would need TWO taxis - one for our cases the other for us! MR MM protested - why two? Our cases had fitted in taxis in countries around the world without a problem.

I said I'd go and get a cab standing in a line outside the hotel. Realising we weren't going to be ripped off the surly taxi driver took one case and put it in the boot of his vehicle and closed the lid.

It fitted! The others were put inside without difficulty and there was still room for us both in the same vehicle. The fixed fare, I had been told, was 8,000 of the local currency. He put on the meter and by the time we arrived at the airport it had clocked up 11,500. I asked for a receipt and after some fiddling with his meter he produced one. MR MM paid him and needed change. He took it. MR MM unloaded the cases into howling winds.

The driver offered no assistance , he just stood there out of the gale waiting for a tip. He was out of luck.

What is it with the breed who drive taxis? Rip-off merchants (mostly) the whole world over is our experience. The airport was busy and an Act of God kicked in soon after we had checked our cases - winds of 125 knots swept down the runway. Nothing could land or take off. Our aircraft, one of the LAN fleet, had been turned around to Puerto Montt which was 2 hours flying time away from Punta Arenas.

We were given vouchers for food - a ham/cheese burger and a soft drink. And over the airport PA system came the strains of THE SKYE BOAT SONG - it was enough to make even hardened well-travelled Scots cry in their scotch! Not that I spotted any.

The plane finally landed just after 8pm and by 9pm we were all on board and off we went into the setting sun and in the hands of a lady captain. An uneventful flight memorable for the lack of any enthusiasm from the cabin crew up front where we sat. We landed in Santiago at midnight, five hours late, but even there things didn't run to plan. We weren't going to be connected to an air bridge - we needed steps and, you've probably already guessed it, there were NONE immediately available - at MIDNIGHT!

After about 15 minutes a set of steps did arrive and the door was opened. But, hold on, we still couldn't get off. Why?

79

Er, because there were NO BUSES to transport us to the terminal building!

At MIDNIGHT PLUS 20 MINUTES? You couldn't make it up! Two buses eventually did arrive then it took almost another hour for the bags to arrive. But our troubles were still not over. More failed promises, more delays followed. There was no transport waiting for us, no one holding up a card with our name on it as we'd been promised.

By now it was past 2 in the morning. We thought we'd try and get a bed for the remainder of the night at the airport. We spotted a Holiday Inn Express (always good value in our experience) across the road from the terminal. We approached reception, explained our plight, but we were told there was "no room at the inn" - they were sympathetic but had no rooms. The Holiday Inn was fully booked. One receptionist did give us what turned out to be excellent advice - that the blue cabs at the airport were official and took credit cards. So we decided to get to the hotel we had been told had been booked for us in Valparaiso and hired one of these cabs.

The vehicle was a top of the range Honda - a limo not a taxi. And the firm was TRANSVIP and it lived up to its name. It was comfortable, clean and the drive was just one hour. It cost 80,000 of the local money (US $170).

As we'd run out of local currency, I paid on the credit card I'd used in Punta Arenas (yes, still had some credit left!). We'd arrived. It was now close to 4am. Surely nothing else could go wrong? Wrong!

We faced yet another hurdle - this adventure was becoming like tackling the Grand National Course at Aintree in Liverpool! We approached the hotel reception but no one was behind the counter. We were tired; utterly exhausted. Our driver was so concerned he stayed with us willing to take us to another hotel if no one came to deal with us. That was very professional of him. The night duty manager, who had been "resting" out of sight had heard voices, woken up and came to investigate. We told him our names, produced our passports and said we "had a booking".

Oh no we didn't! He checked the register and the computer. "Sorry no one of your name has a reservation!" MR MM had spotted a sign for an IBIS hotel close by. He was all for getting our driver to take us there but I asked if the hotel where we were had any rooms available. It did. We decided to stay. It was now well past 4 in the morning. We'd been travelling 16 hours and were quickly to our room.

I went to freshen up and then into bed but MR MM was mortified at the failure to honour numerous promises.

He immediately logged on the internet and emailed Mapfre in Ireland to flag up the failures which he accepted were NOT of their making.

He'd got a reply by the time we woke up (9am local time). The helpful Mapfre lady Krystal said she was very disappointed to hear of the failings and had already been in touch with a supervisor in Chile and had demanded an urgent report of what had gone wrong in Punta Arenas, Santiago and at the hotel in Valparaiso. The adage "It never rains but it pours", came to mind!

We had a full day and an evening in Valparaiso before Arcadia arrived. Before we went to a late breakfast MR MM had been outside to do a recce of the surrounding area. Right across the road from the hotel was a metro type railway system. The ticket clerk gave MR MM enough information to make it appear that would be a good option - take the train that ran along the water's edge and then headed inland to the grape growing region and to mountain villages. MR MM, a wine drinker, reckons some of the best wines (especially reds) come from Chile.

So that is what we did. Walked across the road, bought return tickets and boarded the next train. It wasn't full. We got a seat near the carriage entrance/exit doors and within a minute of setting off a young man and a young lady burst into song - he strumming his guitar and she singing holding a song sheet. This musical serenade was a complete surprise and it lasted probably 15 minutes. She was very pretty and had a nice voice. We'd no idea what they were singing but it sounded nice to me (MR MM is tone deaf) and it was certainly a novel thing for us to see and hear. They came around with a hat for money so we dropped in some coins. They departed and lo and behold another guy with a guitar got on, tuned in and started singing.

Then it clicked, they were buskers and the train was their patch. MR MM reckoned they must have divided the route up so they didn't overlap. The second guy came around with a hat. Some gave others didn't but he didn't appear to be offended if passengers declined. Lo and behold then at another station yet another strolling minstrel boarded and, yes, tuned in, played and sang and then came round with the hat. We were told later there was some sort of music festival taking place, allegedly, although we were not so sure.

After passing through suburbs of Valparaiso and climbing inland the train reached the vineyard area and at one mountain village the track ended. We decided to sit tight and stay onboard the same train. Well, there didn't look to be much to see or do in the place. We disembarked the train at the other end of the line which was by the port and in the heart of town which was a hive of activity.

It was very Spanish looking in its architecture with statues and fountains and pavement cafes galore. We looked around the marina which was full of local fishing boats and the little harbour had rows of tourist souvenir shops.

I found some triangular shaped head scarves, bando type things with beads on the end of tassels. I bought four for a peso each - just the job for covering up the awful looking titanium bridge on my arm. Shopping done we walked back to the hotel. We dined in the hotel that evening because I was tired as I was still weak after the operation and still in pain. Many of the other diners it turned out were crew rejoining Arcadia.

The next day around 11am a taxi took us to the check-in desks for Arcadia which were nowhere near the port or the ship - in fact they were at the opposite end of the bay. It seemed strange but we soon realised why - there was a secure road running around the bay that was exclusively a port facility. It was also the drop-off, pick-up point for the ship's shuttle buses.

So after being off the ship for eight days missing ports and not seeing the glaciers we were about to be reunited with our cabin.

It was raining when we got out of our taxi at the building used to check-in passengers and crew - there happened to be another cruise ship in that day and were sharing the check-in area with Arcadia.

When the paperwork was completed we walked across the building to waiting coaches - our transport to the ship and the first people I saw were two of the ladies from the tap class who had cared for me after I'd fallen. They told me when I got to the Arcadia gangway I must look up. It didn't make sense but all became clear when I got off the coach. There was a handwritten message on piece of cardboard tied to the deck railings saying WELCOME BACK MAGGIE.

We discovered it was all the idea of two avid P&O cruisers, our friends Angela and Wayne from Barrowford in Lancashire. It was a lovely gesture and cheered me up no end.

In Chile there was a man who wanted me to climb
snow capped mountains
We can make love on a mountain top, and on a hard rock, he said
Not In these shoes, I don't want to get frost bite!

BACK ON BOARD.

Our cabin was just as we had left it. Now on with the cruise. Next stop Easter Island one of the remotes places on earth - 2,300 miles from the west coast of Chile and 2,500 east of Tahiti in the South Pacific. Many passengers were unaware we were only "sailing past" Easter Island because P&O did make it appear that we would be calling there in their early literature so many passengers were not happy because they hadn't been informed.

Easter Island is famous for the huge "human" stone images - almost 900 of them - that are carved out of rock. The biggest is 32ft tall carved out of a single block that weighs apparently 82 tons. Others average around 13ft tall and weigh around 13 tons. No one knows why they were carved or how they were moved about the island but they prove their makers were master craftsmen and engineers.

We sailed past in the early evening which was far too late in the day as the light was fading and the sun setting. We didn't even get close enough to land to see anything in detail.

We were around two miles off the shoreline; we didn't see any of these stone carvings called moai - more disappointment.

We were so far off I was told by one of the ship's photographers they used images of the statues they'd uploaded from the Internet to superimpose on the background making it look like passengers were up close and personal to these ancient carvings when they had their picture taken. So that's how it's done by professionals!

Two days later another island and more disappointment at the hands of Arcadia's captain Sarah Breton and her officers. As with Easter Island, the Pitcairn's was described as "in port" in early P&O cruise literature. But that was yet more disinformation in our view. When we arrived off the island the seas were rough, too rough for the islanders to sail out in their canoes so they packed into a rickety longboat with a motor and battled for almost two hours to cover the two miles out to Arcadia. It was the sheer determination of the skipper of that boat that they made it. Pitcairn had a population of just 48 in 2012 and more than half of them were onboard the longboat.

However, when the islander's boat did reach the ship it took several attempts for them to come alongside the ship's pontoon. Passengers lined the decks of Arcadia "willing" the longboat to come alongside. It did and the islanders clambered on board

Arcadia but were in for a shock - Arcadia's captain Sarah Breton had decreed they only had two hours to set up their stall in the restaurant, sell their wares and be on their way ashore. This was greeted with howls of descent from passengers who'd seen the heroic efforts the Pitcairn Islanders had made just to get to the ship. But the woman Breton wasn't for turning. She stuck to her guns. By 11am they must be packed up and on their longboat. Well, passengers scrambled to get to the restaurant to make their purchases but had to line up. Only a few were let in at a time. I queued early and got in; MR MM followed but just before 11am uniformed male officers closed the doors of the restaurant while there were still probably over 100 passengers waiting their turn to enter.

Although the closed doors were meant to signal the event was finished passengers decided to ignore them and pushed them open. Many got through but such a mini mutiny obviously infuriated the ship's officers, they closed the doors again and one burly officer was posted as guard to prevent any further incursions. MR MM has all this on DVD. He commented that the only thing the guard stopping passengers from getting in to spend their money with people living on the margins of society didn't have was a gun! It was a disgraceful episode of which

P&O should be thoroughly ashamed. Did Breton tell them back at HQ? Unlikely! And why the rush?

Then it was anchors aweigh! Now Pitcairn is famous for the Mutiny on the Bounty which has been commemorated in books, films and song. It was in 1789 that nine mutineers from HMS Bounty and their Tahitian companions - six men, 11 women and a baby - landed on Pitcairn and set fire to the Bounty.

The mutiny was led by Fletcher Christian against Bounty's captain, Lieutenant William Bligh whom they cast off in a small boat.

What's left of HMS Bounty was discovered in Bounty Bay in 1957. Bounty Bay was just the other side of the island from where Arcadia had been anchored but Captain Breton refused to sail her liner around so we could have a look at this historic place - an absolute disgraceful decision in the eyes of many passengers.

Many of us by now reckoned that Breton and her senior officers were running Arcadia as their own personal transport and sod the fare-paying passengers. Many of us will never ever be near Pitcairn again and we were robbed of a chance to see where an event that took place so long ago but yet is known to millions to this day happened.

There are around 10 cruise ships call at Pitcairn every year and according to the internet 80 per cent of the islanders' incomes comes from tourism - like landing fees and stamping passports. The islanders will no doubt be hoping that Arcadia will give them a wide berth in future if that's how they are going to be treated when they make such a Herculean effort to get from shore to ship in stormy seas.

I did have time to buy a souvenir - a carved model of a turtle signed by Carol Christian, a relative of Fletcher of Mutiny on the Bounty "fame" - before the islanders were thrown off Arcadia.

SOUTH PACIFIC

Tahiti was our next stop. We decided to take the ferry from Papeete to the island of Moorea - we weren't alone many others on Arcadia had the same idea. The ferry terminal was a short walk from where our ship docked.

Buying tickets was easy and boarding was efficient even though there were long queues of foot passengers. The journey took around one hour. Moorea is stunningly beautiful. But what to do? We met a couple from our original dinner table (the one we were kicked off) and decided to walk with them along the shoreline and see where it took us. We were not disappointed. After about 3k we arrived at the Sofitel Hotel.

Lo and behold, others I knew from the ship were already there having a drink or swimming in the warm turquoise waters. The girls were having a whale of a time in the sea and were very naughty....waving their bikini tops in the air! They were having a good laugh and so were people watching from the bar. I had to miss the swim (forbidden because of my titanium bridge) so did the next best thing - retail therapy. In the hotel shop I found a lovely necklace with matching bracelet. That cheered me up. We had a few rum punches or rather the friends and MR MM did,

I stuck to the non-alcoholic version which was very good and refreshing.

We walked back to catch the ferry to Tahiti so in all 6k of exercise. I loved Moorea - it was like something out of the movies, all lush, tranquil and green with beautiful beaches and a clear blue sea. Papeete on the other hand was not so nice as we discovered when we returned from Moorea. We had a look around but it wasn't long before we were back on the ship - that's how "attractive" it was. May be we needed to explore more. At the sailaway party I met a lot of my tap dancing friends and I did a bit of a one-handed shuffle being scared stiff of falling.

A word of warning - check the return ferry times from Moorea to Papeete carefully. Leave plenty of time to get back to your ship because there is always a chance you could get stranded.

BORA BORA - not a boring place just hot, sticky and raining for part of our time ashore. We had a tour booked but it had been cancelled after my fall. On shore there were some retail therapy opportunities and as we were investigating we bumped in to Diana Moran better known to TV viewers as "The Green Goddess", a fitness fanatic of a certain age. Diana was a guest speaker on the ship and we had chatted a few times over the previous week especially in the Crow's Nest Bar.

She was at a loose end; we told her we were going to visit Bloody Mary's bar/restaurant famous around the world. We invited her to join us. She jumped at the chance.

MR MM sorted out a taxi to take us to Bloody Mary's and it turned out the owner/driver of the taxi was also general manager of the place - a pure coincidence which was only revealed when we got to the premises after he'd taken us on a ride along the coast first.

We wined and dined, well Diana and MR MM did - I just dined. But Diana loves having her photograph taken so there were a lot of snaps taken, mostly for Diana's blog. It was great fun. Diana and I had an impromptu sing along with some local men dressed in national costume and playing local instruments before we rejoined the ship. It was a giggle. Diana loved it, and so did I.

I met a man in Boro Boro. Come I show you my Island
We have swaying trees and tsunamis and a great bar
Bloody Mary's
Let's get into the groove, dance on the sand and sway with the trees
In these shoes?" Not Bloody likely!

FIJI.

For me it's always good to return to Fiji - it brings back memories of my first visit working on the SS Rotterdam.

I recall going ashore with my mates (the ship's photographers) as escorts on a ship's tour.

Anyone not familiar with a ship's tour they work like this: a local escort/expert from the country you're in takes the microphone and stands up front by the driver but there is always a member of the ship's company on the bus.

They're volunteers and carry a numbered paddle that also names the cruise line. It's their job to keep passengers together and to count them out and count them back on the bus. Usually they sit on the back seat of the bus. At stops, the ship's escorts walk at the back of the group and tries to shepherd passengers like sheep by keeping them all together.

Some take the job seriously (they get to see the places passengers pay to visit but at no cost), others treat it as a free day out and have a laissez faire attitude. When I worked at sea I volunteered to escort at every port but, of course, didn't always get picked by the tour office manager. I learnt an awful lot from listening to local guides on tours.

On my tour as an escort in Fiji more than 30 years ago I remember we went to see a traditional village where all the locals wore grass skirts and coconut bra tops - that was the women - the men wore just the grass skirts (nowadays most men wear the LAVA LAVA) and furry things around their lower legs like ankle warmers. We were treated to a display of Maori dancing and spear throwing followed by a display of turtles that they proudly held above their heads.

After our tour the photographers and I went for a meal in a WIMPY bar - remember them? Yes, we ate a Wimpy hamburger in Fiji!

Thirty three years on I was back. We had no tours booked. MR MM was not keen on taking a tour to see local traditions nor did he want to head into the jungle. Once off the ship we found dozens of locals trying to entice us to take a taxi ride tour or a minivan tour for up to ten people around the island.

Nothing immediately impressed so we headed off on foot in to downtown Suva. It only took a few minutes.

It was colourful, dirty and smelly in places while other parts were clean and tidy. Just outside the dock gates was a huge municipal market and it was buzzing. On the pavement outside ladies in multi-coloured dresses sat behind displays of freshly picked flowers and impressive floral arrangements.

The blooms were all very exotic and included Birds of Paradise. We would have loved to have bought some but space in our cabin was very limited with all our possessions - and all my shoes! We decided we should see something of the island

and spotted a black sporty car with double exhausts that was a taxi for hire.

We negotiated a price for a three hour ride around - US$60 the fare. Other taxi men had wanted US$40 an hour which was way too expensive. Downtown Suva looked to be a mixture of old, and not so new, buildings; it was teaming with locals. There was a nice atmosphere about the place although around the harbour area it was quite scruffy. We stopped outside the entrance gates to the Presidential Palace - when we were there this place was a dictatorship run by the military who staged a coup and dissolved parliament in 2006 (the fourth coup in 20 years). but they have since had elections.

Guards in national dress - that is a lava lava - were posted at the drive but were not fussed about you taking their photograph...although they are forbidden to speak. It wouldn't be a job for me!

Further down the road we came to the most modern building we saw all day - that of the inland revenue (Fijians must pay all their taxes!). Around a corner and up a hill we came to the closed Parliament building. Gardeners were working in the grounds but that's all that was going on. Big wrought iron gates were padlocked to prevent anyone entering.

On Parliament Hill there's a monument to those who lost their lives in the military coup. Prisoners from the local jail were keeping the grass cut and the place neat and tidy watched over by an armed prison guard. We passed the National Stadium, which was being renovated; saw the impressive swimming baths and other buildings used for sport. They're a sports mad nation. We were taken to a forest park that was out of bounds for locals; went past cemeteries and through villages.

There were some interesting views from on high especially across to a mountain range and down to the ocean.

When our three hours were up, the driver dropped us at a modern shopping centre close to the harbour.

Just as the ship was about to sail the heavens opened. It rained and rained. It drove the band serenading us undercover into a warehouse. But the music continued under the baton of a conductor with a chest full of medals.

The band's final tune was Now is the Hour. I've often wondered why in Fiji and a few other Pacific island they always play & sing this song...I've now discovered it is a Maori tune with Maori words:

Po atarau

E moea iho nei

Translates into English as "Now is the hour when we must say goodbye...."

It was popular when I was a youngster sung by the likes of Bing Crosby and Frank Sinatra. It was sung by Hayley Westerna (a Kiwi soprano) at the closing of the 2011 Rugby World Cup.

NOUMEA, NEW CALEDONIA

The ship's port lecturer reckoned there was "little to do" in this port. Perhaps that was to try and justify why Arcadia was only in for a morning (four hours). We found more than enough to do in that short time and would have been very happy to have spent longer in this very chic French port with its wonderful marina, good shops and hospitable people.

We had to take the ship's shuttle although the town was within very easy walking distance but we weren't allowed - red tape!

Our intention had been to get a taxi driver to take us on a tour of the island but we were flabbergasted when they wouldn't take us - not because we were inappropriately dressed, or looked like drop outs but because we only had Aussie or US dollars and these taxi drivers (we asked four) wanted the South Pacific Franc. I must say I'd never heard of the South Pacific Franc in all my travels! They turned their noses up at the Dollars we were carrying. We looked for an ATM without success so were basically "moneyless" in Noumea!

We were forced by circumstance to take a walk. Noumea's marina was very impressive with dozens of yachts of all shapes and sizes tied up (do they ever set sail?). We came across a market selling fruit and veg but also had some craft stalls. I bought two pairs of blown glass earrings (handmade by the stallholder she assured me). She took US Dollars.

MR MM saw a colourful cotton shirt locally made and of good quality and bought it. We walked around the marina and came across what looked like a poor quality boat boot sale - even second hand boat toilets! Lots of the items looked like they should be scrapped but people were buying them.

All these items were spread on the ground and there were a few hippy types looking a little potty and not just from the sale of potties!

A short walk away we found out why. I thought the people looked like hippies They were and from a commune with signs advertising cannabis that we stumbled on!

We'd walked right into the commune unknowingly but no one seemed to mind; nobody bothered us. There were wood carvings and statues around the place and a lot of strong aromas drifting by. Thank goodness we are in our 60s now and not in "the 1960s" otherwise I would not be able to remember all this!

We meandered around and came across a couple of nice churches. A wedding was taking place in one of them and MR MM moved amongst the guests with his movie camera. Others were filming so he blended in well in his casual shirt and shorts which seemed to be the dress code.

The bride, though, was very smart in a meringue style dress and hair from the doll Barbie collection - the couple marrying looked oriental. Moving on we headed back towards the port I was taking in the sights and sounds of the surroundings when MR MM shouted " turn around and stand still while I take a photo." So I did.

Then I heard a loud laugh coming from somewhere above my head. I spun around and right behind me were two people - lady and a man all dressed up in medieval costumes with parasols - on stilts. I was shocked; I'd no idea they were there and me being five foot nothing I was a miniature. We had a giggle and they wandered off to amuse other visitors to the city which is capital of the French special collectivity of New Caledonia.

We had to be back on board by 12-00 noon. The one other good thing about this port call was the sailaway party on the deck at 12-30. Billed as the great British and Australian sailaway it was a lot of fun with singing, dancing and flag waving. One thing P&O entertainment staff are good at are the sailaway parties. I was not able to dance like I would like to have done because my hand was still in the sling but I enjoyed the singing and waving. I dressed up for a laugh and it was fun.

SEA DAYS - you either love 'em or hate 'em. On a world cruise you can get up to nine in a row (from South Africa across the Indian Ocean to Australia for instance, or seven from Southampton to New York). Being injured with a broken wrist since January 27, I was at a disadvantage. I soon got tired and was in constant pain. I got an infection in the wounds; it was all very draining.

I spent my mornings resting and when I did venture out I went walkabout. Walk and talk, I called it. I met people and stopped for a chat. I attended some digital photography courses and I went to an I pad class but I had no I pad just a Samsung Galaxy tablet 10.1 - that didn't impress the instructor!

I went to the lectures during the day and that's where I first met Diana The Green Goddess of TV fitness fame). She talked about growing old gracefully. I told her I was having none of that as I intended to grow old disgracefully! Why change a habit of a lifetime?

She looked amazing for her age - a lovely lady. She spoke about osteoarthritis; she warned about broken wrists - too late was the cry although I do not have osteoarthritis. I hardly saw

101

any entertainment at night. We'd have dinner and I was whacked so off to bed early but it was still quite late - around 10-30pm. before we'd finished being served.

I'm normally a night owl and made it to the 1960 theme night out on the back of deck 9. It had been raining; the deck was very wet - I made a quick exit. I couldn't afford another fall. Pity about the weather really because along with some other passengers I'd got dressed up.

I had a red and white op art dress specially made out of original 60s fabric and I had the 60s style shoes I'd got out of the window display when the ship stopped in Recife. I'd been to the ship's spa and got the hairdresser to backcomb my hair in a 60s style bouffant with flicked up ends. The stylist was too young to know how to do this but she followed my instructions. I wore white tights and had a red band around my foreheard. I was a real 60s chick and I looked the part but my heart wasn't in it so I toddled off to bed.

Arcadia then had a '70's night. I dressed up for a 70s themed night as a hippie type. Two of our table companions were game for a laugh - Terry dressed as an Elvis lookalike although Elvis was more 1950s than 1970s, but Terry's look was convincing. Diana, his wife, was big into amateur dramatics back home in Oxford.

They both had parts in the ship's play, and Terry sang and strummed a guitar in the passenger talent show. From memory I think this cruise was their first and they were doing the world.

The Headliners were the resident dancers and singers on Arcadia and put on some excellent shows. I missed them at first but they were repeated and if you're on for the whole voyage you get other opportunities to judge their performances for yourself rather than just listen to the gossips, who may have different entertainment tastes.

I had some acupuncture sessions to try and help me feel better.

On QM2 if you booked a treatment in the spa you got to use the full Canyon Ranch Spa facilities meaning the thermal suite, the hot tubs, the steam room and herbal sauna were all available but on Arcadia there were no extras as an incentive.

You had your treatment, or hair done, goodbye! The bill for my hair and nails and feet was over £1,000 and we weren't anywhere near the end of the voyage - expensive having only one hand!

WRIST UPDATE: My hand is a bit better and the ship's doctor has discharged me from visits to the medical centre unless anything goes wrong. It will be weeks before the titanium bridge is removed but I am now used to it being there although my hand is still painful but getting easier to cope with.

I am unable to dress myself and my hairdressing skills are nonexistent as I can't even bush my hair. I have of visit the spa salon daily. The staff are good and they also help me put on my jewellery - earrings and necklace - ready for dinner . Life is tough for me at the moment and depresses me at times with my wrist, but at least we are seeing beautiful places.

BRISBANE IN THE RAIN

The weather was more like that of the UK rather than that of Australia's Sunshine State. We'd been following the weather in Queensland nightly from the ship because we'd heard about the violent storms that had caused a lot of damage.

We were met at the port by special friends with whom we'd shared at table at dinner when they were on the Aussie leg of Queen Mary 2's circumnavigation of Australia in 2012. MR MM had kept in touch and when they knew we were going to be in town they insisted on taking us out for the day to the Gold Coast. Frank, whose family own a market garden that's thousands of acres in size, also owns a top-of-the-range Land Rover that can take six. It was teaming down when we set off but it did manage to fair up a bit for us to see the fantastic coastline in Queensland.

Frank drove us to Southport and on to Paradise Bay giving us a running commentary of the places we passed. It was an area Frank and his wife, Pat, knew well from their teenage courting days. The Queensland and the Gold Coast are famous for their golden sandy beaches but recent storms had washed as much as three metres of sand away from some and devastated others.

On our visit the seas were spectacular - the high rollers lashing the shoreline.

We stopped for lunch at a waterside restaurant called OSKARS "Burleigh beach house" Burleigh Heads. This was on a bit of a headland as its name suggests and had fantastic views of the ocean. It also had fantastic food. I ate Moreton Bay bug tails for the first time. They were recommended as a delicacy of Queensland.

They're a type of lobster found only in the Indian and Pacific Oceans. They were fabulous! I followed the bugs with a black fig crepe, lime treacle butter and honeycomb ice-cream. All very yummy. MR MM had the wild Barramundi. His was late in arriving for which the maitre d apologised but she said "chef was not happy" with the first one he'd cooked so was doing a second for MR MM. The food was outstanding and we really all enjoyed it so much after weeks of "school dinner" food on Arcadia.

Our four Aussie friends from Queensland are avid cruisers and were booked on a Holland America cruise the following week so they were getting excited about their voyage. But a funny thing had happened as we got out of Frank's people carrier and headed into the restaurant. Ernie, and his wife Roz, were our other two special friends from the Queen Mary 2, 2012 circumnavigation, and were with Frank and Pat - they'd all been pals for years and years.

As Ernie got out to walk the few steps to the restaurant he noticed the sole of one of his trainers had come away from the rest of the shoe. He was not too impressed but as he tried to fix it by clamping it back but it got worse.

Then the sole came off completely apart from the back of the heel - he was flapping around like a sea lion when lo and behold the other shoe did the same. He was so embarrassed and his dear wife didn't believe it was happening because "they'd hardly been worn and were almost new"!

We entered the restaurant and Ernie's trainers left a trail of black rubber in their wake. We sat and had lunch and when Ernie stood up to leave the restaurant after our excellent meal what was left of the trainers "died" - they fell apart completely all over this posh restaurant's floor. Ernie was embarrassed but the rest of us were in hysterics at him leaving bits of black rubber behind him.

In Australia and with other hot countries things dry out in the heat. The glue must have gone. I know what that means. In Cyprus the heat rots glue and also elastic in your underwear so I have to be careful not to wear undies that have started to go as I could end up with my knickers round my ankles for the wrong reasons!

As luck would have it outside in the restaurant car park there was a garbage bin - off came what remained of the trainers and in they went leaving poor Ernie in his stocking feet in the pouring rain. He took his shoelessness all in good heart and sole!

The drive back to the ship was very difficult, monsoon-style rain with visibility just beyond the bonnet of Frank's Land Rover at times. It had been a memorable visit to Brisbane for a variety of reason as you can imagine.

*DES O CONNOR The very mention of his name makes many Brits cringe; others throw their heads up in horror and yet others cry out "Oh, no not Des, not singing!"

He is much maligned but it's a reputation I don't believe is justified. I'd never seen him in concert - just on the TV after he got his own show in 1963 but he popped up as a "celebrity speaker" on Arcadia for "an afternoon only". Yes, a one-afternoon stand. Talk around the ship before hand was "not that old has been!" while others hoped he wouldn't sing. They got their wish, but Des showed he can still work a crowd - he had a packed Palladium Theatre audience eating out of his hands after his performance on Arcadia.

He lives in Queensland these days with his fourth wife and young son, Adam. The octogenarian (he's 82) joined the ship for an overnight in home waters. His appearance was billed as an interview with Des O Connor, by Christine Noble, the ship's cruise director, asking the questions. There wasn't a spare seat in the theatre (so much for the knockers and doubters!). I for one was desperate for a bit of different entertainment from someone who had made a name for himself rather than lots of jugglers and singers nobody had ever heard of yet all reckoned they'd been in West End productions - mostly Les Mis (the singers not the jugglers).

I got a good seat in the upper circle thinking I could escape if Des turned out to be rubbish. Come the hour, Christine introduced Des and there was polite applause. Des started speaking and Christine never got another word in edgeways. He went on for 90 minutes hardly stopping to draw breath. He was hilariously funny and it was all off the cuff. He hadn't a written note anywhere and there wasn't a smutty joke told. Des proved he is still one of the world's top entertainers even at 82 (although he doesn't look his age).

He went up in most people's estimation after his appearance. He was given a standing ovation as he left the stage. Not so much an "old has been", more a breath of fresh air for passengers on Arcadia who'd been starved of any real talent for ages. For the record Des was born in Stepney, in London's East End in 1932; he was awarded a CBE in the Queen's Birthday Honours List in 2008, and was Invested by Her Majesty at Buckingham Palace on December 2, 2008 - a nice early Christmas present!

Well done to Des.

Another O Connor - Tom, no relation - was another entertainer who broke the mould of mediocrity when he appeared in the Palladium Theatre. Some call Tom - I'll name that tune in 500 - a "has been" but again that's unfair in my view. He certainly cheered us up and we laughed at his gags.

THE LAND OF WALTZING MATILDA

Sydney and Australia have always been a big draw for both MR MM and I. He'd not been, I had. So when Cunard published the world voyages of its ships for the 2012 season in 2011 we just had to book on QM2. The circumnavigation was an exciting prospect, especially for MR MM, and the fact we would be in Sydney overnight was a bonus. What to do in Sydney? Soon after we'd booked the cruise I started researching - The Opera House was high on a list of "must see/do", so was the Altitude Bar in the Shangri La Hotel for a cocktail and the Blu Bar on the 36th floor of the hotel which has spectacular views over Sydney Harbour and beyond.

I noticed it was possible to climb the famous Sydney Harbour Bridge either by day or by night. What a challenge, I thought! But could I do it? Here I have a confession. Six years earlier and living in Skipton, a market town on the edge of the Yorkshire Dales, I had undergone major back surgery. I'd had my coccyx removed. Sounds painful; it was. Following the operation, which was carried out on the NHS in Airedale General Hospital, I had to learn to walk again.

Luckily we lived in a converted warehouse on the towpath of the Leeds & Liverpool Canal right in the middle of town. Towpaths are level; ideal for getting me mobile again. At first I could only manage a few yards at a time, and always had to be accompanied, but as the weeks passed I was able to walk further and further.

Even when I had fully regained my confidence and ability to walk I kept up a regime (even to this day) of taking brisk walks on a daily basis.

I thought to climb Sydney Harbour Bridge would not be a bridge too far for me! I was determined to do that climb. I researched the bridge climb on the Internet and found good video footage at http://www.bridgeclimb.com.

I discovered there were three different levels of climb - one goes through the centre, another goes over the top of the bridge and the third does the structure. The climb offered by Cunard was the one over the top. Seeing as I am over the top, I decided to go for that. MR MM, is not a man for heights - at 6' 3" he already has his head in the clouds - and wouldn't join me. I booked it after Queen Mary 2 had left Southampton believing this shore excursion would sell out quickly even though it was an expensive tour (around A$240).

It's actually not that much cheaper doing it independently but places are limited and it does get booked up. With ship's excursions you are guaranteed to get a climb.

Come the day I was surprised to find that out of almost 3,000 passengers only eight of us were doing this tour.

We were escorted and driven by minivan from the ship to the bridge climb offices just a few minutes from Circular Quay on Sydney Cove, the site of Australia's first European settlement in 1788. It was absolutely pouring with heavy rain.

We were ushered in to a Victorian-looking building that wouldn't have been out of place in many British cities. Once inside we were given orders of what was to happen. Our climb was scheduled for 11-0am. It was 9-0am at the time and I was thinking we had a long wait.

We had chance to browse their souvenir shop for mementos and have a coffee which we all declined thinking we may need to spend a penny half way up to the summit.

Bridge climbs are done in small groups so our eight was just fine. We had a bit of a wait, but not that long, before we were taken in to a room for our orientation briefing. We stood in a circle while our bridge instructor asked questions such as our names and if we had health issues. We had to give him a reason why we had decided to climb Sydney Harbour Bridge.

Some said it was a life time ambition while others said they thought as they were in Sydney they would go for it. I told of the major back surgery, how I'd had to learn to walk again after it so to climb the bridge would prove not only had I fully recovered but it would give me a real sense of achievement. Our explanations given, we then had to fill in a health questionnaire before being breathalyzed. Yes, breathalyzed. Any trace of alcohol in your system you were only going out of the door. You could not climb.

They have zero tolerance with regard to alcohol in the body on this bridge climb. Good for them. We all passed with flying colours; all non-drinkers. Ah!ah! says she!

We were then handed blue flying suits and told to take off all clothing apart from pants, shorts and underwear.

Once in our bright blue uniforms we were handed an elastic band to tie our hair back. No hair pins, bobby pins, clips or slides were allowed. Anyone on medication such as asthma had to hand it over and it was carried by one of the instructors. I am asthmatic so my inhaler went up this way just in case. I was sure I wouldn't need it but I was taking no chances.

Next we stood in line to be wired for sound and fitted with ear phones. Then we all had to walk on a moving ladder. If you couldn't hack it you didn't get to do the climb.

114

All the Cunard gang of eight passed. Still we hadn't begun our ascent of the bridge.

We were wired up again, this time to a lifeline which is secured to the bridge. This was a work of art in itself. We had to connect up from a circular ring and all get clamped up with the wire lifeline. We then had to collect a hat, which was clipped onto the collar of the flying suit; a hankie that was clipped to your cuff, gloves clipped to your wrists and because it was chucking down with heavy rain and I mean heavy rain, we had to have wet weather clothing.

So what looked like a bum bag (or a fanny bag for my American cousins) was attached to our backs and we were told to put on the wet weather protective leggings over the flying suit. The bum bag was actually a jacket with a hood. If we wanted a beany hat as well we could have one, again it was attached to the suit. Once in all the gear we were ready for the off...at last!

No time for nerves; two hours had already flown by. Following our leader we headed out through a tunnel affair and then we were walking along a ridge high above the streets. This led us to the first of the two granite pylons that support the bridge. Next thing we were inside the pylon and here we had to start our ascent.

We climbed up, ducking and diving at times and bobbing under and stepping over turning corners and all the time holding our lifeline wire. You hold it near the front and it slides along at your side. Rain was falling fast. We carried on 'till we came to the LADDERS! Yes! the dreaded ladders that we'd had to test drive earlier.

Nothing had prepared me for what they would look like. I am OTT as I've mentioned before and earlier we were asked for a volunteer to be first in the line. Me being me I said "I'm free!" So I was number one in the line-up. At the ladders I was wishing I had kept my big mouth shut as I stood gaping at the huge vertical ladder in front of me. Before we actually set off I had the sense to tuck my wet weather leg pants into my socks as I felt they were flopping around, I was so pleased I had done because when I got on to the ladder I realised the rungs were very narrow. I only have 38 EU/ 7 US size feet but they overhung so I felt I needed to look at my feet.

Once on the rung, though, I dare not look anywhere but straight ahead. I had read on the Internet reviews that said DO NOT LOOK UP OR DOWN. For a fleeting moment I thought I can't do this and panic kicked in. However, I gave myself a quick talking to and said "GO GIRL GO".

I took a deep breath and went for it. Half way up, the ladder splits in two and you have to step across to the next ladder which again goes straight up.

Wow! This was scary but I stuck with the thought don't look up or down so I had no idea how many more rungs I had to climb. Suddenly I was on a platform and the leader was there - we were about to head for the summit.

The climb doesn't go right across the bridge to the opposite bank. It begins on the eastern side of the bridge (at the Circular Quay side of the bridge). At the summit, the climb crosses to the western side of the arch for the descent. You end up at your starting point. Each climb takes three-and-a-half-hours but that including the meticulous preparations. Better safe than sorry.

MR MM's friend in Sydney said it took a decade of negotiations before the authorities allowed bridge climbs to take place. Well worth the wait I can assure you.

Once we started the ascent it was easy peasy for me. I am a very good walker and the climb was a doddle - I could have run up it. The arch of the bridge (which is also known as the Coat Hanger because it looks like one) is a gradual climb of steps. It was still raining but we carried on. There is no turning back once a climb has started.

Climbs are only ever cancelled if it is lightning or it is very, very windy. Rain doesn't count. We soon reached the summit and once on top the rain stopped. We had the clearest, amazing, breathtaking views. The eight of us all huddled together for a group photo which our leader took. You cannot take you own cameras or binoculars - glasses for seeing have to be tied to your head.

The leader took individual photos of us on his camera. Of course you buy these later from the shop at the bridge climb centre. Our group spent time admiring the wonderful views, especially of Queen Mary 2 alongside in Circular Quay, and the Opera House across the other side of the ferry terminal.

This was Queen Mary 2's first time alongside in Circular Quay. The harbour authorities had dredged the harbour to get her in. She was a sight to behold!

Our time for admiring the views over, our leader led us across the bridge all the time talking to us through our earphones. We stood in the centre of the arch for a few moments looking at the highway and all the traffic, the rail tracks and pedestrian walkways below - a Hell of a long way down. Descending now on the opposite side we walked down faster than the climb up then the rains came heavy again.

Our leader chatted away and I was right behind him being a fast walker; the rest were way back. I tapped him on his shoulder as I knew he was talking but we could not hear him. He was shocked because he had not realised we couldn't hear him speaking. What he'd done was he'd turned off his walkie talkie to speak to someone else and had not turned it back on to us. He said it was lucky I was close otherwise he would not have known.

Before we knew it we were back to THOSE LADDERS again. By now I had put the gloves on as I realised on the way up the steel of the bridge was slippy and it smelt of lead paint. So I used the gloves. It was much better. Once over the first ladder and across I was able to concentrate on DON'T LOOK DOWN. Good job as when I had stepped across onto the second ladder a train whizzed by underneath shaking the ladder. I held on for dear life.

I was first down and as we waited for the others to catch up. I asked our leader "does anyone ever freeze with fear on the ladders?" "Yes", he replied "but we are trained to talk them down". We were all down safely without any freezes and headed back to the Eastern Pylon. It all seemed easier now.

There was a lot of painting going on - it never stops - what's that saying about the Forth Bridge? The paint dries in seconds so can't cause any damage to anything below.

Back at base it was off with the clothing. Once again it was a military type operation. We all stood in line all undid the lifeline of the person in front, then the earphones, the gloves and clothing all had to be placed in different coloured laundry bags.

We put back our own clothing, went to reception where we were presented with a certificate and the opportunity to buy photos taken on the bridge climb. No one refused. Lastly, we had a chance to go into a viewing room to see how the bridge was built and see some memorable sights of the bridge such as the Olympic games in 2000 and all the wonderful firework displays.

After leaving with the photos and the compulsory T-shirt we walked back to The Rocks with a guide who took us all for a beer in the Fortune of War, the oldest pub in Sydney - on the house. Cheers!

Had all the drill, and the effort involved, and the cost been worth it?

You Bet!

I loved it, all the Queen Mary 2 gang of eight did. We were all seniors and I certainly would do it all over again. And MR MM was proud of what "the old girl" had achieved especially having had that major back surgery six years earlier.

The Sydney Bridge Climb was undoubtedly the highlight of the 2012 world cruise on Queen Mary 2 - but there were plenty of other memorable and enjoyable happenings like the time we sailed around the Cape of Good Hope; a visit to see the miniature African penguins at Boulders in Simsonstown; a visit to Namibia; the wonderful reception we got at every port we called in around Australia - especially Adelaide, Fremantle (Freo to locals), and Melbourne.

Being able to take a look at Darwin, the Whitsundays and Brisbane proved memorable.

G'DAY MAGGIEMOU IN SYDNEY

I adore Sydney. It never ceases to amaze me every visit and has done since I first set foot here in 1987 onboard P&O's Sea Princess. The city has changed big time of course but there is always something new to discover. On this visit we were met by an old friend of my husband - they had worked together 25 years earlier in Yorkshire before he emigrated.

They met up 12 months ago while I did the Sydney Bridge Climb from Queen Mary 2 but no climbing for me with my broken wrist. This time David, my husband's former colleague, had decided to give us a "mystery tour" of his adopted city.

It turned out to be a real journey of discovery for us. He has use of a top-of-the-range Subaru - well he is the voice and face of the company in Australia. On the stroke of 9am he was waiting. He drove around central Sydney then out to beaches such as Manly, and past Watson's Bay where there's a branch of the famous fish restaurant of Doyle's.

We headed towards The Heads - the entrance for shipping entering and leaving Sydney Harbour.

We stood on the top of the huge cliffs looking out to sea. Bondi Beach was across the water. We had stunning views. We drove to the end of a peninsular to Palm Beach, about 90mins drive from the city.

We past lots of wonderful beaches along the way. But lunch beckoned. David had decided we should all eat at one of his favourite places - Dunes. It's an award-winning diner overlooking the sea and on the edge of a golf course.

My lunch of calamari in a chilli sauce with pasta was fantastic. MR MM and David had beer battered fish. For dessert I had my favourite ice cream - Movenpick maple and walnut.

More beaches and wonderful views followed as we headed back into the city. We were blessed with sunshine all day; so very lucky because the weather had been very wet in OZ due to cyclone Rusty doing it's thing around the country for more than a week. After our fabulous lunch we abandoned the idea of going to Doyle's for fish in Watson's Bay (we were still full) and instead decided to go to the Shangri-La Hotel for cocktails on the top floor in The Altitude Bar. It is aptly named!

We'd arrived around 7-30 pm; too late to see the lights over Sydney coming on. It was busy and we had to wait for a seat - we requested one by a window. We had two cocktails in another part of the top floor which had views over the city but not Circular

Quay, the "Coat Hanger" or the Opera House. A few minutes went by and a waitress led us to small coffee-style table a few paces back from the window tables we had requested in The Altitude. About five minutes later our waitress returned, picked up our drinks and sat us in a window seat with a small table right in the middle of the massive floor to ceiling windows with panoramic views over Sydney Harbour. The Arcadia looked like a Dinky toy below. The bridge was straight ahead and the Opera House was there centre picture, too.

It was an amazing sight to see all the lights on all the buildings ablaze with colour as far as the eye could see. We ordered a lite bite (only light snacks/nibbles are served with the cocktails because it was/is a proper cocktail bar) we went for the smoked salmon and caviar with crème fresh. Delicious!

We sat admiring the view for ages. It had been a perfect end to a perfect day in Sydney. We walked back towards the ship and had a look at some of nightlife - lots of atmosphere, music and plenty of pubs. When we turned one street corner we past a couple who immediately shouted out MAGGIEMOU? I turned and looked. I'd no idea who they were but they recognised the sling on my arm as they had been reading my blogs. They were Kirstie and Mike and joined Arcadia the next day.

SYDNEY DAY TWO

We'd decided we WOULD go to Doyle's after all for lunch and set off with the best of good intentions but first we had some things to buy - like Molten Brown body wash for MR MM from their outlet in the Queen Victoria Building one of the most beautifully preserved buildings in Sydney.

We then went wandering off to see more sights and I decided I need to get something done with my hair, like have it cut as it had been in bad shape ever since my accident. I'd been going to the salon onboard most days but I'd spotted a well-known Sydney salon close by Circular Quay and decided hair was more important than food. Well, a girl's gotta get her priorities right and food for me is low down on the list when it comes to all things hair.

I managed to get an appointment for later in the day. When I came out of Trumps I felt like I had come up trumps! Get it? I felt more human. My hair had got very dry with the drugs I had been prescribed and it felt like a Brillo scrubbing pad. I was now more normal. The salon is right by The Rocks which offers a wonderful shopping opportunity. I bought some new UGG boots embellished with Swarovski button - no plain boring suede for this gal! MR MM got a Aussie kangaroo skin hat called a Skippy and started leaping about like a mad thing on two legs, and a belt with an opal buckle. I hope he's not thinking he can keep up with me in the bling stakes. He's no chance!

We never made it to the ferry for Watson's Bay and Doyle's restaurant! May be next year. We did manage an afternoon with a refreshing beer or two. Well, MR MM did. I enjoyed browsing the pub - The Fortune of War - which claims to be the oldest pub in Sydney dating from 1828.

There were some old photos on the wall and the one that caught my eye was of the old P&O Sea Princess. The ship I'd first sailed on into Sydney. Maybe the photo was taken when I was on her in 1987.

Sailaway was earlier than we have experienced on our previous cruises in to Sydney but in a way it was good. We saw everything in daylight (it only went dusk as we sailed through The Heads and into the open sea). It had started to rain a little mid-afternoon but by the time we set sail it was tipping down. Once we got into open water it became very choppy and very soon afterwards the sea became very rough indeed. It always seems to rain when we're in Sydney but according to our friend David "It never rains in Sydney!"

THE LAND OF KIWIS

Cruising Milford Sound. Another of the "wonders of New Zealand's South Island. Its high peaks rising straight out of the water reminded us very much of Norway and its fjords - stunning and beautiful. Rough seas at the entrance to the Sound but they were much calmer when we got into the Sound proper. As we got deep in I felt as though I could reach out touch the mountains.

That's why navigators like Capt James Cook passed it by believing their ships would be battered by winds against the rock formations that climb 3,900 ft and more and once in they would never get out.

Vegetation clung like limpets to the sides of these stunning cliffs. The clouds also gave us a show - creating a cotton wool blanket that split the mountains in two - a bit like a rock sandwich - their tops and bottoms exposed with a white "filling" in between. There are just two permanent waterfalls but dozens of temporary ones are created during the rains we were told by a Kiwi commentator on the ship.

This transit was a lot like the sail into Geiranger Fjord in Norway only there were no Seven Sisters here! Milford Sound was carved out by the erosive effects of a giant glacier and really should be called a Fjord. (strictly speaking a Sound is a river formed valley subsequently flooded by the sea). There was no danger of running aground with 1,000 metres under keel.

This is the wettest place in New Zealand - a staggering 28ft falls every year. Some of these mountains have names - like The Lion at 4,272ft; The Elephant at 4,977 and The Bishop's Mitre at one mile from water's edge to peak because they keenly resemble such images. Milford Sound is apparently New Zealand's top tourist attraction and the only Sound accessible by road. It was named in 1812 after Milford Haven in Wales by the first European settler, Captain John Grono. A very interesting excursion off the High Seas into this mountainous and water wonderland.

DUNEDIN.

After leaving Milford Sound, Arcadia re-entered The Tasman Sea and battled Force 10 gales around the bottom of South Island past Invercargill and Stewart Island before arriving in Dunedin. The sea conditions took their toll, many passengers were seasick and so ill they couldn't make or face dinner. Our new table companions were two of their number.

The captain's "welcome" party by the municipal swimming pool was cancelled - water was flooding the deck.

I was now not the only walking wounded passenger - there were a couple of other misfits like me with broken bones who had fallen in recent days. I'm hoping I will get some respite from the endless questions..."what happened to you?" It will be a blessing I can tell you.

We took a six hour ship's tour on a train. Not any old train but the Taiere Gorge Railway and what a journey we had! The railway line ran right on to the quayside and was just a short walk from the ship. It wasn't a "steamer" - it was hauled by diesel engines three of them - but the carriages were from a bygone age of steam and all had been restored.

I counted 15 carriages. We were allocated seats in coach L which turned out to be the oldest dating back to 1913. Others were more "recent" like from the 1930s.The train is run by volunteers and owned by the OTAGO EXCURSION TRAIN TRUST and Dunedin City Council in a joint venture. When we found our carriage we were greeted by an spritely lady of a certain age called Ngaire who guided us up a set of four steps. She was very jolly as were the other volunteers we met on the journey. The carriage was divided into two sections with 10 passengers in each. There was room for more but they didn't fill the carriages to capacity which proved a good move - there were spare seats so you could stretch out.

We were in the half of the carriage which had Ngaire as our stewardess. Once all her 10 passengers were seated Ngaire arrived with wine glasses, a bottle or two of champagne and a jug of orange juice. A male passenger got up to help her open the bottle of fizz and began to pour while Ngaire asked us what we'd like - a glass of champagne or mixed with some orange juice. It was hardly 9-30am but no one refused a drink.

The glasses were soon topped up and the people in our section of the carriage were on good form with some lively conversations.

Our first stop was the famous and iconic Dunedin Railway Station - there isn't another like it anywhere in the world as far as I know - where they fuelled the diesels (the passengers from Arcadia were already well fuelled and we had hardly set off!) We couldn't get off at this point - that opportunity would come later said a commentator called Alan on the train's PA system.

As the journey progressed it soon became clear Alan "the voice" was an amusing character, full of fun and he came out with some really amusing sayings. One which I loved and I must use this myself in future was his description of the lady volunteers. He was telling us they would be coming round later in the day with a trolley of souvenirs. How he described them was not as salespeople, or trolley dollies, or tarts with a cart, but as RETAIL THERAPISTS.

I thought that was very funny. His commentary was first class and informative. We were served shortbread tea/coffee around 10-30am and a lunch box around 12-30. In between we sat back and watched the wonderful scenery unfold. Ngaire handed out cans of beer or soft drinks - all part of the service and included in the price of our tickets. We had a stop about half way up the gorge where we were able to disembark for 20 minutes, take some pictures or browse crafts and souvenirs in what was more like a car boot sale in the middle of nowhere. I bought a Paua shell pendent as a memento and to be kind to the people who had sat there all morning in the wilderness waiting for us suckers to come along. Back on the train we climbed higher and higher up the gorge; the scenery on this trip was just amazing and breathtakingly beautiful. We passed through ten or more tunnels; crossed numerous bridges and viaducts; saw rivers, mountains and thick forests. It was when we arrived back at Dunedin Railway Station - which has to be one of the most photographed landmark in NZ - the train stopped for us to have a look at its magnificent architecture and some of the buildings in the surrounding area which were complementary in their design.

Oh, and for chocolate lovers there's a huge Cadbury's factory close to the station and, yes, they do tours. We'd had a great day out and it was one of our best tours so far on this South American and Pacific Adventure on Arcadia.

I met guy in Dunedin who drove a train
He tells me his name
is Billy, puffing Billy
Step aboard, We can go all the way
To the end of the line
Standing room only
"What in these shoes?"   I don't do standing!

AKAROA

An unexpected call here in Akaroa. It was the closest ships could get to Christchurch because of the devastating earthquakes which had destroyed most of the city. We had been due to go ashore in Lyttelton about 20 minutes out of Christchurch but were diverted to Akaroa. It was an unexpected bonus for us at least but you can't please everybody - there were grumbles.

Akaroa has a French feel about it - no wonder it was the French who were the early Europeans to discover what the Maori already had.

Akaroa is Maori for Long Harbour say the guidebooks. The French left their architectural imprint and it survives.

The ship organised tours into Christchurch (84k or a one and a half hour bus ride away).

But we had already decided long before we arrived in Akaroa we didn't want to gloat on the devastation that had befallen Christchurch and so we'd stay put. If we'd believed the ship's excursion "expert" Graham we would have been bored out of our tiny minds - he reckoned there was absolutely nothing to see or do in the village of just under 700 "you must take a tour".

What a fib! We found Akaroa to be beautiful and chic with lovely boutique shops, individually owned, and good cafes and restaurants. There was even a old London Routemaster double decker offering rides. There were plenty of nice routes for walking, and the Akaroa Head Lighthouse was a popular attraction.

The water was teeming with marine life and bird life on the shoreline. The properties by the water had stunning views of the harbour and the rolling hills beyond.

The terrain was very Lake District-ish! and the properties reminded MR MM of those he knew from visits to St Mawes in Cornwall.

In one shop selling French items I asked about a place to have lunch. Without hesitation the lady said try the fish at Bully Hayes. We did and it was excellent. We sat outside at tables and chairs by the pavement and watched the world go by for a while letting our meal settle. The village was teaming with people and not all were passengers from Arcadia.

The village attracts a summertime population of around 15,000. It not difficult to work out why! Akaroa had the feel of a sleepy village where time almost stood still.

Most of the buildings were constructed of wood and many were painted in vibrant colours. It matched the personality of the friendly locals we met. Akaroa was another place bathed in sunshine during our visit.

We walked a lot and passed many of the boutique shops. I managed some retail therapy - one of the most unusual items I spotted was a handbag that looked like a boot and had a stiletto heel.

I just had to have it; it was so different to all the other handbags I have with me on this cruise. I also found some unusual jewellery in silver with semi precious stones - all handmade - so bought two pairs as I didn't want to miss out.

Our sailaway happened as the sun was dropping out of the sky which created some spectacular colours over the rolling hills.

Moral of this story....if you're told by anyone connected with your cruise ship there is nothing to see or do in Akaroa, don't believe them - you're spoilt for choice. We would love to return.

WELLINGTON is not the best known city in New Zealand - that must surely be Auckland - but it is the capital.

I'd researched Wellington on the internet and booked a tour six months ahead of our visit with John's Hop On Hop Off bus tour which we had to pick up at the I.Site - the information office. We took the ship's shuttle into town and walked to the I. Site.(I. Sites are in towns and cities across NZ and are the main tourist information offices staffed by very helpful and knowledgeable men and woman). The one where we picked up John's Ho/Ho was in the Wellington City Council Complex - all very modern, clean and tidy.

Our tour was for ten people. The mini bus - or van as our driver Bruce called it - was very clean and newish. We knew none of the other passengers but did recognise a couple off the ship. We had a very good two hour informative tour. We decided once on we would not hop off and wait until it came around again. A wise move as most of the others were of a similar mind so there was only the odd vacant seat. Bruce took us to the main attractions - the Parliament buildings (one looked like a bee hive), museums, parks, a stop at the movie making centre

"Wellywood" (Wellington has a huge film making industry if you didn't know) where such classics as Hobbit, and Lord of the Rings were made. One lady passenger got off here meaning we had one empty seat.

We had a stop at Victoria Lookout where all of the passengers got out and climbed up to the actual lookout and what a view! We looked down on the city and beyond. Magnificent! After our tour we walked around the city - some of the old has been preserved - but a lot of the buildings are similar to ones that litter skylines in many cities around the world, sadly.

We found a diner called FinC - it was in an old building that had a carving in the stone above the entrance which read "Plumbers Merchants". We didn't care what it had been, it was modern, spotless, the food was good and service excellent.

We attempted to walk off the calories but came across a Movenpick ice cream parlour. This is the only ice cream I eat and it's delicious! Did some retail therapy and bought Manuka Honey body creams. A girl needs her pampering things. Then back on the shuttle to the ship. An interesting city - reckoned to be the windiest in the Southern Hemisphere - where you really need more time to take in most of its sights and sounds. Sailaway was in daylight and we got wonderful views from the ship of the shore and the hills around. Another memorable exit from port.

NAPIER - one of the great destinations and this time passengers really did need to be treated better by P&O planners who allowed only four hours for our trip ashore. Many passengers were upset, others were outraged and some were very angry at this half day in port when other cruise lines they knew spend a full day there. Ships, apparently, pay port charges by the hour in Napier, so you don't need to be a maths genius to work out why P&O stay such a short time....money, money, money it would seem rules!

Napier, what a gorgeous place. This town was destroyed by an earthquake and fires in 1931. It was rebuilt in the Art Deco style. I just love Art Deco and was blown away the minute I set foot in town with its beauty and its charm and it was still not eight in the morning!

We walked around the town which is pristine and all the wonderful Art Deco designs of the buildings and people dressed up in the style of the early 20th century. Fantastic, and what a friendly bunch they all were. Napier could have been a film set. We took a two hour tour (no time for a longer one thanks to P&O). We bought the tickets on shore, again in a minibus for ten just like in Wellington. It was simple, easy and very efficient.

At the shuttle bus drop off point (an Art Deco building by the water's edge) there were a line of desks set up by native Kiwis offering tours.

We wandered down the line looking what each had to offer. We settled for absolutedetours and we discovered the man selling the ticket was John Ford husband of the company's owner Yvonne.

Art Deco Official bus tour www.absolutedetours.co.nz is Yvonne's company name and she was a mine of information. Yvonne and her family were born and raised and have lived in Napier all their lives. In fact when the earthquake struck, she said, he father was just 15 years old. He helped in rescuing some who were trapped. She told many stories and we saw wonderful architecture at every turn. Our ticket for the tour gave us entry into the Art Deco Centre where they show the earthquake and its aftermath. We did not take advantage because I have been in two 6.7 earthquakes over the years and it is something I prefer not to be reliving. However, the rest of the tour was just great.

Yvonne, because she had lived nowhere else, knew every nook and cranny of Napier - and we visited most of them. We were told how some of the buildings shore side had been "gentrified"; how fishermen's cottages had been swept away and replaced by modern buildings - this was outside the main town.

One of the tourist attractions is the national tobacco company's former factory. It has been preserved; its boardroom all carved oak paneling and in beautiful condition. In 1953 a famous "couple" were shown around Napier - they were The Queen and Prince Philip. I met Bertie the Napier ambassador all dressed up as though he was going to the Henley Regatta. He was great; all those we met were just so helpful, so friendly and so open. Just brilliant - a great shame we couldn't have spent longer in Napier. It's on our places to revisit list.

I bumped into Linda, a friend I had made on the ship, in fact she and her husband - from Yorkshire - were on our original table when we had the infamous row/eviction order! She and the couple from Dorset who were also on that table all stayed friends with us. I liked Linda very much. She and her husband, Graham, had been to Napier before and she had purchased an Art Deco brooch.

That reminded me I had one. I said why don't we dress up for tonight's dinner Art Deco-style? We took Napier onto the ship so-to-speak! Passengers stopped us and said they didn't realise it was a dress up night - it wasn't of course, Linda and I happened to have all the gear for a roaring twenties look. I think P&O missed a trick there as they could have had a roaring twenties theme night.

AUCKLAND, once the capital of New Zealand was our last port of call in the country. A couple of MR MM's friends from Leeds in West Yorkshire had emigrated to Auckland a year or so before Arcadia arrived.

MR MM had been in touch via email and they wanted to meet up and show us around. Too good an opportunity to miss. Bill came to meet us off the ship but his wife, Stephanie, wasn't available because of a prior engagement until noon.

That worked out well. Bill talked and walked us to the ferry terminal because we wanted to go to Devonport (not the one in the UK!). But like its UK namesake it has strong naval connections. It's New Zealand's main naval base but is best-known for its harbour side dining and drinking establishments and its heritage charm. Bill left us temporarily and took a ferry back to his home while we bought tickets to ride to Devonport. Hey ho, they offered discounts for seniors, even visiting seniors, on the ferry (NZ$18 return). We were quids in already!

When the ferry docked in Devonport we spotted three Clydesdales harnessed to a wagon - a form of transport from yesteryear that offered rides around the central area.

140

Dan owned these horses and the cart and told us the horses were called Guy, Star and Ernie - Guy and Star, he said, were full brothers and had been bred by him. All had pooh bags so no hope of any Kiwi getting a shovel full to put on the roses! The ride in the cart was a grand experience that cost us NZ$10 each for a 15 minute saunter around the centre of Devonport.

We did some walking and exploring before we met up with Bill and Stephanie for lunch. They took us to a cafe at the Naval Base Museum - a popular place with the locals. In fact we had to scratch around for a vacant tables it was so busy. We grabbed one before the waitress had time to clear the dirty plates - we did the job for her so we had a table. There was a varied menu - we all went for the catch of the day. Well, it couldn't be much fresher than when it's served by the ocean. Stanley Point was the next stop on our whistle stop look at Auckland. The views from here were stunning. It once was the site of guns positioned to defend Auckland. The remains are still there. We said our goodbyes to Bill and Stephanie but still had some time to spare before the ship sailed so we headed to an impressive building from yesteryear right on the water's edge.

It was the Ferry Building dwarfed by the skyscrapers all around. Inside there was a restaurant. The Harbourside Ocean Bar & Grill. The bar had a terrace with views over the ferry terminal and across the harbour. Just the ticket! The ideal place for a sundowner! The Sun Princess cruise ship was in harbour when we arrived in the morning. We watched her depart, and the ferries coming and going as the sun began to leave the sky.

A nice ending to our stay in New Zealand.

In Devonport I met a man called Dan who was fun
He had three horses each with a big bum
They wore bum bags to collect their mess
Does my bum look big in this?
one horse asked
No, you look very horsey and chic, the biz
Thanks says the horse. Now let's go trot.
"What In these shoes?"
These are my best tart's trotters!

I loved both Australia and New Zealand - wonderful countries - if only I were thirty years younger I could live there quite easily.

SOMOA, PAGO PAGO AND APIA

PAGO PAGO......so different they named it twice! Not really and anyway it's pronounced Pango Pango - the early Christian missionaries carried printing presses and moveable type so they could print phonetic Bibles in the local languages. Because the language spoken in the islands was pronounced with an "n" following every "a" the missionaries didn't have enough "n's". It was implied that every time you saw an "a" treat it as "an" - hence Pango Pango for Pago Pago. Clear?

I first called here on a cruise in 1981. It was a shanty town with one hotel - The Rainmaker.

I seem to remember The Rainmaker had been damaged by a cyclone around that time had suffered some damage. American Samoa, for that is what the island is called, was just a rugged rainforest. I remember nobody seemed to wear shoes. No chance of me buying any here! Little has changed.

The Rainmaker is a shadow of its former self - still standing but most of it is shut, and it has been for years apparently. Such a shame because it is in a fabulous location.

There has been some development but a lot of that got damaged in the tsunami of 2009.

There is a huge tuna fish canning industry in Pago Pago but I don't recall if it was there the first time I visited. If the wind is in a certain direction you can smell the tuna factory even before you enter the harbour.

Still it provides employment and food for the masses in countries across the world.

But there's another character from the past who is immortalised here - Miss Sadie Thompson described as a "fallen woman" who arrived in Pago Pago to start a new life. She was from San Francisco - a smoking, drinking, jazz listening young prostitute (her story was made in to at least one film in the 1950) who "set the island alight".

She has an hotel named after her, and her story still fascinates many who visit American Samoa to this day. We'd decided to do a walkabout. Once off the ship and through the quayside market we turned right and kept on going past Sadie Thompson's, past some shops and into a market that sold fruit and veg and clothing, and things to put in your hair like beautiful silk flowers all hand-made by the stallholder I was told.

I bought some because they were the best I had seen on the voyage. We strolled further along the harbour's edge and came to a good spot for a photo for my cruise blog.

As MR MM took a shot a man on the footpath close by shouted "shall I take a photo of the two of you?" I said No thank you - just needed one on my own for my blog.

As MR MM was filming harbour scenes on his camcorder the "mystery" gent and I set off walking and chatting. In our conversation he revealed he worked for P&O and was on board Arcadia until we reached Hawaii - one of his favourite destinations.

And what did he do for P&O? He was a captain - captain of the Azura. His name was Paul Brown who was born and raised in Hull. It was very hot by now and we turned to head back towards Arcadia when MR MM spotted a brightly-coloured building that was an hotel with a bar/restaurant attached. It looked closed but the owners soon swung into action when we asked for some cool, refreshing drinks - fruit punches all round! They were so good - full of fruit including coconut - we had more.

Captain Brown and I had quite a few photos taken together; he was intrigued when we told him Frankie, the resident pianist on Azura, was someone we knew and kept in touch with. Paul left to head back to the ship, we stayed on shore a while longer having a better look around but agreed to meet for drinks on the next formal night. We still had some hours to spare before sailaway but it was too hot to continue walking under the blazing sun so we decided to take a taxi for a bit of a sightseeing tour of American Samoa.

We wanted to see what was past the tuna canning factory - we were not disappointed. The island was lush with vegetation and stunningly beautiful - everything you'd expect in a South Pacific Island paradise like palm trees growing by the edge of the clear blue waters and golden, sandy beaches.

We'd been told of the Bare Foot Bar outside Pago Pago and were within sight of the place so thought we'd give it a whirl.

We found half of the ship's passengers had already beaten us to the bar and there was a queue waiting to get in...but then came the rub - there was a US$10 cover charge per head. There appeared to be no vacant tables and there were too many people in for our liking and given that we had to pay US$20 for the "privilege" we gave it a miss.

Our taxi driver reckoned the cover charge was a new thing to him! We weren't so sure especially as we went further along the coastline and came to another bar this one called The US$2 Beach Bar which had a cover charge, of, er, US$2.

We declined to pay that also. We had water with us - we drank that. But the scenery along the coast road was stunning.

All right some of the houses were in need of repair or in some cases rebuilding but that added to the atmosphere of the island we thought.

Back we headed towards the ship and something clicked in my head - I remember when doing my research on American Samoa that I'd read part of The Rainmaker Hotel had been refurbished and was open as a bar and diner. So that's where we headed. The restored part is now known as Sadies by the Sea. (yes that same Sadie who has a hotel to her name). Bright, airy, modern and busy, mainly with passengers and crew from Arcadia. We went in and ordered two fruit punches after enjoying the ones in the morning. However, the ones here were very disappointing, inferior in fact. No fresh fruit and no fresh coconut! Still I was glad I'd been back to the place even though, apart from Sadies, The Rainmaker was in such a derelict condition. May be one day some entrepreneur will invest and open the hotel again.

I've mentioned how when leaving the ship passengers had to walk through a lot of covered stalls selling all manner of items but mostly clothing of varying quality - some of it "made locally" - in China!

The women in American Samoa, Fiji, Tonga and Samoa are not the only one to wear skirts - the men do to! They're called lava lava in this part of the Pacific and are one piece of cloth that wraps around the body and is tied at the waist. They come in bright colours and more solid colours - like black with a pin-stripe for men who wear them on formal occasions like going to church or for weddings and funerals. And they are a very comfortable garment in tropical climates.

I always try and dress like a local especially anywhere in the Pacific because the colours are a bit like me - lively, vibrant sometimes outrageous! MR MM, who has a colourful streak for ties and bow ties and shoes, thought he'd buy himself a lava lava for a bit of a laugh (and he did). He knew Jean Louis, husband of Spanish Lady (two of our dinner companions), had bought one the year before when they were in Samoa. And Jean Louis had been "threatening" to wear his one night for dinner while Arcadia was in the Pacific. He hadn't by the time we'd reached American Samoa, so MR MM thought he'd keep Jean Louis "company" by wearing a lava lava, too.

The man I met in Pago Pago he said I will
take you to the most beautiful place on earth
On to at the famous Barefoot bar. OK lets go.
What! in these shoes I ain't taking these off in any bar!

148

APIA, is the capital of Samoa which was called German Samoa from 1900 to 1919.

It is not to be confused with its near neighbour American Samoa - the two are different places. It is rather like Pago Pago in American Samoa but more civilised. In fact just how much more developed but not in an ugly way you can see at the sail-in. We walked again. Apia was full of local character and characters.

We dropped in to the local markets - the fish market by the main bus station was fascinating - so many fish unknown to us and some which were. They were sea-fresh having been landed early morning the day of our arrival. Pity the chefs from Arcadia didn't go and buy up the lot. But they didn't. There were a lot of dogs wandering around without collars - don't know whether this signified they were strays. They didn't bother anyone just went their own way.

We passed a corrugated building with large lettering in white which read "Hole in the wall" - it was a bar not an ATM. I think there is a pub of a similar name set into the Bar walls in High Petergate in York, the Yorkshire one not New York. I was dressed in a tropical coloured outfit with flowers in my hair. Two local ladies stopped me and asked if they could have their picture taken with me. Happy to oblige!

149

Evidence of the damage done by the recent tsunami and a cyclone early in 2013 were still visible - especially the large number of big tree trunks along the foreshore road - the trees must have been huge but became victims of the extreme weather.

They were though showing signs of life - green shoots were appearing. We came across an open air tattoo studio where clients were getting their body art work done by a chap holding a hammer and hitting a nail. Oh, he had some dye as well. Looked painful and probably was. The man on the receiving end had something clenched between his teeth and four others appeared to be holding him down on the ground.

By now we'd seen enough and headed for Aggie Grey's Hotel allegedly an "institution" in Samoa. Aggie was the daughter of English chemist William Swan and his Samoan wife Pele. She set up her hotel in 1930 and was a "big hitter" on the local social and business scene, or so the story goes. She died in 1988 aged 99.

The hotel got some if not most of its fame after featuring in the film South Pacific. On the walls hung framed, fading newspaper cuttings of "famous" guests and visitors. We called in hoping for some lunch and a cool drink. We got the drink fairly quickly but had to ask for the food three times so slow was the service yet the place wasn't busy. We'd ordered fresh fish and thought they must have sent a man out in a boat to catch it first!

The staff were unfriendly - maybe they thought passengers from Arcadia weren't "up to their standards"! We wouldn't call again in Aggie Grey's should we ever be in Samoa - overrated and overpriced was our verdict although the liveried front of house staff were colourful in their uniforms.

The hotel has a nice setting though, looking out as it does on to lines of coconut palms, the harbour and the bay.

MEN IN SKIRTS - BANNED!

Hemline - by Western standards the skirts were modest; midi, not mini, but they did show some bare flesh although it was not done to excite either sex on board the P&O liner Arcadia. And although we were sailing in the South Seas, the garments were not garish; they were quite boringly plain in fact. And something worn by men in Polynesia. They are called lava lava.

They could have been emblazoned with images of exotic flowers or colourful birds as the liner sailed the tropical, turquoise Polynesian waters around American Samoa, and Samoa. Indeed one wag, after spying the skirts, said cruelly the wearers looked like the Two Fat Ladies of British television fame. A matter of opinion and one with which I disagree.

In fact the two who donned this attire are arbiters of good dress sense and respectful of fellow passengers sensitivities even though many of them look to have forgotten to pack anything other than attire from Primark or Matalan. I can only speculate it must be something to do with baggage allowances on aircraft and nothing to do with a deficit of style or imagination.

152

Now I have a confession, the two who wore these skirts - or lava lava (the Samoan national dress) - are red-blooded European males who are married and have NO interest in cross-dressing or becoming transvestites. They believed they were dressed to suit their surroundings of tropical islands, golden sandy beaches where palm trees sway gently in the breeze and where people knock back fancy cocktails by the bucket full!

True, they dressed to impress but not to kill and they certainly didn't pretend they were sex-bombs!

But having seen how the Samoan men dressed they decided to follow suit. In fact one of them bought his lava lava in 2011 when he and his wife first visited American Samoa. He liked the experience because it gave him a lot of comfort in the steamy climate. Just why the lava lava is de rigueur for Samoan males. And they've had generations to get their dress sense right.

It's not just the horny-handed sons of toil from the coconut groves who wear the lava lava. I spotted business types, most members of the local constabulary and bankers wearing these skirts and nobody batted an eye lid.

However, when the two passengers went independently with their wives (one of them being me) to Arcadia's Meridian Restaurant for dinner wearing their lava lava they were banned from entry until they followed that night's "dress code" of, er,

153

evening casual or country and western. I ask you country and western in the South Pacific! Give me a break. They were told by one of the restaurant managers curtly: "We've had tropical night already". Only one when we're in the tropics for days on end! Beggars belief. But it happened.

Now on Arcadia, "evening casual" looks to be interpreted as wear what you like no matter its condition. One of those refused entry was MR MM and the other a kind, generous Frenchman called Jean Louis who along with his wife, were at our table. I was unaware that Jean Louis had been refused entry several minutes earlier and had returned to his cabin to meet the requirements of P&O's "style police" who obviously are alive and well and living at 100 Harbour Parade in Southampton (the cruise line's UK HQ) but whose tentacles, and diktats, stretch across the world on P&O ships.

MR MM protested to no avail. He pointed out politely (even though he was fuming inside) that he was wearing what 90 per cent of the men on Samoa did and as we were still within earshot of the island he believed his outfit suited the occasion and our exotic location. It was, in my humble opinion, both Samoan "evening casual" and Samoan "semi-formal" (even "formal" for MR MM's lava lava was black with a pin stripe).

One interpretation of P&O's dress code, set by some anonymous alleged "fashionista" thousands of mile away from where we were, fits all it seems. Well, that's what it looked like from our cabin; No flexibility; No consideration of local traditions or fashions; what a pity. The banning of "skirts" worn by men does, though, raise an important question. What if one of our haggis-loving Highland brethren went to that restaurant on Arcadia wearing a kilt (other than on a formal night) would he be similarly denied entry until he got out of his skirt and "dressed proper?" I rest my case!

Yours, "fallen" hemline. AKA MR MM.

We were four days at sea in very windy but hot condition before we reached Hawaii. En route there'd been another Crossing the Line Ceremony P&O style which to me and many others was no style at all. No passengers take part (elf and safety the reason cited) yet on Cunard liners passengers are positively encourage to have a go. Even the entertainers have been known to take part in the initiation ritual which dates back at least a couple of centuries and go from being a Pollywog to a Shellback.

My initiation into the deep was when King Neptune visited the SS Rotterdam in 1980 and my first time crossing the line.

*On a formal night we met up with Captain Paul Brown of Azura who was on a sailor's holiday and I presented him with a Yorkshire Flag which he promised he'd wave at sailaways on his ship. Yes, Captain Paul Brown does sailaways - we'd not seen Arcadia's master, Sarah Breton at any sailaway so far and we were on the homeward leg of our 99-day voyage.

*We were about to enter America and every traveller knows what that means - facing Homeland Security. It's an experience even most Americans dread. All went swiftly and they were actually friendly Americans. We had a laugh with our man. I couldn't sign forms so left them blank but MR MM was allowed to sign for me in front of the officer. I wore a pretty floaty flowered dress and a big flower in my hair plus my Lei. The immigration men said I looked great. I did it for a giggle and to cheer them up as they can be grumpy!

MR AND MRS GRUMPY

..and there were plenty of them on this Arcadia cruise. Maybe it was something to do with being away for their normal surroundings or maybe they're normally rude and aggressive. In all my years of cruising I've never come across so much bitchiness, or backbiting and I hope I never do again. I have scores of examples. Here are a sample. After leaving immigration in Hawaii I went back to my cabin.

I passed a couple who had their cabin a few down from ours. The woman stared at my arm which was in a sling in the Lei. I overheard her say to her husband: "Well, Nobody is going to mistake her as a tourist"! He said "how ridiculous"! Am I bovvered, I thought? There are some very rude, boring people on this ship. One guy stopped me after a sailaway party to tell me he hated the colour of my hair. It was horrid. So I told him "you weren't the person who I had in mind when I dressed this morning"!

He huffed and moved on shouting no wonder you have a bad arm! I was wearing the multi coloured wig I'd bought in Recife at the time. He just didn't get it! After my accident in The Beagle Channel I found the constant rude comments made by passengers about my wrist really tiresome and it did get me down.

It got so bad that we had a table for two at lunchtimes in the main dining room just so I could get away from the constant barrage of questions about my wrist. The most common being the quip:"oh what have you done? Take more water with it next time!" I reckon the passengers who said that - and they must have numbered over 100 - have brain cells missing.

Even out on the deck reading a book people would shout "excuse me, excuse me what have you done"?

They even tapped me on the head when I was laid down sunbathing and asked the same questions. One guy even approached and shook my foot to get me to look up from my sun lounger and asked the same question. Is there any wonder I got to the end of my tether? Even walking in the streets of Noumea in New Caledonia we passed a couple of middle aged passengers and because the pavements were so narrow we stepped into the road so they could keep the path.

The man said "broken your wrist then?" To which MR MM replied: "No, it's her foot!" and we carried on walking. They were left looking non-plussed.

But the worst incident happened in the Belvedere Restaurant - the self service place on board Arcadia. We had been in port all day, were late back and decided to skip dinner and just have a snack. I was discussing with MR MM what I'd like from the buffet because he had to bring my food, serve it and cut it up when I heard a woman's voice from a table down the line shouting "excuse me. excuse me". Thinking it was someone wanting a waiter I ignored it.

Then a tap on my shoulder. It was the man with her. "We want to know what is wrong with your arm?" "Nothing", I replied and ignored him. MR MM stood up preparing to go and get the food from the buffet and said to the couple "she has had two doctors' opinions and isn't in need of a third!"

MR MM then went to get the food. That remark must have really angered them for the woman shouted louder than before:" Oh! get her! who does she think she is?" She spewed out more bile and I was livid. I stood up and turned to them and said: "Enough, just leave me in peace to have my dinner". The man with her said: "Now, now, don't be like that we only wanted to know what was wrong with you." I asked why they needed to know and said :"you can see I have a problem why do you need know about it?

"Do you ask everyone you see with an injury or who are disabled what their problem is?" To which he replied: "because we care about you!" I said "no you don't, you do not know me from Adam you are just being bloody nosey!" To which the woman replied: "Oh! listen to her she is not from our neck of the woods (not sure what that had to do with it other than she was trying to talk all posh like MRS Bucket from that British TV sitcom).

More words were exchanged and I told them to back off and leave me alone as I was trying to make the most of the bad situation I was in. They still didn't shut up. The woman said: "you always draw attention to it as you wear fancy flowers in your

159

sling or have something on your arm". I said:"listen here, If you had something stuck in your arm that looked like a Meccano set you would cover it up as well. Now back off and mind your own business."

I turned back to our table to find MR MM back with the food and cutting it up. While all this had been going on I hadn't noticed two other passengers had joined our table. MR MM was speaking to them. I apologised for my outburst but they said they hadn't witnessed it.

Shortly afterwards the couple left the table behind us and as they passed our table she gave me a "two finger salute" and went "na! na! na! na"! You couldn't make it up. It was just unbelievable. Are these really the sort of passengers that P&O attracts these days?

HONOLULU: I GOT LEI'D IN HAWAII !

March 17 is the day the Irish celebrate their patron saint - Saint Patrick. And how! That was the day we docked in Honolulu. MR MM had no desire to go to see Pearl Harbour so we decided to take a walk. After leaving the quayside we headed across a main road and straight ahead. It looked as though the streets were in a grid system like in New York. We took our chance and were not disappointed. We walked through what looked like the University quarter and then came across the distinctive building that is the base for the YWCA (the Young Women's Christian Association). The coffee from the refectory smelled and tasted delicious.

From there we headed for The Iolani Palace, the official residence of the last ruling King and Queen of Hawaii - King Kalakaua and Queen Lili 'uokalani. Since 1978 it has been a museum and is open to the public - but being a Sunday it was closed at least to those not on official tours. We found KAWAIAHAO CHURCH, also known as the Westminster Abbey of the Pacific.

Being Sunday the place was packed but we found some seats right at the back after being told we were dressed OK - MR MM had shorts which are frowned upon in some places of worship. The preacher was an evangelical type - his sermon spoken with real passion. Reminded MR MM of sermons by the late Rev Dr Ian Paisley.

And the congregation were in good voice. One hymn was sung to the tune of Danny Boy - appropriate we thought for St Patrick's Day. On this part of our walkabout we also went to the State Capital Building, the island's Parliament.

What an impressive if modern structure. We were fascinated by its architecture. Well worth a look if you are ever in Honolulu. But we were in Honolulu and just had to visit its most famous attraction - Waikiki Beach. But how to get there?

We saw a bus stop on a main road and waited. Sure enough along came a bus with Waikiki Beach on its destination board. We jumped on. "A dollar each" said the driver. We had the correct fare (they don't give change so if you had $5 that's what you'd pay).

It was a 30 minute journey and it took in some of the suburbs towards Waikiki. But we jumped off before the beach because MR MM spotted a detour sign and a lot of vintage cars and people dressed in green - little green men and women!

162

It was a smart move because we had stumbled, by accident, across the starting point of the St Patrick's Day Parade, Hawaii style. And what style - it had a real party atmosphere with vintage cars, marching bands and dozens and dozens of people dressed for the occasion. Very impressive. It kicked off bang on noon. We stayed put on the same spot to watch it from beginning to end and it took over one hour to pass us. The crowds of onlookers numbered 10 deep as far as the eye could see.

We were handed green necklaces and shamrocks by the Budweiser team (didn't realise they were Irish!) which was just the ticket.(we kept them around our neck when back on board - we were "honorary" Irish for the day!).

The parade gone we still had to make it to Waikiki Beach. Once again we set off and walked. We just followed the crowd. They had the same idea. We eventually got to the Hotel Moana on the Beach - an old colonial type hotel that looks rather similar to the Peninsula in Hong Kong.

We "tested" the cocktails and then ordered lunch. I had blackened fish which was delicious and spicy. I needed a spice kick after weeks of very bland food on Arcadia. More walking followed and some retail therapy. Hawaiian matching top and skirt for $19 or two for $35.

163

I only bought one which is not like me at all! Shame as it is quite nice but we will be in Honolulu next year God willing! We left port at midnight - to see the Honolulu skyline all lit up was something to behold.

IF YOU GO TO SAN FRANCISCO

San Francisco and the weather was perfect - no mist or haze so wonderful views of the Golden Gate Bridge. We sailed in at 7am and I was up on deck watching from around 6-15am. Bitterly cold but I was lovely and warm because I had the right clothing on unlike most others who rolled out of bed and wore shorts and fit flops. Anoraks were not even enough to keep the biting winds at bay. I wore my full length duvet coat and my UGG Boots, gloves and a hat plus my hood. So no chill factor for me. Once the sun was up the temperatures rose to a pleasant 20C.

We docked at Pier 35 almost next door to Fisherman's Wharf (Pier 39) and went to look at the sea lions that are famous (or infamous) at Pier 39. I could have watched them all day. They were so funny playing and falling into the sea. Very smelly though so you can't hang around too long. We made our way to the ferries and got one to Sausalito - a 15 minute ride away. We sat on the top deck. It was freezing with the biting wind coming off of the sea.

We sailed past Alcatraz. MR MM and I had both been to San Francisco before so done all the usual tourist bits like Alcatraz.

But we'd never been to Sausalito. What an impressive and beautiful place - everything about Sausalito screamed quality - the marina, the properties, the shops, the cafes and the seafront walk.

All rather twee in many ways but a very restful place with no hustle and bustle. You have to check the ferry timetable closely. We discovered when we got to Sausalito the last ferry back to Fisherman's Wharf was at 2-55pm. We took an earlier one. We got senior discounts without any trouble. We'd decided to have lunch at Fisherman's Wharf. The whole area was buzzing - street musicians played just a few metres apart. There were crowds galore. Its trams, its candy floss sellers, its junk food, its shops selling tat reminded me of Blackpool but with sunshine!

That's not being disrespectful to Blackpool which has undergone some major redevelopment in recent years, especially on its seafront. It's classy now to what it was.

We'd decided to eat at a large restaurant called Fisherman's Grotto. It looked nice from the outside, had proper tablecloths and it had linen napkins and I wanted to have Dungeness lobster which it offered. But later we wished we'd given the place a miss. We seated ourselves (the place was empty) but a waiter eventually came, he was Chinese. Then another waiter arrived who sounded Eastern European.

They were not very helpful. We ordered my lobster and MR MM had Calamari. Mine arrived - it was a huge looking lobster in its shell and had a side dish of melted butter. It had been steamed. It sat on a bed of white lettuce and looked very bland and it turned out to be very bland indeed. It was a bad choice. I hadn't given a thought to how I was going to break into the claws when I ordered it with having my broken wrist to contend with, and it's not something MR MM likes doing but he did his best. It was not a good idea for me to have lobster after all plus it was totally tasteless, very disappointing and expensive at US$42 for the lobster alone.

I would not recommend this place. Looking back I suppose the warning signs were there before we entered the place - there was no one dining. It was more Fisherman's grotty than Grotto! After the meal we caught the tram to Union Square - $1.50 for the two of us at senior rates and the tickets were good for several hours. Excellent value!

We headed for Macy's so I could stock up on Clinique makeup - it is cheaper in the USA. Only trouble is Macy's 10 per cent visitor discount doesn't apply to makeup or perfume. Shame!

Did a bit of shopping and walked all around the Union Square area before taking the tram to Nob Hill. Cost $6 each.

This is the tram that takes you to the steepest street. Something new we discovered - the Fisherman's Wharf area and Pier 39 closes at 10pm . We went for a walk at that time and it was like a ghost town. I felt sorry for crew members leaving the ship for a wild night - if they stayed around Fisherman's Wharf they would be very, very disappointed.

Second day in San Fran we caught a tram (a wonderful means of transport) and went to the Bay Bridge area for the markets at Pier One. It was only a few stops down the line but MR MM loves travelling on trams.

This part of the San Francisco waterfront is far more classy than the piers around Fisherman's Wharf. It was buzzing with atmosphere. In the open air street market good quality crafts were on sale. All the stallholders were licensed craftsmen and women who'd made what they were offering. There was some nice handmade jewellery, some interesting paintings and unusual ceramics. It most certainly wasn't junk.

Across the road the old Pier building has become an indoor market - a lot of the shops and stalls sold organic this or eco that. It was heaving. The cafes were bursting at the seams they were so busy. We decided to walk back towards the ship because on the way down on the tram we had spotted a few what looked like interesting restaurants on the waterfront.

We looked at their menus and settled for one that was called - The Waterfront! The food was of a very high quality and the service matched the food.

A bonus was the stunning views out to a jetty with yachts in a marina. All the waiters were in livery, they were exceptionally polite, skilled at their jobs and all had a smile. And at just US$ 16 each for a main course the price was right, too. Highly recommended. This dining experience at The Waterfront certainly made up for the disappointment we'd had 24 hours earlier at Fisherman's Grotto.

We walked off the calories by going once again to Pier 39 to see the sea lions. Just a short walk from Pier 35 there is a Safeway supermarket. I was able to stock up on fresh blueberries to have with my breakfast. I have to say I haven't enjoyed many things apart from the ports of call on this cruise. I am restricted with my broken wrist so activities since my fall in the tap class have been non-existent. However, I have really love the sailaway parties. I like to dress up in the theme of a place so when we were in our second port of call in Recife, Brazil, back in January and before my fall, I'd bought a wig like the ones the locals wear for carnivals. I started a trend. Now about 10 ladies, and even a few guys, dress up for sailaways.

The cruise entertainment staff on Arcadia are just amazing, so full of energy and fun and they get the whole ship going. The sailaway from San Fran was very good; we all sang as we went under the Golden Gate Bridge. Most of those dressers up had a hippy and flower power look. It was great. Memorable for all the right reasons.

MEXICO

P&O cancelled our planned port call in Acapulco at Christmas yet other lines were still using the city. P&O claimed it was for "our safety". So the lines that are still using it were putting their passengers at risk? I don't think so. Huatulco, is the latest resort area created from scratch by Fonatar, Mexico's national tourism development agency.

Huatulco Bays are situated at the foothills of the Sierra Madre Mountains in the State of Oaxaca. Along the shoreline are nine bays and 36 beaches. Playa Santa Cruz was where the ship docked and it was a short walk to the bustling beach and cafes and there were shops galore! The port has a long quayside and by the dock gates a sniffer dog checked passengers bags. We'd been warned not to take food ashore. However, as most people would not have been fed for 30 minutes many ignored the warning and packed a take away just in case they needed sustenance. The dog sussed them of course - good boy! I reckon passengers who took food hadn't reckoned on the Mexican authorities being as strict as those in Australia about taking food items ashore. How stupid. The food was confiscated;

what a pity they didn't levy an on-the-spot fine or confine those offenders to the ship by refusing them access ashore.

Playa Sana Cruz is an eco built town like most of this area specially to attract and cater for the tourists. It had a certain charm and I found it very pleasant and relaxing, with friendly locals and lots of beach activities and beach side cafes along with a marina and a village square.

Jewellery, silver in particular, was very nice especially when set with Indian turquoise stones. There was a nice little church in the centre of the plaza that we popped into and spent a few quiet moments.

But I needed a new dress for the sailaway party as "Pan's People" (that's what those of us who dress up at sailaways have been "christened") would be dressing up for the sailaway. For this sailaway to be authentic we needed something like a sombrero (we had a cult following which included Neil Oliver, the best Cruise director at sea). I found a cheap dress for US$20 and some really nice long shell bead necklaces and earrings for US$10. I bought a large straw hat and I decorated it with bits of glitz out of my own things.

I used a strip of shiny gift wrap and some sequined material I had spare from a dress I had.

I stuck it all on the hat with one hand and viola! I had a hat! The real thing were over $65 - and very heavy.

We had a very good day out in this port; I liked the place a lot. And, yes, the usual suspects dressed up for another wonderful sailaway party. Later that evening details of an alleged incident spread like wildfire. A guy ended up getting very drunk and threw a glass of red wine over another passenger and was rude to entertainment staff (who were the best people on the ship in my opinion) who went to calm the situation. The passenger who told me witnessed the incident and said he was restrained in handcuffs and locked away for the night. I never did find out if he was put off at the next port. Some very rude people onboard.

I met a guy in Mexico
He wanted to show me the way to go
Ten tequila sunrises and a dance on your hat
" In these shoes" I want none of that!

PANAMA CANAL

The transit was from West to East - a first for me. It didn't look that different from going the opposite direction. It was hot at the back of the ship so I stayed upfront on deck 6 where there was a good breeze. We came through here in 2011 and work was underway on the widening of the Canal - it is ongoing but difficult to work out what is happening because much of the construction is out of sight. People tried hard to spot a few alligators and wildlife - with moderate success.

It is always interesting watching the "mules" - the powerful train engines that keep ships stable as they enter and leave the locks. Miraflores Lock has a lookout point and when we've passed through on Cunard ships hundreds of spectators have gathered to watch from this vantage point. For Arcadia's transit I noticed only one guy there and he was a cleaner sweeping the terraces. A transit through this feat of engineering should be on everyone's tick list. BTW we had Island Princess for company throughout the transit - plenty of views of her back end!

EXCLUSIVE: Left behind on the banks of the Panama but don't tell the passengers!

Four charity bike riders and a bevy of photographers, all crew members of the P & O liner Arcadia, were stranded on land in the Panama Canal. A news blackout was ordered by Sarah Breton, the first female captain of the cruise line P & O, on the incident in the Panama Canal but that was lifted following the midway broadcast on April 1 - this is no April Fool's joke!

The Captain admitted the photographers and bikers were still on shore and claimed delays by "official agencies" had caused them to be left behind. These crew members didn't have their passports, they had no money and only the clothes they stood up in.

Arcadia was nearing the end of her 99-day world cruise and had transited the Panama Canal on Easter Sunday. In the run-up to the transit of the Canal, crew had been fund-raising for the Macmillan Cancer Support and the four volunteer cyclists had donned the distinctive green T-shirts for their charity bike ride.

There were updates on their progress as the ship made its way from the Pacific to the Caribbean and when the liner reached the Gatun Locks - the ones before entering the Caribbean - the four cyclists were clearly visible. They even waved at the ship.

As a mark of their achievement Captain Breton even blew the ship's whistle in salute.

175

But the ship sailed on out of the locks and towards the open ocean. The photographers from Arcadia, were seen at both the Miraflores Locks (the first to be negotiated on leaving the Pacific) and at Gatun Locks as they filmed footage of the liner's journey to put on the ship's video of the canal transit to sell in the photo gallery.

Passengers were told over the ship's public address system by Graham Howell, the port lecturer on Arcadia, that the cyclists would be picked up after the transit of the locks. He said they were going to be brought back on board by launch. Passengers first learned something was amiss when DJ Martin passed on comments from a passenger about the cyclists being left behind on his popular Radio Arcadia show in his Easter Sunday broadcast. Attempts by passengers to find out more from crew members were greeted with "we've been told to say nothing on the Captain's orders".

It was the talk of the ship. Probably realising she couldn't fool passengers any longer, Breton decided to say something. She used the midday broadcast and tried to put a positive spin on the incident by first praising the cyclists' efforts and telling passengers that already £5,170 had been raised for Macmillan and "the pledges were still being counted".

After more of what appeared to be a "softening up process" for the bad news she then admitted the cyclists along with the photographers had been delayed because "official agencies" had delayed the boat that was due to bring them all back to Arcadia. And by the time these "difficulties" had been resolved it was deemed sea conditions were too rough to make the transfer of the photographers and cyclists from launch on to the ship. This just didn't ring true! No explanation of who the "official agencies" were or what the "difficulties" she mentioned in her broadcast were.

She said they would all join at Arcadia's next port of call. But the next stop was the next day Curacao on April 2.

How they would travel without their passports was not explained. The liner's next call after Curacao was Bridgetown, Barbados, on April 4, (which was when and where they were repatriated).

Speculation was rife aboard Arcadia that the real reason "official agencies" delayed the boat due to bring the crew members back to the ship was because they wanted a bribe - a bung - but none of the crew members had any money to pay a bribe. How it was sorted out only Arcadia's "top brass" know and I'll bet they'll never tell. It cost P&O even if a bribe wasn't paid because the stranded passengers needed food, accommodation and air tickets and clothes. It put a dampener on what should have been a wonderful charitable event for a very worthy cause. And what happened to the bikes - they'd been bought brand new in San Francisco?

Ah, the perils of life at sea!

CURACAO.

We'd called in Curacao on the world voyage of Cunard's Queen Elizabeth in 2011. Then the capital, Willemstad, was a dump; there was dereliction all around but yet the place still had its charm. What a difference two years had made. Willemstad had been spruced up and what a good job those involved had done. Now it felt like a capital and yet it had maintained, even strengthened, its Dutch heritage. It was still though work in progress.

Willemstad is divided into four historic districts two of which are the Punda and the Otrobanda. You access from one to the other across a floating bridge in St Anna Bay.

It's an interesting structure built in 1888;and 16 floating pontoon boats support this floating bridge. To open and close it two powerful ship's motors are used. It was named after Dutch Queen Emma but known locally as the "Swinging Old Lady". In recent times the bridge has been restored to something like its original construction - all asphalt removed and replaced with original wooden boards.

Riffort was constructed to protect the harbour from invaders but it lost its military purpose in the early 20th century. Today it is a classy mall and has a split name Rif Fort. Ships dock either outside the harbour and close to the Rif Fort or inside the harbour close to the impressive Queen Juliana Bridge. Arcadia tied up inside the harbour. On our last visit we thought the Rif Fort area was very clean and tidy but the main shopping area on the Punda side looked tired; there was a lot of graffiti and the buildings needed of a lick of the colourful paint - the trademark of buildings in Curacao that give it its Dutchness.

This time we found tidy streets with pavement cafes and new shops and a shopping centre. The Church in the middle of town looked nice and bright in its yellow and white colours. Beyond the church a very scruffy area had been restored. A little park with modern structures now formed a centre piece near the church. Curacao is a haven of duty free shops. Many good jewellers and diamond stores and real designer watches on sale. Plenty of electrical goods like mobiles and cameras at very reasonable prices by European standards.

We went to the floating market and into the old town, passed through the municipal market before heading to the fort area where we'd spotted a little restaurant that had an interesting menu. We also found a Douwe Egbert's coffee shop (real Dutch coffee!).

On our walkabout town we discovered the Caribbean Princess was due and going to tie up at the jetty on the exposed part of the town by the Fort. The seas were rough but she made it in eventually. We ate at the pavement restaurant close by this jetty and didn't realise until we'd had our meal it was part of the Renaissance Hotel which had a huge casino.

MR MM went in and investigated (he didn't have a bet, he couldn't - I keep the money!) He said it was "heaving" and it was just two in the afternoon.

The food was very good. We popped into a jewellery shop that had some nice gem stones in its window display. We ended up buying a pendant, or I did as if I really needed another pendant. But when did "need" ever enter into the equation? We quizzed the shop manager about the vast improvement in the town. He gave us a bit of a history lesson.

Apparently around 30 years ago there had been riots in Willemstad and, he said, most of the Dutch people left the island never to return to their properties. That was why it always looked run down and scruffy at the back of the town. He said the government decided to restore the neglected properties and redesign part of the centre of Willemstad.

Now we knew why Willemstad had taken on a new look. It was very impressive. The history lesson over, and being a "few dollars lighter" after our visit to the jeweller, we headed back to the ship. A very enjoyable time we had in Willemstad. We will revisit I am sure.

OH! WE'RE GOING TO BARBADOS IN THE SUNNY CARIBBEAN SEA

But no time for us to soak up the sights and sounds of this holiday playground. It was straight to a clinic to see a surgeon who was (hopefully) going to remove the titanium bridge which had been on my right lower arm for over 10 weeks. It was put in place on Jan 29, 2013, in Punta Arenas, Chile, after I'd fallen the day before in a tap dancing class on board and smashed my right wrist to smithereens.

In recent weeks it had become uncomfortable and I went to see the ship's doctor. He X-rayed it and decided it was not fully healed. He sent a copy of the X-ray to P&O's medical chiefs in America asking for a "second opinion" but he never received a reply so he made arrangements for me to see an Orthopeadic specialist in Barbados. Transport was arranged by P&O's agent whom we met and handed over US$20 for use of a minivan. We were not alone. Two crew members in urgent need of dental treatment were also in the van along with a lady passenger who needed to consult a specialist.

The medical clinics all looked to be in one part of Bridgetown where the streets littered with sign boards for all kinds of private medical practices. The agent left us at the clinic. We had to call him to pick us up for the return journey.

I hadn't to wait more than a few minutes before I was ushered in to see the consultant. He examined the X-ray taken on the ship and decided the injury was not fully healed but he said the bridge should come off.

Before I'd been discharged from the clinic in Punta Arenas I'd been given a tool kit that was to be used to unscrew the contraption.

After inspecting the tool kit the consultant went ahead with the removal. It was like having your teeth pulled out without an anaesthetic! It was excruciating!!!! I gritted my teeth and clung to the couch. MR MM was very brave and filmed the whole thing without fainting. Poor wuss! he doesn't like Doctors - ahhh!
I was urged to wear a brace. The consultant wrote down the address where I could buy one which I passed to the ship's agent's driver when he picked us up. However, while he'd been away the ship's agent's driver had collected a few of his mates who needed dropping off here and there. We were given a "guided tour" with commentary along the way. We went off into the rural area of Bridgetown and headed up hills and inland.

We saw lots of shanty towns; some nice views looking down towards the coast.

Eventually we arrived at the rehabilitation centre. The staff were very helpful and caring. A girl measured me up for the brace. We left with my new arm accessory attached.

We had another detour back to town to drop off another mate of the ship's agent's driver. We had a laugh with the driver so we gave him a decent tip in US dollars. He'd been like our personal "tour" guide. It was the least we could do.

By the time we got back to the ship it was 2pm. We had really very little time to do anything but I was determined to get a Rasta-style hat for the sailaway. Not far from where the ship was berthed we came across some stalls outside a building that looked as though it was a market. One stall had knitted hats. Just the job for a sailaway outfit. Rose was the lady at the stall and she said she had hand-knitted all the hats she had for sale. I bought one in the loudest colours so I could make a real spectacle of myself at sailaway. And I did! That was our run ashore in Barbados - no time to look at any of the stunning beaches but at least we'd got to see something of the interior.

MORE ACTION AND ANGER ON ARCADIA.

There was a protest on a grand scale on the Arcadia's South American and Pacific Adventure as it was billed.

Or the Arcadia world cruise 2013 as it is called by all the crew. The anger was directed at P&O over the itinerary, or non-itinerary - the missed ports of call. Over 400 passengers turned up for the first meeting who felt cheated by P&O who'd cancelled Argentinean ports at the last minute and after we'd all paid for our cruise in full. Last minute being 12th of December, 2012, by letter - not email - right at the height of the Christmas postal rush. I learnt about the cancellation from an internet cruise forum!

Most of those at the meeting booked the voyage on Arcadia for its South American adventure - the main thrust of P&O's marketing of the voyage. Many Australians were on the segment from Southampton to Brisbane. All the ones I met were hugely upset at P&O for cancelling a whole country - Argentina - from the itinerary.

There were more than 600 doing the full 99 days - a large number considering when Queen Mary 2's full world in 2012 attracted only 250 passengers for the whole 108 days. But the cancellation of the Argentinean ports wasn't the only gripe with P&O. Once onboard a note was put on our beds telling us P&O had cancelled the call in Acapulco - "for safety reasons" yet other cruise lines were still using the port.

What started out as a natter or a moan on the deck between three people gathered steam and it was decided passengers should gather for a meeting to hear the views of others.

Some thought maybe a dozen would probably turn up but word, like Chinese whispers, spread throughout the ship. By 9-20am on the morning of the first meeting The Crow's Nest was full to capacity with standing room only. Amazing! Over 400 turned up which goes to show how many unhappy passengers there were on this tug boat. It was decided a letter should be written and handed to the executive Purser. Three guys volunteered for the job and another meeting was arranged. Even more people turned up for that. Names and cabin numbers were all added to a petition. Hundreds of names collected. I bet 80% of world cruisers were there. All livid with P&O.

This second meeting also discussed the non-return of port fees from the missed ports. People felt "ripped off", cheated and conned into buying a cruise that P&O knew well in advance it could not honour because one of its liners had been barred by the Argentineans over 12 months earlier because it flew a British flag. A protest letter was sent to the then boss of P&O, Carol Marlow (since sacked) but in reply she gave just platitudes. Many on the full voyage took legal action in the County Courts in the UK and got settlements.

TIME TO SAY GOODBYE ARCADIA.

Ponta Delgada - what a lovely place. It's in The Azores - a "remote" place many knew only from listening to BBC Radio 4 weather forecasts. We'd not been before so we wanted to see as much as possible only the weather was "iffy" as they say so we held off making a decision about whether to visit the green lake and the blue lake that are such a feature in the crater of an extinct volcano. We thought we'd try out the free wi-fi advertised in a cafe in the modern cruise terminal.

After we'd bought a coffee (and a pasty for MR MM) we found it wasn't that fast after all so we walked into town. Around the port there were plenty of taxi drivers touting for business. They wanted Euro 40 to take us to the lakes but the storm clouds still lingered so we again put off a decision. We found Ponta Delgada had a certain charm about it and shopping looked to be inexpensive compared with much of the rest of Europe. A word of warning - the pavements are often narrow and they are tiled black and white similar to those in Madeira and Lisbon and become very slippery when wet.

We saw some wonderful Portuguese-style architecture; people taking rides in a landau - they looked very elegant. By noon the clouds mostly cleared and the sun shone.

On our walk along the foreshore we passed an A board advertising a one hour open top bus tour that took in coast, country and town. A young lady standing by the board had tickets. They cost Euro 10 each and tours ran every hour. We took the one o'clock bus which wasn't very busy (well passengers from Arcadia would be eating their lunch on board - couldn't miss a meal might go hungry!) We got the upper deck front seats and MR MM videoed the ride.

It was a very good tour with excellent commentary and gave an insight to Ponta Delgada. Highly recommended and it didn't break the bank. After our bus ride it was time for something to eat but where? The pavement cafes were bursting at the seams with passengers we recognised from Arcadia (like us they were desperate for a decent meal).

Some passengers we knew at one pavement cafe recommended the fish. We found a vacant table and waited, and waited, and waited and when a waitress eventually arrive she said the fish was sold out. We got up and left.

We had looked at a very nice restaurant earlier on that was down some steps in a cellar. Its sign painted in green letters read Mercado do Peixe and underneath it claimed "Fish is king". Just what we wanted, fish.

We weren't bothered it had no outside seating we just wanted some fish. There were tables available.

What a good choice this turned out to be. The tables were covered in white linen clothes and set with good quality cutlery. The food was superb and the service was fast and efficient and all in an authentic, rustic cellar setting. It had many sections this cellar. You could imagine in days of old smugglers of liquor (not people) would hang out there.

All the food was cooked fresh and you could watch the chef at work. We had wonderful fresh calamari; MR MM had a few glasses of wine and we had two coffees and used their wi-fi and the bill came to just Euro 24 which we reckoned was the best value meal we'd had ashore all cruise. Another good port call - our last on this cruise. The sailaway was always going to be special given it was the finale. The weather was perfect and "Pan's People" (those of us who have dressed up for almost every sailaway since Tenerife) were at full strength.

Out came all the wigs, hats, beads, dreadlocks, bangles, flowers and the hula hula skirts for the very last time. It was very funny. Even Madam Captain who had been "invisible" most of this cruise put in an appearance. Not that she looked at us - she mostly only talked to the staff - we were mere fare paying passengers. Although she did deign to pose for photographs with a few passengers.

*I think some of the crew must have been demob happy after we left Ponta Delgada. Why else would they put up a sign saying "Welcome on board party" when it was a Farewell Party as everyone was getting off in Southampton? *We declined the offer from our waiters in the main dining room of the menus from the whole cruise -Thank you but no thank you. The food had been so unmemorable we didn't want for ever to be reminded just how plain it had been. Those questionaire/comment forms so beloved of cabin stewards. Ours handed me the form on the penultimate day at sea and said "excellent would be great". I thought you must be kidding!

Looking at the form I realised he (or someone) had already penciled in "excellent". He'd been the worst cabin steward we had ever come across at sea. His idea of cleanliness wasn't mine; we asked for ice in the cabin on day one - he always had to be reminded; he never washed the soap dish out and I had to get the room fumigated at one point because we were being bitten by bugs; toiletries were never replaced without asking. He was hopeless.

Others along the corridor had a similar experience and his supervisors knew about him not being up to the job but he remained in post. MR MM went to get a new comments form from reception as they call the purser's desk on Arcadia. He was asked why he needed one. He promptly showed a receptionist the one which had already been tampered with and said "that's why!"

Word got back to our steward and he was not happy that MR MM had got another form. He questioned me. I told him the one he gave us had already been marked under housekeeping. He did not speak to us after that. We'd paid our gratuities but we didn't leave him a cent as an extra tip. We do not believe in just tipping for tippings sake. People have to go the extra mile but many just expect one regardless. Not from us they won't.

It was a different story with the waiters at our dining table. We looked after them well because they had gone more than the extra mile for me especially after I broke my wrist. They always saved me a corner seat so they could serve me properly without my damaged arm being in the way. It also allowed them to cut up my food, something I couldn't do myself for more than 10 weeks. We remained on good terms with four from out first table but ignored the two who had the problem with us and had told us to leave.

Sailaways were one of the highlights of this cruise especially after Neil Oliver joined as cruise director in Australia.

He was just so enthusiastic at wanting passengers to have a good time - his enthusiasm was infectious.

The ports that we did make it to were fabulous but I can't say the same about Arcadia. We'll not be sailing on her or any P&O ship in the future if what we experienced on Arcadia is par for the course throughout the fleet. The food on board was boring and stodgy - Spuds-R-US could have been the ship's slogan. As for many of the passengers - they were just so nosey and often made very rude comments instead of keeping their own counsel. Never before on our world cruises - or shorter voyages - have we experienced anything like the level of rudeness.

MR MM and I missed not only the whole country of Argentina and also Acapulco, but because of my accident we never got to see Chile, Chacabuco, Puerto Montt, or Santiago and we also missed the glaciers of Poi XI and Amalia. So disappointment all round. But in 12 months time we will be back on the High Seas on board the Cunard liner Queen Elizabeth for its 118-day voyage around the world. Something to look forward to in the months ahead.

But it wasn't going to be all plain sailing, no pun intended!

THE WRIST SAGA CONTINUES

Six months passed after the fall and I was still in pain every day. I went to see my doctor who gave me painkillers and some pain relief cream. They didn't work. I got an appointment at the hospital but the waiting time was three months. The pain just got worse so bad in fact I went to A&E. The wrist was X-rayed and I still had two fractures. Another plaster cast put on my arm. When will it ever end?

After further examination I was told my wrist was "deformed". Not the sort of news you expect to hear after it was supposedly "fixed" in Punta Arenas, Chile, in January.

July and August came and went and still no improvement; still lots of pain in my wrist despite having the plaster cast and having physiotherapy. By mid-September I really was at my wits end. I did some research and managed to find a wrist specialist who was working as a consultant hand surgeon at the Royal Devon and Exeter Hospital, and at the Royal Cornwall Hospital in Truro, Cornwall, in the UK. He's Dr Constantinos Kritiotis who also practices at the Iasis private clinic in Paphos. He flits between the two centres every month.

I booked an appointment and even before he looked at the X-rays taken at the general hospital Dr Kritiotis told me what the problem was - my wrist had lost some bone and one side was longer than the other and needed surgery to correct it. This prognosis was confirmed when Dr Kritiotis looked at the X-ray. My wrist needed a titanium plate fitted to hold it in place.

Within 24 hours I was the clinic and all dressed in my white theatre gown and white stocking when I had an ECG done.

Surprise, surprise! it showed I had heart problems. No way I said I am very fit and added I eat well, I am not over weight and I don't smoke. They insisted I had a stress test. So there and then the gown came off and I was strapped to a treadmill. Standing in nothing more than a pair of paper pants and the white support socks up to my thighs I looked a right bonny bugger as my mother would have said. I past the stress test with flying colours. But that wasn't good enough. I needed to have an angiogram before they would consider doing the operation on my wrist. At the Paphos clinic they have no facilities to do such a test. I had to go to the American Heart Institute in Nicosia the next day. What a fabulous place that was! A futuristic building with state-of-the art medical facilities all to do with the heart.

The angiogram showed I was 99.5 fit and healthy but had a very slight narrowing of one artery due to my age. What does the doctor mean I am getting old? That can't be right, I am the oldest teenager in town! That was the green light for me to have the wrist operation. It meant yet another plaster cast on my arm for three weeks but there was a bonus of sorts - I'd time to study the internet (using one hand) to look at tours and ports of call we would be making on the Queen Elizabeth's world cruise in 2014 which was less than four months away. I had to be fully mended by the time we boarded.

I was fully confident that after the operation Dr Kritiotis had fixed my wrist permanently. I can't feel the titanium plate or the six screws that hold it in place. Will it set off the alarms at airports I wonder? Not supposed to but we will see. Our voyage would take us to 23 countries and we'd have 40 ports of call. I researched Japan over and over again; made contact with people who do Tours by Locals but in the end decided to use the ship's tours - some tour guides wanted more than Cunard.

Once the cast came off I could already see my wrist looked so much better. Scaring yes, and a piece of flesh missing where the titanium bridge had been drilled in to my lower arm. Next came the physiotherapy - 40 sessions before I was fit again just in time to leave for the cruise on the 29th December, 2013. I had my last session the day before we left for Southampton with instructions of exercises to do for a month.

So a good result after a year out of my life.

MAGGIESHOEMOU

There's always space in the wardrobe for a new pair of shoes.

I have yet to meet any woman who doesn't like shoes. Men are not so fussy but ladies, well it can be an addiction. Put on a pair of high heels and you instantly feel better; you'll walk taller and you'll hold yourself better, and feel slimmer. Well I do! High heels also make your legs look great. They're like a love affair - they attract you to them, they mould themselves to your feet and they make you sway and fall head over heels in love with them. They give you pain and make you wince, but be brave you are a head above the rest in your higher than high heels.

I've loved stilettos from childhood when a neighbour let me wear her patent leather ankle strap shoes. I loved to dress up and longed for spiky heeled shoes. Of course the shoes in those days being the 1950s had kitten heels as well as higher heeled stilettos. All had pointed toes. Eventually on my apprentice hairdresser's wage I was able to buy my own shoes for the princely sum of £1-2s-6d. from a shop famous in the UK in those days called Dolcis.

I loved and cared for my shoes and I wanted more! The first pair I bought were black and red. I also has white PVC boots - I was a "Mod".

That was the start of a love affair that has lasted longer than any male relationship. It has stayed with me through thick and thin, sick and sin. My shoes are my comfort zone even when they are killing my feet! I've no idea how may pairs I have, I don't count them but I do recycle by giving them to charity shops - my shoe policy is one pair in, one pair out. Same principle applies to clothes - buy a new dress, give one away to charity. I gave some shoes away on our last world cruise to the entertainment staff.

I was probably over generous to one charity organisation called Martin House. It's a hospice for children and I worked next door to their charity shop in the village of Boston Spa on the West Yorkshire/North Yorkshire border. It was at a time when I had just married MR MM. He had to increase his house insurance when I moved in as I had so many pairs of shoes and boots, many of them designer. Feeling guilty, I decided to give some to Martin House for a charitable evening of formal wear. So what did I do? I gave all my GINA evening shoes and all my matching bags to them! Plus a lot of evening dresses.

Now the dresses I didn't feel I'd need them so that was fine, but my shoes, well I must have been so blinded by the sight of my newly married husband that I had lost my head, or I was feeling charitable towards those less fortunate than me. Even so I have regretted doing it although it was for a very good cause - children with cancer. Weeks later I went to Vidal Sassoon's Hair salon in Leeds where I had worked some years earlier.

My friend there was cutting my hair and we spoke about a new store that had opened in Leeds called Harvey Nichols.

The staff at Sassoon's were raving over the shoe department and especially the GINA shoes. I could have cried when the stylist told me how Gina shoes were the "must have" shoes. OOCH! It hurt to know I had just parted with 13 pairs. Ah! well I can only say they went to a worthy cause. Gina shoes, Renata , Charles Jordan and Kurt Geiger were all my favorite brand names. I loved the heels and the soft leather and the gorgeous colours and the clicking of the heels. If the heels got scuffed Gina had a service where you could return them and have them recovered.

All the heels were covered in leather, you don't find that so much nowadays. I wore heels for work and for dancing the night away. I was rarely in flatties.

Nowadays I tend to buy sexy heels in the UK or I shop online for shoes from the USA. I like quirky shoes such as Irregular Choice, Poetic License, Iron Fist, and Rocket Dog or Dune and

Faith. I also like LK Bennett - their heels are comfortable. I buy shoes on my travels, and I recently discovered after a visit to the United States that Miami is fabulous for glamorous shoes. I had a back operation in 2007 (probably due to standing in high heels all day when I was younger) and after the surgery I could not walk at all, let alone in heels.

I discovered Fit Flops - sandal type shoes. They are good for your back and work out the glutes in your butt.

Fit Flops (not to be confused with regular flip flops) were invented by Marcia Kilgore. She originally founded Bliss.com (spa and cosmetic group in America) and sold the company and formed one called Soap and Glory which is found in Boots Stores in the UK.

In 2005 she got the idea of a shoe that would give you a workout as you walked. I bought her shoes after my operation and they became welded to my feet. I found I wore them daily, even popping my feet into them to go to the bathroom during the night. I have had ten pairs in different designs plus a pair of her Snugger boots in silver. I bought the Snugger boots, which look like moon boots, to wear on the maiden world cruise of Queen Elizabeth in 2011. I wore them out on deck whilst crossing the Atlantic. It was bitterly cold in New York and while the boots were great the coating peeled off so not my best buy but they still have the good work out type sole.

There's a down side to wearing the Fit Flops. When I put on a pair of heels my feet are uncomfortable because my feet spread wearing Fit Flops for long periods.

I have since stopped wearing Fit Flops for that reason. I like to be a trend setter not a follow of fashion. Nowadays so many people wear Fit Flops I hate to look like the average person. They're popular on cruises - you can now buy them onboard.

In Singapore in 2010, I was staying in an hotel waiting to join QM2 on her world cruise segment back to Southampton.

One day when the elevator came to our floor in the IBIS I looked down and saw four pairs of Fit Flops gazing up at me! All the ladies in the elevator were wearing them. I never wear shoes out (I have too many) but I gave it a damn good try with Fit Flops. I walked them to death. One day in the spa resort where I still work a client stopped me and said I see you are wearing Fit Flops, I looked at her feet and said Snap! It turned out she was on her honeymoon and she was the PA to Marcia Kilgore in London.

Her Fit Flops were very special - encrusted in Swarovski crystals - £180 per pair! Marcia had given her them to wear at her wedding. Nice, and a limited edition from Harrods but by then I was tiring of mine as they did not have high heels. If they made them in high heels they would be the most comfy heels in the world but comfort is not part of the game when it comes to sexy high heels.

It's rather like no pain no gain. If they fit and are comfy from the word go we should buy the whole range, but it never works like that. I always have to "walk my heels in". I do this by wearing a pair of thick trainer socks or even MR MM's socks. I walk around the house in them with the socks on 'till I have stretched them so they are a snug fit. It can be a sight for sore eyes if you turn up at one of these breaking in sessions.

I often will have a bikini on and the socks and the shoes! Not a pretty sight but we do live in a hot climate.

I take the shoes and I scuff the soles outside because most of my cruise heels never see daylight. I wear them at night and on a carpet-covered floor so they never get scuffed underneath, and I never wear them out. The only shoes I ever wear out completely are my walking shoes. I wear Sketchers or Reebok. MR MM and I walk 4k every morning before breakfast. I had a pair of oldish Reeboks that I kept in my cupboard in the hair salon.

We get VIP clients and one young lady stopped me one morning and asked if I knew where she could hire trainers to wear in the gym. She said she'd forgotten hers. I explained there was no such facility but asked what size shoe she took? She said 38EU or size 5 in old money. Same size as mine, I said, I'll lend you mine. She jumped at the chance and she had them all week.

Before she departed with her new husband to return to London, she brought them back and gave me a gift of Elemis products.

I can't say who she was except she's a very sporty young lady with Royal blood. She wasn't to POSH or upper crust to wear my old trainers.

My latest shoe love affair is with Vivienne Westwood's Melissa polyflex eco friendly vegan shoes. They are so comfortable and very colourful - like me. "If the shoe fits buy it in every colour" I say. So I did! I have six pairs one in each colour.

Three are her Ultra Girl Orb range and three are her Anglomania range They are ballet type pumps but quirky and I love them for daily wear.

Vivienne Westwood only puts her name and finishing touches to these fabulous comfy sexy, ultra stylish shoes as do Karl Largerfield and other top designers. The actual shoes are made by Melissa a Brazilian company that has been around over 20 years. They made the original "jelly shoes" and today their shoes are mega stylish and wearable, recyclable and most of all comfortable even their high heels!

Iron Fist is another brand I buy online and they are vegan eco friendly with so much glamour and detail. They are based in San Diego, USA, and make some of the most unusual shoes around. I have a small collection in my wardrobe. It was fashionable to have matching shoes and bags years ago but I do not go for that look any more. I think it's "aging". I do, however, have a large collection of evening bags that I take on world cruises.

I have around 30 because I like to co ordinate bags to my dresses. I always take around 40 pairs of shoes on a world cruise. I also take boots with me, a pair of ankle boots and a pair of UGGS. Thirty pairs of my high heel shoes match my 100 plus dresses.

I like things to blend in and I remember going on Safari in the mid 80s. There was no way I would have worn sensible shoes (I don't do sensible) that did not match my safari outfit. I found a pair of Charles Jordan ballet pumps that looked like animal skin so I bought them to traipse around Kenya looking the part as trainers were not for me at that time. The shoes did have a matching bag so I bought that as well and the shoes & bag cost more than the holiday.

On a world cruise I also take walking type shoes for sightseeing; day shoes for around the ship, and ballet flats with some sort of embellishment on them in case we have a rough night at sea and I can't wear my heels. Gym shoes, beach shoes/flip flops/thongs, but the main ones are my stiletto heels. I have them in silver, gold, pink, sparkly red beaded pewter, multi-coloured with flowers, black with diamantes, cobalt blue embellished with gemstones, black satin, pink satin, silver snake skin, bronze, purple and black and white. OH, and Magenta suede with embellishment... to mention but a few. On the forum where I have posted my blogs I am well known for having a lot of luggage and a lot of shoes. I am Maggieshoemou on www.cruisecritic.com.

One reader superimposed a photo of a container leaving the docks with the words Maggieshoemou's shoes. It was very funny. I pasted a laminated poster on my cabin door on Queen Elizabeth on our 2014 worldie which read:

"I love Cunard but I love my shoes more!"

I added lots of photos of shoes to it. People kept knocking on the door to see if I was selling them! My shoes are nearly always a talking point on cruises, especially Cunard voyages. On Queen Elizabeth's 2014 world, one of the professional groups to come on board were The Manhattan Dolls (a great group not to be missed if you get the chance). They were staying in a cabin along from ours. Three girls all very attractive and years my junior.

They had seen me out and about in my shoes and just loved them. I was flattered when they asked me to pose with them for a photo to show off the shoes.

I did 20 fashion shows on Queen Mary 2's world cruise in 2012 for H Stern jewellers who have an outlet store onboard. Each time I wore a stunning pair of heels to go with the very expensive diamonds I was modeling. Almost everyone in the Chart Room, where we paraded the jewellery, wanted my shoes. An opening for a real shoe shop on Queen Mary 2! Where do you store all those shoes when you're not travelling in a suite? is a question I'm often asked.

Answer: In collapsible shoe boxes bought at IKEA's Southampton store. I put three pairs in one box and I stack them up on top of each other in the cabin. The evening bags go under the bed in another IKEA under bed storage.

I usually wear them all over the four months on board. Once back home I have now got them in the same boxes to protect them but they get little wear when I'm not cruising! My Vivienne Westwood's though get worn daily. I would never wear Crocs or Birkenstocks (tried them once very uncomfortable), DR Scholls, Doc Martens, or any ugly shoes, laced up shoes or boring shoes.

I am not saying these are not good for the people who do wear them but for me they are a non-starter. I love colours and something different. I like style but I have to admit I like a bit more comfort these days.

I can't stand all day in high heels as I used to do when I was younger. The heels are now reserved for cruises or special occasions. However, the day I have to stop altogether having sexy glam shoes is the day I will throw in the towel. I often look at people's feet on a cruise and I am always fascinated by the type of shoes many wear. I can never understand why a woman would wear a pair of ordinary day shoes with an evening dress when you can get flat or low heeled shoes for evenings. I also wonder why they wear plain black shoes when they could wear patent for instance, or black satin with a bit of bling on them. Anyhow I guess the saying is right:

"You can tell an awful lot about a person by the shoes they wear."

Well, my shoes are a dead giveaway. Colourful, playful, sexy, outrageous and sometimes unstable. Just about sums up me and my shoes!

I once met an Englishman who said
"Won't you walk up and down on my spine
It makes me feel strangely alive"
I said, What! "In these shoes?
Oh!, I doubt you'd survive"

HI HO,HI HO! IT'S OFF TO SEA WE GO

10TH JANUARY 2014

Bags are packed and waiting for a "removal van" to arrive and transport us to the docks to board Queen Elizabeth - we have 19 pieces of luggage, plus the kitchen sink! Queen Mary 2 arrived in Southampton around 6-0am and at 6-30 she sounded her distinctive whistle and woke the whole City up. What a great sound to wake up to - better than any alarm clock. We set sail this evening in tandem and there's a special send-off planned to mark the 10th anniversary of Queen Mary 2.

She's another Capricorn lady like myself, built to last and glamorous with it! So I will not be letting the side down. My dresses are packed. No dumbing down of dress codes for me on our 118-day voyage around the world.

We've been packing for a week and the day of departure has arrived. We've booked a nine seater taxi (a people carrier) to take us to the QE2 terminal. A few minutes ride normally. However, for months road works have been causing major traffic snarl-ups around the dock areas and are going to last well in to 2015 we were told. When our driver, a softly-spoken Irishman, told us of the horrendous hold-up (we could see for ourselves traffic had been stationary outside the Premier Inn for more than 30 minutes).

Nothing moved and then when it did only a car or two at a time got through the traffic lights outside the Carnival Corporation HQ. Our man said he would take us a long way round but it would be quicker than taking the most direct route.

Where have I heard that before? We told him to get us to the ship as fast as possible. He did by weaving in and out of traffic (cabbies are experts at pushing in!) and giving us a tour of Southampton at the same time. He got us to the terminal in 25 minutes. We found out later that other passengers who'd left the Premier Inn at the same time as us had been two hours getting to the ship. We'd been blessed. MR MM gave our cabbie a big tip (much more than he normally hands out). You can know the price of everything and the value of nothing! We felt we'd got real value from our cab driver so did he honorable thing and tipped very well.

It took less than 40 minutes to check in, be given our cruise cards and pass security. A very smooth and efficient and friendly operation. We're diamond members of Cunard which gives us priority boarding along with other benefits. We carried two bags on board and the rest arrived soon after we'd got to our cabin.

We were rather overpowered with the speed of delivery and once the cases were in the cabin we couldn't turn around for bags and suitcases. I thought OMG! what have we done? Brought too many things? Who would have thought that?

Unpacking is an art form for me. I get the cases with my dresses unpacked first in the hope they haven't got too creased in the couple of hours they'd been in the cases - I packed them last just before we left the hotel. While in Southampton I'd done some shopping and bought new coat hangers that matched my hair colour. They were slim line and non-slip and were inexpensive - £4 for 8 in Primark.

We always take out the heavy wooden hangers and the fastenings they sit on to make more hanging space in the wardrobes. The steward takes them away and they only return the day or so before we disembark.

He also takes away most of the suitcases and puts them somewhere below decks. Where? We don't care as long as they are returned when required. Working as a team my husband/butler (I had to join him in this) managed to unpack most of the contents of the cases and bags but it did take several hours.

On the question of numbers, singles doing a full world cruise will generally have six or seven pieces of luggage; couples probably 14 or more. Our count at 19 was not the highest - that went to a couple who got married while on board who took on 29. Going away for four months isn't like leaving for a two week break and then you're back home.

No, you need lots of little things you take for granted (see my list of things to take on a world cruise that gives you some idea).

Now Cunard are normally good at organising events but whoever decided to hold a welcome on board cocktail party for world cruisers at 2pm on departure day wants a rocket.

We couldn't make it because of unpacking, dozens of other world cruisers were stuck in traffic and hadn't made it to the ship and, of course, there were no senior ship's officers there - well they have other more important things to do heading towards departure time than make small talk with passengers. Very poor organisation. The planned pyrotechnics display went ahead despite it raining bucketfuls and it was spectacular - the best we've seen in any of our Southampton sailaways.

The Southampton weather though doing its worst didn't put too much of a dampener on the proceedings. What did, at least for Queen Mary 2, was a passenger becoming ill which delayed her departure while he was medi-vaced to hospital. Word got round the passenger had suffered a heart attack before Queen Mary 2 had slipped her lines.

How unfortunate for him and the ship. Queen Elizabeth cast off while Queen Mary 2 remained alongside her berth.

The rain did have one effect...on the Verve Clicquot I'd bought for the sailaway. I had to drink it fast to stop it getting diluted with rain water. Well, that's my excuse. Cheers!

Dinner on departure day, especially the start of a world voyage, can be something of a hit and miss affair for other table guests. Some may have travelled vast distances to reach Southampton and be exhausted so skip a meal. Yes, some passengers do skip meals despite what many others might think. It was like that on our table - only three turned up.

Our table is in what I call the "first class" section not that there is such a thing in the main dining room but it is in a good location - opposite the grand staircase and the next table to the one that the Captain uses on formal nights so I can give him the eye if I feel like it.

Dateline 11TH JANUARY, 2014

I'd volunteered to do a "meet and greet" for members of a cruise forum to which I belong. It's Cruise Critic and is not what its name may suggest - to slag off a cruise line, or complain. It's a chatty and informative forum that has members in many countries - it's not exclusively for Brits.

Months before we set sail I'd offered to do the meet & greet for the roll call from Southampton and someone else would take over after New York. However, the other person bailed out so as there were no other volunteers I said I would do them for the whole world cruise. No one objected. It will keep me out of mischief and is safer than tap dancing! Over 50 attended the first meet and greet, and I kept them entertained and made them laugh.

I dressed for the occasion as one would expect me to - My "Captain Maggie" cap had lots of Cunard badges on it. Bling, bling! Aye, aye, Captain!

Church services at sea are something we always attend. For our first on this world cruise there was a large congregation and Captain Christopher Wells, who took the service, sang Onward Christian Soldiers with gusto! Crossing the Atlantic (seven days) on Cunard without a port stop means there are plenty of opportunities to dress up with at least two if not three formal evenings and a theme night or two.

The London Ball was one such night. We had Pearly Kings and Queens. I wore my long royal blue evening gown with a Union Jack headdress and a Union Jack scarf bought on Ebay. (you can find all dressing up stuff on Ebay for little money). I wore my sequined Union Jack shoes, made by Iron Fist, and I carried a Union Jack clutch bag. So I guess I was Miss Union Jack. I am getting more high maintenance as I get older so need more time to prepare for such balls. As Dolly Parton once said:"It takes a lot of time and money to look this trashy!" There's hope for me yet!

Dateline 12TH JANUARY

Queen Elizabeth is "off course" and heading towards the Azores to avoid storms that are lashing the route we should have taken but Captain Wells, an honorary commander in the British Royal Naval Reserve, decided it would be prudent to take a different line to New York. Just as well with seven metre waves and the weather forecast to deteriorate further. Our cabin was now organised and all 40 pairs of shoes in situ so I can easily grab them should the ship go down! I'd float I reckon.

Last night was a theme night - the Elizabethan Ball. I had to look like an Elizabethan. I had bought a dress but it's also the hair you have to get right. It is believed the Elizabethans never washed their hair and put powder in it to clean it. I had to do the same. There's a product on the market called Matting Powder. I use it at work - it gives the hair a messed up look.

Well, I did that and sprayed it and ruffled it up and it felt like a dirty old moggie's coat! It was so matted I looked like I'd been dragged through a hedge backwards.

After the ball I spent over 20 minutes washing it before I could go to bed. What am I Like?

Anyhow back to THE DRESS. I am not sure if I was Mary Queen of Scots, Anne Boleyn, or The Queen, but I looked the part all right. I went down to the ship's photographers to have a professional photo taken before the crowds arrived because I was so pleased with my outfit. I didn't want one of MR MM's out of focus snaps! On the way to the studio passengers kept saying how beautiful I looked. Some took my photograph they were that impressed (or did they think how odd?). Mind you they were all wearing glasses!

People bowed and said "Your Majesty!" It was very funny. After dinner I went to the ball but there were not many people there and only two of us had made the effort to dress up apart from the entertainment staff. I was happy and I'd had a good old laugh.

As a point of interest the Elizabethan dress was made of crushed velvet with a chiffon panel and ribbon and pearl trim. The skirt had a wire hoop in it, shoulder of mutton type sleeves, plus a huge stand up collar that also had a wire inserted to make it stay up. It cost a "small fortune" from my favorite online store EBAY - £29-99. It arrived flat packed in a very small plastic bag. It was lightweight, crushable and did not crease.

The headdress was on an Alice band and had pearls hanging down to the forehead, it was included in the price of the dress.

Dateline 13TH JANUARY

My birthday. These past few years we've always celebrated it while being on a cruise. On the Queen Mary 2 world voyage in 2012 we were in Madeira on the 13th. MR MM had organised a surprise lunch for me at Reid's Palace Hotel. We dressed up - he in his morning dress and me in the dress I wore when MR MM went to Buckingham Palace to be Invested by Her Majesty The Queen with his MBE. That was in 2004 and, yes, the outfit still fitted without requiring any alteration, surprisingly!

MR MM had arranged for us to be picked up in a chauffeur driven limousine and had, I discovered, given instructions that the driver must not be wearing sandals or shorts but dressed in a suit. He was. We were shown around the hotel by Carla Jesus, one of the managers of Reid's Palace. MR MM went off filming around the hotel grounds (he'd not been to Reid's or Madeira before). I was taken to the table that had been reserved for us outside the restaurant and not far from the swimming pool.

A waiter brought the lunch menu, I looked at it and thought there was something strange - it had my photograph on it.

I put it down thinking this must be a joke, or was it a stunt by that TV programme called Candid Camera?

MR MM reappeared, the waiter opened a bottle of champagne and I picked up the menu again and asked MR MM what it was all about? He confessed to having been in touch with Carla for several months as they plotted the menu cover for my birthday - not the food, but the layout. MR MM had been through some of my old photographs from when I worked at sea - including one with my late mum when I took her cruising - and had incorporated them in the design of the menu to make it look like a newspaper. It was impressive and a first for Reids. Carla told me when MR MM emailed her months before and explained what he wanted to do she was immediately "taken" with the idea - and so were her bosses. That was probably the most memorable of my recent birthdays.

On Queen Elizabeth the 13th was a sea day. MR MM organised with Anna, the chief bar tender in the Commodore Club, to rope off a section at lunchtime so I could have birthday drinks and canapes. He also asked for a number of bottles of Veuve Clicquot to be put on ice.

I invited people I knew from previous cruises as well as some passengers I'd met through cruise forums.

MR MM had bumped in to Father Aidan Logan, a Roman Catholic Priest with the American forces. Father Aidan had been stationed in Germany but his tour of duty had ended and he was sailing back to America rather than taking the plane. Father Logan held a Mass each morning and while we are not Catholics we attended each day and were made very welcome. MR MM invited Father Logan to my birthday drinks party and he kindly said a few nice words and offered a prayer - I was blessed!

We went to lunch in the Verandah restaurant. This is the specialist dining venue that has a cover charge - entrées of $6 for instance. The food is of the highest standard and the service impeccable! We don't pay the cover charge being diamond members of Cunard. We can take two lunches each segment. To get to diamond loyalty status you must have sailed 150 nights with the company. Loyalty benefits begin though when you first cruise and they increase the more voyages you make. Diamond is the top one at the time of writing. There are also internet, laundry and dry cleaning discounts along with invitations to cocktail parties.

The Verandah restaurant is brilliant. I love the art décor theme of black & white and it is a bright airy space overlooking the ocean, Lovely art work, too.

I was unable to walk off the calories because so far the seas have been so rough it's been dangerous to go out on deck. In fact they have been closed off it's really been that bad. Then it was on to dinner and more food! I am not into eating huge meals so I had to pace myself having had lunch. More fun at the table and one of the ex Cunard ladies at our table (EX QE2 girls from 30 years back) produced a silver bag with little party poppers , mini crackers and mini bottles of bubbles - as in "I'm forever blowing bubbles!" Which we all did to the surprise of the waiters. I am afraid after the dinner I was a party pooper and retired to bed! MR MM went to the show.

Dateline 14th JANUARY, 2014

I have still not been to any talks or any shows. I always find crossing the Atlantic very tiring as the rolling and bumping around of the ship sends me to sleep. I am not alone, many passengers say how sleepy they feel. It is rather like being rocked to sleep in a crib, I suspect! The movement at sea on Queen Elizabeth and Queen Victoria is more pronounced than on Queen Mary 2 - she cuts through the Atlantic rollers so easily but she was built as an ocean going liner and not a cruise ship.

Dateline 16th JANUARY, 2014

I still have had no fresh air since we left Southampton and I am feeling zonked out. I need to exercise but dare not go to the gym in case I fall off the tread mill.

My fall last year has left me nervous. Just went walkabout inside the ship and heard a talk dolphins which was interesting. We have an ocean view cabin. I don't bother with a balcony any more as we rarely ever used them. I am used to having my own 40 square metre balcony at home so a 2x2 on a ship does nothing for me. Plus I prefer to be out and about on deck in case I miss something!

Dateline 17th JANUARY, 2014

The seas have calmed quite a lot this past 24 hours. We've left the Atlantic storms behind and hopefully they won't return at least on this Transatlantic crossing. But I might have spoken too soon. I now remember when we were on Queen Elizabeth's maiden Transatlantic we were battered by a Force 11 the day before we reached New York. The decks are open again now the storms have abated. It was good to be able to breathe some fresh North Atlantic air. I've been for some brisk walks, well wrapped up of course because it is still cold.

I'm pleased we are travelling on to warmer climes - it wouldn't do for me to leave the ship in New York and then fly back to the UK. In the summer may be after a crossing but not in winter. Still not everybody has that choice.

I have been to acupuncture three times now. I often have a few acupuncture sessions on a cruise because they make me sleep well afterward. I've now managed to see a show (well part of one) called Vanity Fair and performed by the Royal Court Theatre - but I fell asleep - it must be something in the water! I think it was a good show.

There are some extravert characters on this crossing (I include myself); plenty of Friends of Dorothy who have some extravagant jewellery. The Cunard Queens are a favourite with the gay community and they especially like the Transatlantic voyages - Southampton - New York or in reverse.

We've had another theme night - The Starlight Ball. I dressed a bit vintage, some might say like a "has been" movie star! And, yes, I did manage to stay awake. In fact so long I went with the fun-loving former Cunard girls at our table to hear the karaoke singers in the Golden Lion Pub.

We had a good laugh and became the backing singers to some poor soul doing his best to kill the "Wonder of you". Poor old Elvis would be turning in his grave.

I staggered back to our cabin as the swell of the ship had come back with a vengeance. We rolled around all night. We arrive in New York tomorrow around 9-0am. It's a later arrival than normal because we are hours behind schedule after Captain Wells decided to sail south of our planned route to avoid the fierce Atlantic storms.

I hate to think what sort of sea state we'd have been in had Captain Wells kept to the planned route to the north. We passed over the spot where the Titanic went down which shows how far south we'd sailed.

I am not upset that we arrive 5 hours late with our sail into New York. It will be nice to see the shoreline in daylight. In the past when we've sailed in we've passed the Statue of Liberty in darkness at around 5-0am. We've also left in darkness. Our late arrival also gives me the chance to have a lie in and not be out on deck long before the sun rises over Manhattan. I can't wait to see New York, New York in the morning.

I met the guy in New York

He told me I'm taking you for a walk

In the park where we'll ice skate on the lake.

WHAT! you want me to do it in these shoes?
They don't have blades.

NEW YORK NEW YORK SO GOOD
THEY NAMED IT TWICE

After a week of rolling and bumping around in the Atlantic Ocean on board The Queen Elizabeth we arrived in New York but only two hours later than originally planned. The only fault we found was on this sail-in there was no ship's commentary from the likes of Bill Miller or John Maxtone Graham - both experts on New York, its illustrious history and its skyline and on ships.

That was a dampener not only for us, but also for many who had not sailed in to New York before. They were left to work out landmarks for themselves. It's fairly easy with some buildings but the two men I've mentioned bring a sail-in to New York "alive"! Such a let down by Cunard we felt.

It was bitterly cold out on the open decks and soon after we'd docked it started to snow. Huge flakes but they didn't settle. Immigration entering America can be testing even for the most patient. The queues were very long but it took us only around 30 minutes to pass through the system which was very good considering the number of passengers who were disembarking. The ship was cleared within three hours.

Once through passport control we walked straight out into the cold air. Well wrapped up and dressed for the climate we headed off on our own towards Times Square. Having done the tours in NY and the HO OH buses in the past we just needed a good walk after been inside for a week. Fresh air was what I needed as I felt drowsy after lack of sunlight and no exercise.

The Big Apple is easy to do on your own. Just over 20 minutes walking and you should reach Broadway and Times Square. You cross quite a few junctions on the way. The hustle & bustle is what's thrilling. On one side of Times Square is the Marriott Marquis hotel - it's a good landmark. We've stayed in this hotel in the past. It has a fabulous rooftop revolving restaurant with views over Manhattan.

Our first call is always at Macy's - a department store like no other, especially the New York branch (Macy's are in other American cities like San Francisco) which is a rabbit warren of a place. We are fans of The Metropolitan Museum of Art which used to have a shop in Macy's - it's now a Starbucks. We asked at customer services where the museum outlet had gone and were told it had relocated to The Rockefeller Plaza. That involved another walk and on the way we passed Bryant Park winter gardens famous for its ice rink. The Metropolitan Museum of Art sell some very interesting and unusual items - I bought a pair of earring modeled on Faberge' eggs. We were attracted to the Pig & Whistle, a famous Irish pub near Radio City.

We pigged out on the special of the day - an Irish Angus beef burger! Well, you can't do NY and not have a burger! It was cooked as we wanted it - medium rare - and was all meat. It was a treat for us. We don't do burgers as a rule.

When we're next in New York we'll return to the Pig and Whistle and see if they're on the menu again they were that good. More walking and sightseeing and then to the ship. Back on board we spotted Bill Miller, the maritime expert whom we've heard give a running commentary when sailing into New York on previous cruises. His cabin was six along from ours. MR MM greeted him and bemoaned the fact he hadn't joined in Southampton so he could have given the ship's passengers his first hand knowledge of New York on the sail-in.

"They didn't ask me in time. I was on another ship", he said with a tone of regret. Bill did give a commentary during sailaway but we missed it because we were at dinner (second sitting). We could have skipped the meal but we had new passengers due at our table so thought it only right and proper to be present. And we have probably seen the two best sailaways from New York anyway.

In 2008 we witnessed the sailaway of Queen Mary 2, Queen Victoria and the QE2. It was the only time all three Cunard Queens had been in the same port at the same time. A fantastic sight.

We were on the maiden world of Queen Victoria and had sailed in tandem across the Atlantic from Southampton with the QE2. That was some crossing, and the sailaway was just as impressive.

The other special Cunard sailaway from New York happened in 2011 when Queen Mary 2, Queen Victoria and Queen Elizabeth left - it was another "first" - the first time all three ships had been in the same port at the same time and sailed away together. We were on Queen Elizabeth and it was her maiden call into New York.

FORT LAUDERDALE

An impressive cruise terminal at Port Everglades. It's usually full of cruise ships especially in January. We've been to downtown Fort Lauderdale before. It's impressive, clean and has a good beach. But we went to Miami on a ship's tour. MR MM had not been for 36 years but remembers in those days in the late 70s it was not a particularly nice place to visit - it was very rundown. When we knew we were calling in Fort Lauderdale, MR MM spoke with a Yorkshire friend and his wife who have lived in nearby Delray Beach for more than 30 years.

MR MM was advised to "steer clear" of Miami Beach, but we were not going to be put off. Our tour included a guide but we were left to do our own thing for several hours. So we were accompanied yet unaccompanied if you follow my meaning. The coach took us through the Art Deco District, which was very impressive and we drove through other parts of the south beach area. We were not disappointed. In fact what we saw from the coach, and on our own, was pretty impressive. It rained for a while we were by Miami Beach but it was warm rain. When it stopped the sun shone. I was so happy!

On our walkabout I found a shoe shop. Not any old shoe shop but one that had lots of exotic numbers all around the shelves called simply The Shoe Shop. I could have spend all day in there, but didn't of course, just long enough to buy an exotic pair to add to my collections. MR MM was tempted and made a purchase but his were just "ordinary". That ship's tour to Miami Beach was brilliant. We were dropped centrally and it was easy walking. We even walked on the famous beach for a while. A most interesting visit to a place that's known around the world for sometimes all the wrong reasons.

We walked a good way along Ocean Drive and were impressed with everything we saw - the buildings and the people. An interesting sign outside the Hotel Clinton in South Miami Beach - "we have beer as cold as your ex's heart!" We skipped dinner so we could take part in a "Mexican-style wave" as Queen Elizabeth sailed past the blocks of apartments that stand on the port side of the harbour entrance as you leave for the open ocean. Residents of these flats generally give a rousing send off to liners, especially the Cunard Queens. They hang out the flags of various nations and blow klaxons, whistles and ring bells.

It all adds to the atmosphere. They cheer, too, and passengers generally respond.

The Cruise Critic forum to which I belong has a member called Dreamflight Pat. Pat worked for British Airways as a trolley dolly (an air hostess) who ended her career as a Cabin Director (a fancy name for a purser). She's a lovely lady and co-founded the Dream Flights charity that every year takes disabled children and young people to Florida for a holiday of a lifetime. Pat lives in the south of England but decided to join Queen Elizabeth in Fort Lauderdale. "It would be warm", she said!

Pat had a friend who was staying in one of the apartment blocks and it had been arranged that Cruise Critic members would line the deck and shine torches in salute. It would also be picked up on the webcams that are located on these buildings and are watched by people around the world. We all did and yes we were picked up even though it was pitch black.

*Burn's Night clashed with Australia Day. Burns took precedent. I added a tartan sash to my outfit. Well, you have to make an effort.

*Most comedians that tell gags on cruise ships tell one about passengers not being able to go more than 30 minutes without food!

*Some passengers do pig-out. And they are the ones who are "targeted" by the spa staff. I noticed a poster which claimed we would gain between 7 to 14 lbs in a week on a cruise.

So how much in16 weeks on a world cruise, I wondered? Like a lot of these claims I take them with a pinch of salt. Oh, we shouldn't be eating salt! In times past I have looked in to lectures on hair, feet and how to improve your health but never stayed to the end. I think a lot of it is questionable; and little more than a sales pitch.

*To get an invitation to sit and dine at an officer's table on formal nights is a highlight for many passengers, especially if it's one to sit at The Captain's table although the captain doesn't always attend in person, sending some of his junior officers to host the table on occasions. The beauty for passengers is that the officer hosting the table picks up the tab for the wine consumed.

*I don't drink wine, and MR MM doesn't normally bother either preferring to stick with water. We got an invitation to a hosted table but turned it down. Why? Would you believe it was to the ship's principal doctor's table and given that I'd had 12 months of seeing nothing but doctors I couldn't face dining with one. Nothing against him. We did get a personal invitation to dine with Queen Elizabeth's chief engineer whom we'd met at various receptions. He liked us so we got an

invite to his table. It was a "cheap evening for him - we both just drank water. But the company was excellent.

*Bingo is not something I have ever played but I did on Queen Elizabeth. One afternoon I got the idea I wanted to see how the game was played.

I persuaded MR MM to join me so we could both see the numbers and mark off any that may be on our card. Just one card I bought not the multiples that others around us seemed to have. Guess what? Bingo, we won! Not one game but two and had US$50 when we walked out. Beginner's luck!

ARUBA.

Doing tours independently of the cruise ship can be risky. If you're late back the ship could have sailed without you. Ships only wait for passengers delayed on a ship's organised tour. In Asia and the Far East we tend to take the ship's excursions because we feel safer about getting back on board - on time or not. However, in the Caribbean I think it's worth organising your own excursions. One of the countries I'd researched was Aruba - one of the so-called ABC Islands. I have faith in the comments posted on Trip Advisor and one was for a tour of Aruba with a man called Bully (his real name is unpronounceable to Europeans he said).

Bully is a licensed taxi owner/operator who has good reviews on Trip Advisor, and on the Cruise Critic website. So I booked him and hoped I'd get three others to join in before we got to Aruba. But if I didn't it wouldn't break the bank if there were just the two of us.

Bully charges US$45 an hour which I thought was very reasonable.

He is licensed to take a maximum of five passengers although his cab is a people carrier and could take more but he would be breaking the law and run the risk losing his license if he did. Not something he was prepared to do. Bully for Bully!

I had no difficulty in getting three others. Bully gave us his grand tour of the island and stopped at places of interest where he would take photos of us on each other's cameras so we all got the picture. He was humorous and full of knowledge about Aruba. It was a fun half day tour. The tour over, MR MM and I walked the short distance from the ship in to Oranjestad the capital of Aruba.

We saw nice examples of Dutch style buildings; the city was clean, colourful and it has a street car that takes passengers around part of the centre without charge. It's sponsored by some of the larger stores and hotels, I believe.

Oranjestad was classy yet had not lost its rustic charm, thank goodness. It has high end shops, and top of the range hotels were prominent along with casinos. There's a branch of Diamond International. We looked in stayed a while but walked out without buying, much to MR MM's surprise and to that of our credit card! It was hot and MR MM wanted to try the local Aruba beer. We climbed some stairs to a bar on the first floor of a wooden structure not far from the port gates.

It wouldn't have been out of place in a frontier town in the America west. The beer was so good he had two!

We had a sail away party on deck but it was not well attended. The resident band on Queen Elizabeth is called Nexus.

The musicians are from St Lucia and play a lot of Bob Marley and some obscure musical stuff - obscure even to me a music lover! A case of passengers voting with their feet by shunning sailaways?

COSTA RICA: LIMON

I met a man in Limon
He was giving me the come on
let's go swing half naked through the jungle tree tops
I said " In these shoes?" I think not!

This port in Costa Rica is on many cruise itineraries and rightly so. It's a fascinating place - the cruise terminal being one of the attractions. There's a great bazaar, or flea market, with all sort of goods and services on sale - some of those doing a roaring trade were the three offering manicure, pedicure and massages.

I had a mani-pedi (manicure and pedicure). I recognised a lot of other passengers from Queen Elizabeth were also having similar treatments. It was all done very professionally with high standards of hygiene and it wasn't a rushed job. As an extra I had a flower with sparkly bits put on my big toes. All that cost US$27. Browsing the stalls in the market I spotted one selling T-shirts with a Mola sewn on the front. Molas are squares of appliqué hand sewn like a collage.

They are colorful and often have parrots in the picture. They are made by local Kuna Indians on the San Blas Islands, an archipelago which stretches some 200 miles along Panama's coast. Years ago cruise ships would call at San Blas before going to Puerto Vallarta. The Kuna Indians would sail up to the ship in canoes. They always smelt of curry! The women (with babes in arms) were wrapped in colourful clothes and they all shouted "money, money, money"!

May be this was where Abba holidayed before they hit the big time! Passengers would throw coins over the side of the ship, the men would dive for the money and bring it up in their teeth.

Back to the Mola on the T-shirt. I bought two with Molas on them because they should last for years. I have heard of people who cut them off and frame them when the T-shirt has shrunk or faded or become washed out. The two I got cost US $18 each instead of US$20. The next day on the transit of the Panama Canal similar ones were on sale for US $25 each. We had two stops in Costa Rica. The other being Puntarenas.

Ironic really because almost a year to the day I had been in a clinic in Punta Arenas, in Chile (although the spellings are different), having urgent surgery on my wrist after I'd taken a fall in a tap dancing class on Arcadia. Puntarenas in Costa Rica is on the Pacific coast.

We didn't tour here - we're a bit too long in the tooth to be zip lining, kayaking or just being jungle bunnies!

We went walk about and thought this Puntarenas was a very interesting place. Costa Rica, as a country, reminds me of how the Caribbean islands such as Barbados and St Lucia were in the 1970s - shanty towns and scruffy, but with a lot of atmosphere and character.

Puntarenas was tidier than Limon, it had better pavements and more shops. We found a very busy fish market that stunk to high heaven as you would expect. It was just off the main drag. The locals welcomed us and were happy to pose with their catch of the day for photographs. They were a jolly lot, laughing and dancing. We walked back towards the ocean and stumbled across a TV crew filming an outdoor cookery programme - The "food goddess" of Cost Rica, doing her thing with a stuffed leaf filled with goodness knows what and topped with a salsa mix.

Fortunately we were not offered a taste. Moving on we went to the local stall sellers and looked at their wares. I bought a new sun hat to add to my collection. Back to the ship where I persevered once again at the sail away dance off. I wore the new hat with a huge flower I had bought in Curacao last year, and a colourful dress. I was all ready for action. Only six of us turned up this time!

I'd suggested to the entertainment staff they would do better if the band played music most people recognised.

But my comments fell on deaf ears. My big hat went down well, though, so I kept them entertained. I did however, decline the complimentary belly dancing class that took place at 5-30pm. Thought I had better not tempt fate.

On the way to San Francisco, we experienced our first casual night on Cunard. It was a casual Caribbean night with dancing on the deck. I wore a floral number as I don't do casual so next best thing - a Karen Millen tropical patterned dress, silk flowered bag and the shoes were the show stopper - a pair with 4 1/2 inch high heels and covered in silk flowers with a bow on the heels I'd bought online from Iron Fist.

MR MM AND THREE "DOLLS"!

We were six days sailing away from the City by the Bay. Our position was off the Mexican coast and close to the port of Cabo San Lucas. The weather was getting cooler again but MR MM got hot under the collar when he was "propositioned" by not one but three gorgeous, talented young ladies. True! But more of that later. These waters off Cabo San Lucas are good for whale and dolphin watching. In fact when we were on Queen Elizabeth on its maiden world voyage in 2011, Julian Burgess was Captain and after leaving port (we called in Cabo that year) he took us on what he described as "coastal cruising" for a couple of hours up the Mexican coast line specifically to see if we could catch a glimpse of whales and dolphins. We were not disappointed! Shame Cabo wasn't on our list of port calls on this voyage. Still may be another year. It is a nice resort. Reminded MR MM a bit of Whitby with sunshine but without the swing bridge or the Abbey or The Magpie Cafe!

Lots of passengers are getting ready to leave the ship when we hit San Fran. But they have to spend the first night on board (we are there two nights) for some reason.

240

For all (or most) of the disembarkation and the embarkation takes place on the same day when a liner is overnighting in a port.

Expect it makes sense. I remember on our world on Queen Mary 2 in 2012, and docked in Circular Quay in Sydney, one Australian couple who lived on The Rocks (an upmarket part of the city these days) couldn't take their cruising gear off on the first day although they did go home and they went to work before returning that evening to Queen Mary 2 for dinner.

As we edge ever closer to our Californian destination, the launderettes are packed out with all machines, I say all, (all three), working from 7-30am to 8pm. There are the usual stories of selfish people hogging machines, and others who put "out of order" signs when there is absolutely nothing wrong with them. Now I don't do domestic - that's for MR MM. And he has first-hand knowledge of the out of order scam not only on this cruise but on our previous world voyages.

The other day he was in the laundrette and spotted out of order notices, official ones with Cunard on them. But he is a suspicious chap and so tested the two machines - a dryer and a washer - to see if they genuinely were out of order. Lo and behold they both worked.

So he took the notices down and brought them back to the cabin. And it's NOT the first time he has come across this deceit.

On Arcadia's world in 2013 he accumulated no fewer than six P&O "out of order" notices on that voyage. So far on Queen Elizabeth we only have the two. But he is ever alert. Amazing how stories that have been doing the rounds for donkey's years still have credence with some passengers. Like the one about the two women who got into a fight in the laundrette and one attacked the other with the flat side of a hot iron and was put off at the next port.

No one ever says they witnessed the incident, on what ship it happened and at what port she was kicked off nor whether any prosecution took place. It's a pure myth. The other tale is the one about a woman passenger who took a cocktail dress and put it in the washer only for it to vanish. That night, as this story goes, another woman was seen wearing the dress at a reception and its "true" owner approached the woman and accused the wearer of stealing the dress only to be told "prove it!"

I ask you, would you put a decent cocktail dress in a laundrette on a ship when there are proper laundry facilities? I know I wouldn't. Another myth. But would you credit it, some MR MM has seen believe both tales. He once got into an argument with a fellow passenger when he tried to point out the nonsense of the iron attack story so now just keeps his mouth shut and his thoughts to himself but has an "inward smile".

This is turning out to be an interesting cruise with a real mixed bag of people onboard. Some real characters, and lots of interesting people. I like sailing with mixed nationals. Captain Christopher Wells is fantastic, he's funny, personable, friendly and personally makes the 12-00 noon announcements and tells us all some news of the area we are sailing in. But his stint on the world cruise ends in San Francisco.

He then heads off on holiday and will rejoin the Cunard fleet later in the voyage only next time he will be in command of Cunard's flagship Queen Mary 2.

We have had some good speakers onboard. Bill Bryson the author and Bill Miller ships' historian whom I have heard many times on Cunard. I don't go to many talks , as I prefer to listen and watch them on the TV when I am getting ready for dinner.

Now I did promise I would reveal why MR MM got hot under the collar (well flattered at his ripe old age) the other evening when he was "propositioned" by three very attractive young ladies - The Manhattan Dolls. They are a girl group with a difference. They sing songs made famous by the Andrews Sisters - to remember them you have to be of "a certain age"!

But they also sing numbers from other girl bands. For instance the Shirelles and the Ronettes.

Their cabin is a few along from ours on deck 4 and they passed our door several times a day but always stopped to read the notice I had pinned to it which showed some of my 40-odd pairs of shoes. I expect it was all too much for them to comprehend! I was going out one time when they were passing and they stopped to chat and asked me all about my shoes. They, too, loved shoes and they insisted I have a photograph taken with them.

Then they spotted MR MM wearing his hand-painted world cruise tie (or one of them) which showed the flags of all the countries we'll call in up to the halfway point which will be South Korea. He has one for the return leg. All are hand painted on Chinese silk by Julie Raiises in Derby, England.

The "Dolls" were blown away with the colours and "insisted" MR MM also be in the picture. He couldn't resist three pretty girls and little old me looking not one bit out of place at their side. One for the album I guess!

I hadn't been to the theatre much at this point in our voyage but I did go and see the Manhattan Dolls, and would do again if they were ever on a ship on which I was a passenger. I was flattered that they asked me to have a photograph taken with them as it should have been the other way round - they were the stars and were young and gorgeous.

I have promised to cut a friends hair - "have scissors will travel!" I have also to get my names arranged for the meet and greet of over fifty passengers from the Cruise Critic roll call the day after we leave the City by the Bay.

IN THE CITY BY THE BAY

The arrival in San Francisco was fairly uneventful; dull almost - it was still dark and well before dawn so the iconic Golden Gate Bridge was more a rusty red and visible only from a few metres away. MR Movie Maker though got up at 4-30 am to do some filming. I told him he was mad getting up at such an unearthly hour as I rolled over and went back to the land of nod. I thought he must have either acquired night vision on his video recorder or been eating too many carrots as I did not know what he expected to see.

Off he went anyway only to return with my morning cuppa of lemon hot water at 6-0am and declare we had been in port for some time, and immigration had boarded the ship. After he'd disappeared again he then re-appeared to announce we needed to go to the immigration . So dragging myself up and out of the cabin to join the long lines waiting to be inspected. It was a one hour wait. Not bad considering the amount of people in the line.

I have a scheme with all immigration officers. It's this - I dress up and wear clothing that's better than nice so they comment, and I am always very smiley and chirpy. Like giving a real big Hi! and a smile.

It usually works. This time the guy, or I thought it was a guy as "it" had very short hair like a man and no make up, and was flat chested.

But I really couldn't tell if it was Martha or Arthur! Surname on ID badge suggested to me the person was male so I thought yes, a man. I smiled again but not much of a response. So as he/she inspected my passport MR MM joined me. The person looked up and said:

"Is this man with you? and are you married"?

I replied:"I hope so as he has been sleeping in my bed for the past 15 years!"

To which said person laughed and sent me on my way so I thought good! Then as I can speak the lingo, I said have a nice day and the human laughed again. Turned out the person was a woman not a man! I always wonder why women want to cut off their hair and look like a man. Is because they can't be bothered with it? It took three hours for immigration to clear the ship. Of course there were the usual moaners saying they were never going to come on this ship again as it was ridiculous having to queue up for immigration. I always wonder what these people think it is all about?

I said to the guy in front of me, who insisted on telling me how awful it was, "if you had arrived in Heathrow or Manchester you would be queuing up just the same.

247

You have just entered a new country so this is how it is". His wife told him to shut up, eventually.

Once off the ship we went shopping - to Safeway's for provisions. We know where most supermarkets are around the world. I wanted blueberries for my morning porridge.

I'd only seen them in puddings on the ship and didn't like to especially ask for them although I could have done. I got five boxes and put them in the fridge. I have all the mini bar stuff removed when we go on board. We don't drink fizzy drinks full of sugar, or fizzy water for that matter. The fridge is kept for the important things like tonic water, face mask from Lush and blueberries and may be the odd bottle of vodka.

We've been to San Fran before and done the Alcatraz, Sausalito, the trams, the cable cars, Pier 39 and Fisherman's Wharf, and eaten in fine restaurants. I find San Francisco such an easy place to get around.

Tickets for Alcatraz are sold in many tour offices around the pier area and the Ferry for Alcatraz. Pier 35 is where lots of cruise ships dock, but in August 2014 a new cruise terminal is scheduled to open at Pier 27. It looks a super-duper affair and should provide San Fran's cruise port with state-of-the-art facilities for both passengers and immigration staff. So may be immigration will become a pleasant experience!

248

Getting to Alcatraz can be done on the Internet or at the booths selling tickets but bear in mind often all the tickets for your arrival day may be sold out. If you are berthed two days then make your booking as soon as you can after arriving for the next day. Sausalito you can do on your own by ferry. It's a quaint village (or is it a town?). There are big discounts for seniors on the ferry but you have to ask for them at the ticket booth.

After the highlight of Safeway's store, a short distance from where the ships berth, we dumped the shopping back in the cabin and went off to explore. We took the tram to Union Square.

We intended getting off at Bay Bridge to visit a craft fair that is often there opposite the Farmers' Market in the old Ferry Building, but we could see from our tram that it was not operating that day so we stayed on 'till Union Square. We needed to go to Radio Shack for some film for MR Movie Maker's old faithful camcorder. This was easy. We'd then aimed to get a cable car up to Nob Hill.

The trams and cable cars have different prices - the trams are very cheap. US$2-50 for about 4 hours travel time but if you are a senior it is only 75 cents. They do not give change so we usually give $1. It is so inexpensive. The cable cars are $5 one way per person for a short journey. We set off walking and before a car came we were half way to the top of a very steep street. We decided to carry on on foot. I think mountain goats would have struggled!

But we made it. Once at the top we visited The Grace Cathedral which is fantastic place for worship with its artwork and stained glass. There were very long coloured streamers hanging from the Gothic beams in bright colours. They reflected in the sunlight coming in through the stained glass windows. At night there is a light show and the streamers make patterns on the floor of the Cathedral. All very unusual. They suggest a donation for your visit of ten dollar each. We obliged. We'd have spent that on the tram ride. After leaving the Cathedral we walked to the summit and down the other side. We passed through Chinatown and the Italian Quarter. After several hours of walking we arrived back at the ship. Our next big excursion was a date with Clint!

It was an early start - 6am - for our 11 hour tour of Monterey and Carmel. Our ship's tour left San Fran on a dark, cold and very wet morning. As we headed out amongst the fog and drizzle it was rush hour but we were heading in the opposite direction and going against most of the traffic. We went along the Pacific coastal road.

The weather picked up and by the time we reached Davenport after one and a half hours the rain clouds gave way to bright skies.

The tour guide chatted a while and then stopped and piped music came on. It was quite loud and the choice of music I found strange for early morning. It was like honky-tonk/ Speakeasy music. Sort of bump your rump stripper music. I thought any minute someone was going to get up in the aisle and wave their anoraks over the heads and start stripping off! Or at least do a burlesque type dance. I was on the starting block ready for action when the music suddenly changed to a sedate Swan Lake, which went on forever.

By now I was looking at the inside of my eyelids. Somehow the grey sea and the rain did nothing to compare to the Azure Aquamarine Turquoise of the Mediterranean. Suddenly I came back to life when we stopped at a hotel/restaurant named The Davenport Roadhouse. It looked like something out of the Wild West.

Davenport seemed like a one horse town. However, it was a gem of a place and they served really good coffee and pastries, cakes and cookies. Not that I often eat such things, but getting up early and having only my porridge and blueberries for breakfast, I had hunger pangs before we reached this little oasis of a town. So my see food diet kicked in - I had seen it so eat it!

I had a raisin and cinnamon cookie. Most people ate brownies with pecan on top and two people behind me had coffees with cream and a double shot of Amaretto plus the cakes! Sounds delicious for a 10-0am mid morning snack if you have no conscience whispering in your ear! Guess where they were from? Fully refreshed we carried on along the coastal highway passing through Santa Cruz, and eventually on to Monterey. Weather had really become nice and sunny; the town looked lovely. We passed Dennis the Menace Park - apparently the author of DTM was born in Monterey.

The town is famous for canning sardines but many of the canning factories are now shops or restaurants. Also it houses a world famous Aquarium but unfortunately we had no time to visit it on our whistle stop visit that gave us less than an hour's free time - not long enough to do an aquarium and see something of this famous town. We went to lunch in a place called Bubba Gump Shrimp Company (the meal was included in the price of the excursion).

This was a very quirky place and I think it had connections to the film Forrest Gump. The food was fab! We had all ordered from a menu that had been passed around on the coach on the journey from San Francisco and the guide had phoned in our orders to the restaurant. It was all very organised. We had five main meals to choose from. I had the coated shrimps and MR MM had battered fish pieces. We all had Caesar salads as starters and a chocolate fudge cake topped with cream for pudding.

I ate a little of that but not being into sweet things I left most of it. The meal was very good and I liked the location of the restaurant right by the water's edge. There were signs over the door as you entered one which read: "You can tell a lot about a person by the shoes they wear"!

I thought ah! they knew I was coming. So true! My shoes are all colourful and outrageous! After lunch we had free time to explore for around 50 minutes. Lots of small shops all along one main street. So easy to do in the time available. The rest of the town was seen from the tour bus. The shops were mainly gift shops, jewellery and galleries.

Some nice things to be had so the credit card suddenly escaped from my Pac Safe bag (thought they were meant to secure your money!). I had found a new trinket which was waiting for me to buy. So I did! Once back on the bus our driver took us along the spectacular shoreline; past some very impressive (and expensive) homes which had stunning views over the water. They had big picture windows and none seemed to have blinds or curtains. Anybody passing could look straight in and see their entire lounge and even spot a crease in the cushions.

I guess the folks that owned them either lived in a tent in the back yard, or they lived somewhere else. They were certainly not married to an untidy partner. I was intrigued looking into the houses but most folks were looking for otters in the sea. They did not see any so I didn't miss anything, but I saw how the other half live. Not a speck of dust to be seen even on the light bulbs.

Now I know all about "show houses" and show offs! We drove on to Carmel-on-Sea. What a wonderful neat, tidy, pristine place. Reeks of class and quality! No £1 or $1 shops here. Plenty of "looking" shops and window shopping.

We stopped at the Carmel Mall, which was not a Mall as we know it, more of a mini village in the centre of the town. It was fascinating!

We walked around the town; It's quite hilly. We headed down a steep hill towards the sea but turned back.

We reckoned we would miss the bus if we continued. We said goodbye to Carmel -on-Sea - a place that was graffiti free, and free of litter and free of street signs and no sign of Clint! MR Movie Maker is more reliable!

It was dark when we arrived back in San Fran after a three hour drive from Carmel which meant we had a wonderful view of the Bay Bridge with its led lights show. The Bay Bridge has become more of a feature for many than the Golden Gate, especially at night. The draping of lights over the Bay Bridge was an experiment. It proved so popular that when the authorities said they could no longer afford the electricity to run the lights, motorist agreed to pay a higher toll to keep them on. Brilliant gesture. Thanks to them all.

We arrived back on board at 7-0pm after 11 hours away and we set sail at 8-0pm. Queen Elizabeth was now under the command of Captain Alistair Clark who had relieved the ebullient Captain Christopher Wells, RNR, who'd gone on his holidays. We don't think our new man will be cast in the same jolly mould as Captain Wells but we will reserve judgment. The sailaway was fantastic and spectacular.

In Monterey there was a man
who wanted show me all he cans
Sardines!
It all seemed a little fishy and maybe slippy
So I said
In these shoes?" NO CAN DO!

HANG LOOSE IN HAWAII

Aloha! Honolulu, what a wonderful place - lively, great climate, classy and chic. You can't be in Honolulu and not visit Waikiki Beach! We did but were a little restricted for time. We'd signed up with a group of passengers (13) to go on a private tour to a Luau. We were not sure what it entailed but thought we'd go to find out. We had only a few hours to spend in down town Honolulu. I bought a few things like Macadamia nuts and blueberries coated in dark Hershey chocolate! Yummy! We walked along the sea front and took a few photos. We had been joined by another couple from the ship. Locals smiled and said Aloha and gave a us a "hang loose "sign.

To make the hang loose sign you stick your thumb and little finger up and at the same time fold your three other fingers into the palm of your hand and then shake your wrist from side to side (the pinkie finger and thumb are not to be mistaken for the British two finger "rude" version) It means "hang loose" and it's where the saying "Hang Loose in Hawaii" comes from. I purchased a new dress on the quayside for US$20 and wore it for the Luau.

We had no idea what it was all about but the lady from Adelaide who'd arranged it had been before and reckoned it was brilliant.

We had all booked independently online. The Luau was called Germaine's and is famous apparently in Hawaii. We were the first to board a 50 seater coach and realised there were going to be more than 13 of us. We set off from the cruise terminal on something of a "mystery tour" picking up other people from hotels around Waikiki. MR MM was getting restless and I knew what he was thinking.

He hates this sort of herding around. When the coach was full we got on the way but it was rush hour Hawaiian style.(traffic jams) The journey out to the site was 27 miles and took over one hour. The guide on the bus was very informative and funny. She explained what the evening involved and the more we heard the more I could read MR MM's mind.

It reminded me of the nights out we had in the 1960s when I went off on package tour holidays to Spain and went on a tour, stopping at hotels along the Costa Brava to drink cheap "champagne-style" sparkling white wine and Sangria, watch a Flamenco show, eat rubbish food, and then throw up on the way home! Not me though, honest! So it looked as if this Luau could be something similar from the guide's explanation of the events

257

to come. We were told there would be 400 people there including passengers from 6 coaches. We were coach number one.

We had to practice saying "we were coach number one". By this time MR MM was wincing in his seat and I think he would have jumped off if the bus had slowed down enough. We were told of events that would take place and given tickets - one for our meal, three for three free drinks and one for a raffle. More wince and grimacing from MR MM. What had we let ourselves in for? We arrived at the Luau and were herded towards a photographer who took our pictures, for a fee of course. We were given a shell Lei.

A ritual we were told is to kiss your partner at this stage. No explanation who to kiss if you didn't have a partner. Photo taken we were free to explore the site. It was right on the beach and there were long trestle tables and bench seats. Our table was reserved so we found our places. MR MM wandered off filming and as it was getting dusk he got stunning images of the sunset over the ocean. He then went and got our free drinks; mine was a Blue Hawaii - a vodka based drink that reminded me of Elvis in the Blue Hawaii movie. So once we were all onto our first drink we had been told we could collect our free gift for bookings online. We all got a rather nice cool bag.

The music had started up and the dancing girls in their coconut shell tops and long lashes and not much more, were parading around making us feel old and fat!

The guys all had another photos taken with the girls on their own cameras for viewing later back home in the local, and showing off no doubt. It was beginning to have the makings of a fun night.

More singing and the compare/singer sounded just like Elvis so I thought yes he is here! It is Blue Hawaii so I had another one of the gooey drinks. This time it tasted too sweet so I watered it down with a splash of vodka and tonic I had in a bottle - my "emergency" supply in case there was nothing available for me (alcohol wise I can only drink vodka, or Champagne).

So Elvis was alive and was in the room! Not that he sang a song we knew but he sounded OK after I'd downed my complimentary Blue Hawaiis. By now the Luau was hotting up.

Audience participation was the next thing - shout as loud as you can "Who has the best guide on their bus and what number is it"? Now we knew why we had to learn our bus number. ONE! ONE! 50-odd of us yelled out. "What number was it again?", asked Elvis. One, One, One! By now half of our table were standing on the bench trying to shout louder than the other 350-odd people.

And so it went on. We didn't win the prize for the loudest shout - can't think why! There was yet more dancing from the girls and the guys all dressed in next to nothing.

Biceps bulging and that wasn't all; women shouting; men cheering. It all got very silly and by now we were on a roll. Laughing 'till we cried and joining in the madness.

In between all the noise and laughter we had to use our food ticket. The food was all Hawaiian and most of it was inedible to me as I eat mainly fish. The specialty was a roasted pig that had been cooked buried in the ground for a whole day. There was a fire dance as the king of where ever ordered his servants to open up the ground and retrieve the pig. A similar lamb dish Kleftiko, is cooked this way in Cyprus, but without the half naked men dancers to serve it.

May be that is where the Cypriots are missing a trick. Strip off and eat fire when serving the Kleftiko. They may sell more! We had to line up and serve ourselves using polystyrene plates with the matching plastic knife and forks. Fine dining Luau style! I can't say I enjoyed the food, but tried some chicken and a bit of the pig. The dessert we were told was made from coconuts.

"Do not eat more than three pieces", warned our guide as she implied it would give us "the runs". One of the dishes was called Poi and another was called Pe.

So many had poi and Pe followed by Senokot cake. Guide told us later the coconut can cause you to go to the bathroom more.

I kept my fingers crossed we didn't end in a traffic jam on the way home as some on our coach had ignored the guide's warning! There was more cabaret - most of it was very good.

National dancing by Pacific Islanders from Fiji and Tonga and Maori dancers from New Zealand.

The final act being fire dancers who, we were told, were world champions but never having met a fire dancer I cannot confirm this. There was a grand finale. But Elvis left the building without a song from Blue Hawaii so we all piled back on the bus.

Our guide entertained us all the way back and we had to sing along with her(cringe again). No traffic so we were back at the ship in less than half hour.

Back on board at around 10-30 pm and the sail away party on the deck was in full swing as we set sail at 11-59. A great sail away and the lights and skyline of Honolulu were spectacular. We DID enjoyed the Luau. It was different and we all joined in the fun. In fact it was a fantastic experience you do once in your life I guess.

Plus one of our table mates, a full world cruiser from the Cotswolds called Chris, was crowned "King of the Hula" for doing the best dirty dancing with a sexy maiden. He was a great sport. You'd never guess he is partially sighted. He just went for it, bless him! Great guy, and a good sport. He kept his crown of palm leaves on his head 'till he went to bed and maybe he slept in it for all I know. I forgot to check that out. Well done Chris - what a star!

Forgot to mention, the day before we arrived in Honolulu there'd been an hour's hula dance class.

I went along as I felt it safer than tap dancing. It came in useful though at the Luau they wanted ladies up on stage to do the hula dance. I went up and the dance was the one we had learnt on the ship! It was funny as well. The words to the dance are so silly and you do the actions. It is all about going fishing! So all that sexy hip wiggling is about catching little fish going home and cooking them. Not being the domestic kind of girl, I prefer to think it was about dancing to catch a handsome millionaire!

Then I met a man in Hawaii
He said to me Hang loose!
I know you love a good roller
Come surf the break with me
I said In these shoes - I'd rather surf the Internet!

Lahaina Maui: Another beautiful tropical island that has volcanic mountains and looks a bit like Bora Bora or Tahiti.

I had been on the Internet last year and came across a journey on the Sugar Train (Lahaina Sugar train.com). When sugar cane was no more some enterprising souls stated to run a passenger services for tourists on the track. It is successful. The station was a one mile walk from where the ship docked. The tickets cost US$20.

It was a great fun ride into the countryside on a real chuffing Billy! The carriages came originally from the UK. It rattled and rolled along into the countryside passing through a pristine looking golf course. Not a long journey but scenic.

At the end of the leg you can disembark and catch a later train back but we stayed on for the return journey so we had time to explore the town.

On the return leg we got good views of Queen Elizabeth out in the bay, and of the mountains inland. We could have been in Scotland. Ah, no, we had sunshine and no midges! There was an onboard commentary and guess what? The guide sounded like ELVIS.

He burst into song playing a guitar and his first song was, yes you know, BLUE Hawaii followed by the Hawaiian wedding song. OH! yes, Elvis lives and he is singing on a train on Maui. But don't let on! Lahaina is a nice little place with lovely restaurants and shops and has a village atmosphere.

This is the place for whale watching and there was no shortage of tours on sale on the quay. This is a tender stop and the tender ride's around 20 minutes. There were whales everywhere. We could see them from the shore side and from the ship. We were going to have lunch ashore but changed our mind after we realised we had not brought the credit cards ashore and the problem with a tender port is if you forget anything you can't just pop back aboard. So lesson there for us - always double check before going ashore.

Sailaway was in daylight. I dressed up in my hula hula skirt which I got last year on the cruise. I wore it and my colourful wig. I practised my hula dance steps again in Lahaina. As we'd left the ship earlier in the day there were four ladies - all seniors - dancing to a band on the quayside. The hula dance about the fishing started up and they asked people to join in. So I did. I dropped them a few dollars.

A LIFE AT SEA ON QUEEN ELIZABETH

Most people take a one, two or three week cruise but by now we had been on board Queen Elizabeth for 40 of our scheduled 118day voyage. Some potential world cruisers wonder if they could cope with a long voyage and ask themselves: What would I do all day? Would I get bored?

The following is my take on world cruising having done six - two of them as crew, the others as a passenger:

There is no urgency "to fit it all in" in a tight time frame so most days pass by doing nothing much. I potter around the ship chatting to whoever I meet. I walk and I use the gym. On Queen Elizabeth I teamed up with another lady and we walked and talked (multi-skilled, me!). After 10 laps of the deck we'd go for a cuppa (green tea for me), talk some more and then it was lunchtime. On Sundays at sea MR MM and I go to Church. In the afternoons I may lay around one of the pools and read a book. I have a dance every lunchtime as the resident band, Nexus, entertained for 45 minutes. A few other passengers generally join in because we believe this exercise burns off a few calories.

I find time to go to the sauna and swim in the pool, but not every day.

The ship's daily programme, delivered to your cabin the evening before, can be a very useful guide. It lists events that are taking place like port lectures (which can be very informative), times of guest speaker appearances. Some are worth going to others I avoid if the subject doesn't interest me.

American Bill Miller is a maritime historian. I've listened to his lectures on other cruises so gave him a miss on Queen Elizabeth but I did go to a talk on Maggie Thatcher by author Bill Bryson. There are far too many lecturers on ships that I've been on who talk only about World War 11. This is probably because in the Pacific many ports have interesting things to see about the war like Pearl Harbour.

I much prefer to be outside rather than sitting in a theatre where folks are often coughing and sneezing although I sometime listen to the classical concert in the Queen's Room after lunch. One good talk I went to on Queen Elizabeth was given by Patricia Pearce MBE. Pat used to be a trolley dolly with BA flying long haul. She's co-founder of a charity called Dream Flights that takes 108 sick children to Disney in Florida each year.

Pat, who'd joined in Fort Lauderdale and sailed to Sydney, wasn't scheduled to be a lecturer - she was asked when Cunard discovered her charitable work.

She's written a booklet about the history of Dream Flights and had just 30 copies with her - they sold out fast after her talk which left many who heard it with tears in their eyes. Pat's a very inspirational lady and good fun, too.

For those that are interested there are cinemas on ships but often a good film clashes with something else of interest. There are numerous dining options from buffet to waiter service.

At lunch time I like to dine in the main dining room and eat the spa selection which lists the calories of each dish. If I go to the Lido (buffet) I tend to eat a lot more. I don't often take desserts, potatoes or bread rolls. You have to be disciplined on a long cruise because you can eat 24/7. I take breakfast in my cabin brought from the Lido by my butler, MR MM.

I often spent some time in our cabin doing ordinary things like washing my smalls. I've altered a dress length by sewing the hem. I sometimes take a nap or read my book or do my manicure.

All the things you do at home After all the ship is your "home" for a few months if you're doing a worldie. You really can do as much or as little as you like on board a ship like Queen

Elizabeth. There are classes and lesson every sea day - dance, bridge, art, singing, crafts, acting and spa talks. I avoid the spa talks that are designed to part you from your hard earned on board spend.

So not going to talks on "How to achieve a flat stomach" - just eat less and exercise is the answer to that one - or "Burn Fat faster" - answer eat the right fat burning foods or "How to relieve swollen ankle and tired feet". Answer: Put your feet up and relax otherwise only your wallet will be relieved!

There are often Ladies' Pamper Parties where you get a dab of Elemis eye gel for free, or some hand cream for free on the back of your hand - it will only costs you half your On Board Spend.

These days the programme is full of all these spa talks. I know they have to promote their treatments and I do work in a spa but I find most of these talks so unrealistic. Interesting only, I guess, if are wanting some relaxing pampering treatments and you have not experienced these treatments before. I always find the spa staff are very professional and well trained. Watch out for special spa days where you can save on treatments. These are often on port days and worth taking advantage of.

I have done most activities on ships over the years - napkin folding, scarf tying, dancing and painting. Nowadays I do just what I fancy on the day.

There are some very good cookery classes on Queen Elizabeth but not being a domestic Goddess, I don't do those either - I leave MR MM to pick up some tips he can put into practice when we get home. That's a sample of daytime activities. At Night, more choices, more options. We tend to go for drinks in a cocktail lounge (The Commodore Club is our favourite) before dinner. But it's like any bar anywhere in the world, it's the people that make it and give it atmosphere - drinkers and those who serve the drinks.

Service in the main dining room late sitting (8-30pm) got slow on Queen Elizabeth. So slow we were missing seeing the parade of outfits in the Queen's Room which mostly happened around 10-15pm. In fact MR MM, who is normally a patient chap and doesn't like to kick up a fuss, told the senior waiter at our table to "sharpen up his act". Service did improve, but not by much and not for long.

The cabaret in the theatre starts at 10-30pm and for popular acts all the good seats have been taken if you arrive last minute. If we're going to a show, and service is slow at the dinner table, we will make our excuses and leave as soon as we have all finished the main course.

It's the only way to get a decent seat. If we have an early port arrival, and we are going on tour, we will have an early night and even forgo the show. Cruise lines often repeat acts. - On Queen Elizabeth for instance there were three sets of jugglers; many of the singers were also doing the rounds of the cruise ships. They sing the same songs year in year out - mostly for Le Mis. If I wanted to hear the songs I'd go to the show when in London. The Royal Court theatre singers and dancers are probably the best I have seen. Especially the singers. I enjoyed their shows, but they come around each segment. Generally we see them only once.

One day runs into the next. It's amazing how the weeks sail by, excuse the pun. WHO do you find on a world cruise? Everyman and his dog, (no, not the ladies but there are a few about!). The first leg of the cruise on Queen Elizabeth took us across the Atlantic into New York. Passengers on that segment were mainly British and Americans and some Germans.

There were 80 Germans doing the full 120 days from Hamburg and back. From Southampton to New York, many passengers were younger people heading for a shopping spree in the Big Apple and many had booked a last minute cheap fare that was on offer from Cunard.

There are usually a fair number of gay men on a Cunard Atlantic crossings as it is an iconic thing for them to sail on Cunard's "Queen" ships. The queens love the Queens and often stay in Queen's Grill accommodation - the most expensive suites.

They are usually fabulous, flamboyant, and fun! I enjoy their company and their dressing up makes mine look dull at times - sequins, and diamond brooches are common place along with a few glamour real mink coats. There are always a few characters on a ship and I have to say I am right up there with them.

People who stand out are often fun. One lady on the first leg was an ex-ballerina, slim, wore a drab coloured smock like artists wear and teamed it with a felt hat. Usually a pillar box type hat or a flat cap with sequins. She never took them off and wore them from morning 'till night. She may well have slept in them for all I know. Her hair was always hidden underneath and I wondered if she had any.

On the final day I saw her and her hair was hanging down to her waist in a ponytail. It was gorgeous hair but it had been hidden away all week. She was still wearing the same pillar box hat!

From New York to San Francisco we had some real characters onboard - mainly Americans and what fun people they were. I got really friendly with a lovely glamorous lady I'll call Charity. She was my age; tall, very slim, or thin would be a better description. She said she was thin through anxiety, stress and being bi polar. She did not drink alcohol as she reckoned she was always "well medicated" which I guess is the American term for been drugged up to the eyeballs!

She had been a fashion model and if you picture the photo of the glamorous senior couple on the Cunard brochure, this could be Charity! She had fabulous clothes and HUGE hats - and that was just for sunbathing! I didn't see her wear the same hat twice.

She never left the ship in port, she just sat around the pool networking, holding conversation non-stop with every single person out there. She wore fabulous floaty long pants and beautiful tops always topped off with a massive hat that extended beyond her slim shoulders. Charity had big, bold jewellery and bright red lips and nails. Only thing that let down her image - she chewed gum all the time. I liked her a lot and missed our chats after she and her other half left the ship.

Her husband was the opposite in casual shorts and Pringle knee high socks. Very eccentric but a lovely couple. There was Ci Ci (not real name) Ci Ci did not know if he/she was Martha or

Arthur. A guy who was in the wrong body. Lovely person. Married and was my age and wanted to be a woman. His was a really sad story.

He had come on the cruise so he could dress as a lady. Fantastic sense of humour and a great guy. Problem was his size 12 feet. He put them down "like plates of meat", as my late mother would have said!

She/he wore the high heels though and wanted to learn to walk like a lady. A passenger offered to help as she said she taught trans genders how to walk properly. He had his own hair but it needed my attention. I offered to sort it for him/her but he didn't pursue the offer. He also asked me about makeup as "all this girl stuff" was new to him. He was fantastic fun and I hope he finds himself soon.

Then we had the swingers! A couple of swingers and I don't mean from the chandeliers! They were married but were always looking for other partners. The lady looked like Tootsies (remember the Dustin Hoffman film?); her husband was always trying to "come on" to other women. Tootsies "made it" one night and was caught in a compromising situation in the elevator. Oh, the gossip!

We also had Daisy onboard. She was so funny and sweet. She hailed from "Up North" of England and sounded like a cross between Hilda Ogden and Mickey Mouse; very friendly, chatty and dressed very theatrically. She always had flowers and a headband. She was in her 70s but talked in a squeaky voice. I had a lot of time for her and I made her laugh. She was on her second world cruise after losing her husband.

She made me smile when she was going to dinner with the Captain. Whooo! She said to me, I saw the Captain so I said I wanted to sit with him for dinner. Can I sit with you Captain? "Yes", he replied and she added "can I sit next to you?" . "Yes", he replied. And so she did!

No one else would dare ask to sit with the Captain but she did and good for her! I teased her afterwards and asked if she'd felt the Captain's knees under the table? "Whooo!" she went "you are naughty. No but I would have liked to have done!"

She also made me laugh. When her toe nails needed re-varnishing she realised she had no nail polish remover. I said they sell it onboard. Whooo! I'm not paying their prices she said. So I gave her a bottle of mine. I had to smile - it's typical of some older people, they can afford a world cruise or two but shy off at a few dollars for something like nail polish remover. Anyhow, she's a good lady. I made sure I chatted to her each day.

Cunard likes to think it's strict on the dress code. On formal nights passengers are not supposed to go in to most bars or restaurants (besides the Lido) if they are not properly attired.

One night instead of going to The Commodore Club we went to the Midships Bar for a pre-dinner drink. Everyone was dressed in formal gear when a British guy arrived to order a drink. He was dressed in a T-shirt and shorts. He was quite rightly politely refused service.

He started to complain loudly; said he'd paid the same as the rest of us and he would dress how he liked. He would not be told by anyone what he could or couldn't wear "so there"! MR MM turned to him and said he was not showing respect for the people who were dressed correctly and that when he booked the cruise he entered in to a contract with Cunard to abide by its terms and condition which included the dress code. Fellow passengers applauded. The guy had no answer and slunk away.

Five minutes later two Aussies arrived as though they'd just got in from the Outback (but without "Skippy"). They too were told they were not dressed correctly. They just left. Cunard staff do monitor the dress code on a formal night and if passengers don't wish to dress formally they know they have restricted access to many of the ship's facilities like bars and restaurants.

They are allowed in the self service buffet and on Queen Elizabeth in to the Winter Gardens. I can't understand why anyone would want to dress down.

Seeing men in full black tie is so sexy! How can any lady not like dressing up and feel like a movie star with "James Bond" at her side? One thing I've noticed - women dress down more than men. Not many, but some do and it annoys me. I've seen women on formal nights wearing a pair of day trousers and a plain T shirt type top and ordinary shoes.

Why don't they just wear black pants and a sparkly top if they are not into dressing? You can buy them cheaply enough. There's nothing wrong with a nice long black wrap skirt and a beaded top. Simple really! BWT "Daisy" has already booked Queen Elizabeth's world cruise for 2015 which means a least one passenger will be a fun person.

GO WEST THIS IS WHAT WE'LL DO

Pago Pago The South Pacific Polynesian Islands - A "dream" destination for many cruisers and wannabe sailors. And so it was for passengers on Queen Elizabeth. She docked in Tutuila in Pago Pago pronounced Pango Pango. Why? Forgotten already? The early Christian missionaries carried printing presses and moveable type so they could print phonetic Bibles in the local languages - good thinking! Because the language spoken in the islands was pronounced with an "n" following every "a" the missionaries didn't have enough "n's". Every time you see an "a" you should treat it as an "an" - hence Pango Pango for Pago Pago. Clear?

Now I've been here a few times in the past 30-odd years and little noticeable change has taken place over that time. MR MM and I were last here in March, 2013, and returning felt almost like we hadn't left. Stepping off the ship we were met by the tropical heat; the quay side had the same stall holders there in the same places selling the same items like sarongs, flower headdresses, grass skirts, tropical patterned shirts, and the usual local crafts.

You can pick up some nice costume and fun jewellery here and great flowers for your hair. As we past through I noticed a new native couple were present - a man and woman dressed (or half dressed should I say) in Tribal attire. He was wearing a palm wreath on his head and a grass skirt with tribal tattoos all over his body. He was a big boy, and most of the women here are just as big so many of the ship's passengers were in good company and wouldn't have felt out of place!

The two people I mention were there to pose with passengers for a photograph. I noticed a few did without realising the cost was US$30 (although there was a sign clearly pointing out the charge) making the ship's US$27-50 price per photo cheap. So be warned if you ever pose for a photo in any country you may have to pay. Wandering off through the maze of traders we knew where we were going - to see a very nice slim lady.

No, not the infamous vivacious goodtime girl Sadie but the lovely Lena. Lena has a stall in the Fagatogo covered fruit market area along the road from the port. In Pago Pago you can only go along the coastal road either to the left or to the right as you leave the ship's terminal. Head right and you walk into town. It's a small place with limited shops, a bank and business premises. All very compact.

This fruit market I mentioned where Lena works you can't miss it - the fruit is laid out on the ground outside.

Enter and you find stalls selling the same stuff as the quay side traders but for less money. There was a band playing this year but I noticed not as many traders - it looked half empty.

MR MM bought a nice cotton tropical patterned shirt here last year. Unfortunately this year all the shirts were not of the same good quality cotton. Seems they have downgraded quality for quantity but the price remained the same. Still the reason we were there was to see Lena. Her stall is in the top left hand corner of the market. She sells sundresses, but they are nothing out of the ordinary.

What she does sell though, and the reason for me paying her a return visit, are flowers. Lena makes flowers for your hair - the same style as the locals wear in their hair. They are not cheap imports from places like China but made in Pago Pago. They are very colourful and are made out of dyed palm leaves and silk flowers.

They are on a large clip and they are very, very unusual in my travelling experience. Pago Pago has the best hair flowers you will find around the world in my opinion. I went to buy yet more flowers for my hair. Lena remembered me from a year ago by my hair colour!

After a chat I purchased three flowers - cost US$5 each and one which was well over the top (again rather like me) cost US$8.

Not a King's Ransom. I didn't try and bargain because these people have little or nothing. I paid what she asked. I was happy, Lena was happy. We were all happy. Lena gave me a key ring of a flip flop as a memento.

We had decided in advance that this year in Pago Pago we would take a taxi around the West of the Island. Last year we took a taxi East. Then we were going to have a beer in the "famous" Barefoot Bar out of town but discovered when we got there they wanted US$10 admission each. "Blow it, said MR MM, I'm not paying that."

So we hot-footed it for a while along the coast near to the bar before returning to our taxi for a sedate drive back to the town and the ship.

Be warned, taxis can be very expensive here so you need to negotiate. It's no different to many ports around the world where the taxi drivers turn out to be robber barons if you let them get away with it. Not that I want to be a cheapskate and deprive a poor family from putting food on the table but there are limits. Last year we paid US$20 per hour. The car was very old and battered and had a door that would not open. It had no handle on the outside and on the inside there was a wrench on what looked like the place where the handle should be. The boot was battered as if it had a bump.

The interior was well worn with the plastic covering of the door peeling off. Well, we had said yes to the price and off we went. The car didn't let us down.

So this year Go West was the motto! Go West where the skies are blue, go West this is what we'll do. I feel a song coming on! There were dozens of cab drivers touting for business so we left the car ride 'till later when the crowds had died down thinking the prices would drop, and they did eventually. On our walk to the market we came across a driver with a nice car in an area away from the masses.

He wanted $160 for three hours. So we passed on that. After buying the flowers for my hair from Lena in the fruit market and having had a look at what else the little town had to offer, we headed back towards the dock gates to see what the taxi drivers now wanted to take us on a tour. There were still around a dozen men trying to get business by the quay.

We stopped at one in the middle because he had a friendly smile. How much to Go west? Showing him the map of where we wanted to go. We told him where we wanted to go and didn't let him tell us where he would take us.

After figuring out how far we could get in three hours we agreed a price - US$20 per hour - same as 2013. No cars were visible, they were parked across the road a little walk away. "Do you have good reliable car?" I asked, "Yes, Madam", was his confident reply. Off we went to the vehicle. Guess what? It was the exact same car we had the previous year! What were the odds on that? Long I suspect.

The door still would not open and the wrench was still fixed to where the handle should be. A different driver but the same car. We could not believe it, but we were OK as we had confidence the car would get us there and back. We had faith 12 month before and we had faith again it wouldn't let us down.

We wanted to see John Williams' first Church built close to the spot where he landed on the Island as a missionary. We got in the car and headed out of town (we were in God's hands). We passed the airport and the site where a jet crashed some years ago and then went along hugging the coastline before the driver "insisted" on taking us to see an hotel close to the water.

We couldn't argue as we were out in the sticks so-to-speak. We had a cursory look and then told him to get us to John Williams' Church. We followed the coastline and passed through areas that had been badly damaged by the Tsunami in 2009. Work was going on to reconstruct a bridge, while some houses had been repaired others were still waiting to be reconstructed. We eventually arrived at the village - it's called Leone - where Missionary John Williams had landed on what is now American Samoa. We went into the church. It, too, had suffered some Tsunami damage.

There are dozens of churches on Pago Pago and many are John Williams Churches but this is the most famous one. Leone is also where the first Catholic Church was build on the island. John Williams came from Tottenham in London and was eventually murdered after returning to the Polynesian Islands accompanied by his wife. Our driver - one of John Williams followers - retraced our route back to town and at our request dropped us at Sadie's-By-the-Sea.

We wanted to go in for cocktails and a bite to eat before heading back to the ship. We always find it nice to have some "non-ship" food at certain points in a voyage. As we paid our driver a couple of passengers from Queen Elizabeth who had already been fed and watered approached him and got him to take them back to the ship. So the old banger did good business the day Queen Elizabeth called in Pago Pago.

Sadie's-By-the-Sea, by the way, is part of the old Rainmaker Hotel. It used to be a very up-market place and when I first went there in the early 80s it was well-known by the "in crowd".

Somerset Maugham stayed there before settling in Apia, Western Samoa.

The Rainmaker went banco some years ago and was taken over by the Government.

I understand a German entrepreneur has acquired part of the hotel complex and he has restored some of it - the rest remains in a state of disrepair.

We had a bite to eat and I had a fruit drink but didn't linger because I was not feeling all that well. I had been fighting a chest infection for over a week. Hardly surprising as the A/C on the ship can be freezing and when you step outside you are hit by a combination of heat and humidity which can be debilitating. Not surprisingly many passengers suffered with colds and chesty coughs for much of the Pacific part of the cruise.

Remiss of me to forget to tell you about our Crossing of the Equator (or Crossing the Line as it is more commonly known) which happened before we reached Pago Pago. Cunard, unlike some cruise lines, actually encourage passengers to take part in this ancient yet fun occasion (unlike P&O who told us when we were on Arcadia in 2013 that "health and safety" prevented anyone but ship's crew taking part!).

Many of us thought that was a load of tosh. For as long as I have cruised, Crossing the Line has always been a fun day (except on Arcadia in 2013). It's where King Neptune, the mythical god of freshwater and the sea, comes up from the deep and onto the ship and gives the Captain and the crew permission to "cross the line".

If you're a new person or it's your first time Crossing the Line, then you are eligible to be "initiated". It is a silly, fun thing where on Queen Elizabeth even the straight-laced Captain, Alastair Clark, took part and got "gunged".

Those taking part (volunteers all) get to kiss a large smelly fish before they dive in to the swimming pool to clean themselves of the gunge (kitchen slops made by the bucket full).

Passengers and crew crossing the line for the first time are known before the ceremony as Pollywogs (how long before the politically correct brigade demand a name change?) and after their "initiation" they become shellbacks. This is how I have always known the ceremony be on cruise ships and I was first a Pollywog in 1980 and the same traditional ceremony took place on Holland America ships as it does today on Cunard. Why, you may be wondering, was it so different as I have already mentioned on Arcadia 12 month previously? For starters the Arcadia event took on a whole new ball game - literally.

No passengers were allowed to be involved just cruise entertainment staff.

They'd dressed as pirates and played silly games in the pool chucking in balls and retrieving them in their mouths and then dropping them in a bucket. The team with the most balls won! Pathetic! Why was this so? Well, if you want an answer you should address your question to Arcadia's "invisible" Captain Sarah Breton at Carnival House in Harbour Parade, Southampton, UK.

Just shows what a difference a Captain can make! Captain Alistair Clark, Master of Queen Elizabeth, was dragged to a table by the poolside, laid out and then had buckets of the coloured gunge poured over him. He was then led into the pool and all this while he was still wearing his uniform and shoes. What a sport! Did he mind ? Didn't appear to! All good harmless fun and much appreciated by hundreds of passengers who, in boiling hot temperatures, stood gazing on the ceremony that lasted over 45 minutes.

I for one am glad to see Cunard stick to good old sea-faring traditions. One more reason to choose Cunard for a world cruise, I believe.

NO DAY TO REMEMBER.

We went on an unexpected tour yesterday to the island with No Name in the middle of nowhere!. We were woken to find the Queen Elizabeth had grown wings and was flying upside down over a sea bed of snow capped mountains. Arriving precisely at one minute past no time at all and a few seconds. We disembarked and walked backwards up the gang way. Stepping out onto the soft white snow that scorched our feet, It was very hot. We had to wear our UGG boots on our hands to keep our feet cool. All the buildings were very colourful and made of ice cream. There were pale green pistachio bungalows with hazelnut tiled roofs. Strawberry coloured apartments with vanilla shutters, and the trees were all bright beige. The flowers were all wonderful shades of black with purple leaves.

We went on a glass bottomed boat to view the birds in an aviary and saw huge myna birds swimming backwards. It was not much fun and we did so enjoy it, we were all very happy or unhappy. We had our breakfast as it was dinner time, and we ate yesterday's lunch - all washed down with some very sweet bitter lemons. Later when it was still earlier we went back, or was it forward, can't quite recall. It may well have been sideways but there again it could have been upside down.

Either way we arrived back, or maybe it was forward, and joined the rest of the world in our small transporter travelling around the moon, or were we on the planet of good times? That's where we are. So tomorrow or may be yesterday we will be back, or there again we may be forward.

287

Or is it aft or afternoon? Forward or stern. POSH or not! Does this ship every stop flying long enough for us to get back on? Roll on tomorrow when we get back to normal. Happy days or was it just one day we missed in our lives?

For the uninitiated this was my take of crossing the International dateline where you lose a day when sailing Eastbound. The International Date Line is an imaginary line of demarcation that runs from the North to the South pole and passes through the Pacific Ocean.

TONI IN TONGA

Another of our South Pacific ports of call, one new to me, was Nuku 'alofa in Tonga. We arrived in a tropical storm some passengers described it as a monsoon. It was, as we say in the North of England, "raining cats and dogs...and elephants, too! This was a maiden call for Queen Elizabeth in what were known as The Friendly Islands because, allegedly, of the reception they gave to Captain James Cook when he first set foot there. And the Tongans, who are proud people, wanted to give the ship and her passengers a right Royal Tongan Welcome. And they did despite raindrops bouncing inches off the ground.

A man dressed in a grass skirt came out from under a gazebo and did a dance before blowing in to a sea shell. The sort of thing many of us did when we were kids and went to seaside resorts like Scarborough in Yorkshire.

Only this Tongan got a muffled sound from his large sea shell. The Tongan Police Band were on hand to provide a musical welcome however they were sheltering under a canvas covered structure. Nevertheless, their music was appreciated as was the dancing by some local maidens who, like the shell-blower, got soaked. When I was researching the port calls on the world cruise I decided to take a close look at what was on offer in Tonga (I remember that it used to have the heaviest by weight monarch in The Commonwealth).

I ended up looking at Trip Adviser (always I reckon a good honest guide) and the Cruise Critic website (another useful reference point). I spotted a tour that was highly recommended. It was for Toni's Guest House Tours. I liked what I read on both sites and made contact with Toni. We were in touch a number of times over six months. He had two vans to take guests around the island. One nine seater the other could accommodate 11 passengers. I said in an email to Toni that I would book the nine seater vehicle and get seven other passengers to fill the seats.

But from the Cruise Critic roll call I got 20! Not to worry that would be all right because that was the exact number of seats in Toni's two vehicles. All was well. He arranged to meet us at the port.

By the time we had tied up at a recently installed pier paid for with Chinese money the rain had abated and we headed off to find Toni. I had assumed Toni was a "local". Never gave it another thought and we were looking for a dark skinned man called Toni.

We couldn't find him at first then he "appeared" through the port gates. Hang on, are you Toni?" I enquired of a man with a fair complexion who had his grey hair tied back in a ponytail? "I sure am", he said in a broad Lancashire accent.

You could have knocked me down with a feather! I was speechless (for once). Not that we are still fighting the War of the Roses we Yorkies and the Lancastrians. It was just an accent I didn't expect to hear on Tonga and not from the guy with whom I'd booked our tour.

But what a "treasure" Toni turned out to be. He hailed from Leigh in Lancashire but quit the Red Rose County 23 years ago and headed to Tonga. He had never been to the place, obviously, and picked it because of its remoteness. He had ideas of giving it six months to see if he liked the place. He confessed to having returned to Lancashire only once since arriving on the island. He'd found his island paradise in Tonga.

One in our van asked him: "What brought you here?" Quick as a flash Toni replied: "Air New Zealand!" Must have been asked the same question a thousand times before. Anyway, Toni was a laugh a minute. His Lancashire sense of humour was infectious. Mind you some of our number needed to listen carefully or they missed his words and needed a translator. "Luke to yur left! Luke over thur" he said. Sounding a bit like the Beatles would say "thur".

He was so funny we were howling with laughter. He took us to the "hysterical" sights as he called them. One was the Trilogy. This is a three stone structure rather like Stonehenge but bigger and safer, so Toni told us, because it's "mortared in!" Get it? This is the first place in the world where the sun rises.

I remember seeing it on TV at the Millennium 2000. Toni was very funny indeed and also very knowledgeable. He'd spent years researching and learning the history of the islands. He was also very basic. Didn't pull any punches when telling you how it "really is" in Tonga.

According to him Tongans are a set of scroungers; they never work; they expect to be helped out by each other and they go into stores and "borrow" the food. All the stores had iron grill across the front and you could not enter. Food stuff and such was passed through the grills. They are "wife beaters" allegedly, "child bashers", and "lazy sods". Now you may think that sounds harsh. He did, however, explain why this is their way of life.

He understood these people and he explained how those in authority are trying to educate them not to beat their wives weekly just to look manly, and he explained why they can all "borrow" from a shop or walk into your home and borrow your things never to be returned. It is how the island had always been. He loves it all of course. Speaking at dinner that night back on board Queen Elizabeth, a lady said their Cunard tour guide had told them the same stories so there must be some truth in them. Toni probably had a blunter way of getting the message to us. He was fun. He was 72 years old going on 50 and looks like an aging hippie. I asked him if he had been a hippie and he said "No". But he could qualify now as an "aged one" because he said he had not cut his hair in twenty years.

He wears it in a ponytail. I did offer to get out my scissors and give him a haircut but he, in his own inimitable Lancashire way, said "Nooo". At least I took it to mean that!

I like characters like Toni (I think of myself as one) and we got on so well. Toni gave us a fantastic tour of the island and told us so much even about the flora and fauna. We went along the coastline and saw amazing blow holes and at the end of the tour he took us to one of his guest houses (he has several) where it costs as little as NZ$25 per night.

If I had to tell you it was on the most secluded exotic private beaches I have seen anywhere in the world (and I've travelled just a bit) I would not be lying! It really was paradise on earth! We declined lunch but had drinks and then went to the secluded bay at the bottom of the garden and frolicked in the sea.

It was stunning! The property was lovely, and Toni said he had over 50 people to help him with his businesses (a major employer of local labour our Toni).

The gardens were pristine with beautiful birds of paradise and flowers everywhere. He had dogs that were like him, friendly, and his helpers were lovely.

The bedrooms were clean and airy. I loved how the sheets were folded into the shape of palm leaves and laid across the bed! Nice touches like that made Toni's guest houses different I suspect. Toni has other properties he rents out to tourists. All are inexpensive and yet in very pretty locations.

We saw some of them on the way back to the ship. After taking us back to the ship following a fabulous day out, Toni drove off in his little van to go back to his world of peace and quiet. Toni is a fun guy and is a non-drinker but he did confess that back in his Lancashire days he had been known to take the "waters". But that was then, this was now. I recommend Toni's tour to anyone going to Nuku'alofa and, no, I am NOT on commission before you ask. Just happy to tell it as I found it.

In Tonga I met a who was hot to trot
He danced on hot coals and said come on baby light my fire
I can see you are hot stuff
I said In these shoes, I think I've seen enough!

The sailaway was as impressive as the sail-in. Again we had the police band, the dancers and again the rain came by the bucketfull. But that didn't deter hundreds of locals lining the banks of the harbour to wave us off. For the Aussies on board Queen Elizabeth there was a special musical "treat" when the Tongan Police Band played Waltzing Matilda. I saw some crying into their XXXX. Honest! The ship's sailaway party, though, had to be abandoned because of the torrential tropical rain. Talking of sail away parties, Cunard really should get their entertainment staff different uniforms. The rig for the girls is grey skirts and navy blue tops!

No fashionista would pair these two drab dull colours together! They also have to wear tights (the girls that is) or what our American cousins call panty hose. They also have to wear awful polo shirts in navy. This is only the females, the guys wear the same colours without the panty hose (I hope).

They look like they are in school uniforms or about to attend a funeral. I asked one of the girls "do you have navy blue knickers to match"? She laughed said "no just vests", and I said "are they Liberty bodices"? I doubt she knew what I meant but went on to say she would love to get rid of the uniform when in hot weather. She hated wearing the tights, and the clothes made them all too hot.

I can't understand why they have to wear dull heavy weight clothing in the tropics and in the Caribbean. A grey skirt matched with a navy polo shirt has to be the most unflattering combination for any woman of any age to wear even on the golf course!

Come on Cunard, get the girls looking more brightly coloured, lightweight clothing and get rid of the dowdy old fashioned look they have to wear when dancing at sailaways in hot temperatures on open decks as part of their jobs. What's wrong with floral dresses or a pair of white trousers and a colourful top or even a T-shirt? Where are the Cunard "fashion police" when you need them?

RETURN TO KIWI LAND

TAURANGA AND THE BAY OF PLENTY: We joined nine
other people for a private minivan tour. This had been arranged
by an Australian lady from the Cruise Critic roll call. The name of
the tour for anyone interested is "Archer's Tours." Jim Archer
owns the business he started 13 years ago. He was very
professional. Tourism is the biggest industry these days in NZ.
Not sure I believe that...what about all those sheep? I remember
first going to Auckland in 1989. The country was in recession
and no one had much of anything. Now it looks very prosperous
indeed. The main reason for our tour was to visit the thermal
geysers of Rotorua.

I'd missed out on seeing these years ago due to bad weather.
I was on a cruise in the days of good old P&O on what was my
favourite ship Sea Princess when P&O were a class act. Sadly
times do change and not always for the better! However, NZ has
changed for the better. What a fabulous country. So off we went
to Rotorua. First stop was to look back at Tauranga from the
shoreline. Unspoilt, almost deserted. A long beach which had
beautiful sea shells.

Go on can you say it fast - she sells sea shells on the sea shore? A couple of older guys were fishing from their deck chairs. The fishing line was attached to a motor and then fired some 3km from the comfort of their seats on the beach in to the ocean. Once they'd cast the line they just sat and nattered to each other and then to us when we got close until they decided it was time to haul in their "catch". They appeared out of luck when they brought in their line on our visit.

They said they'd have another go to see if they could land Moby Dick. A lazy man's way to fish I guess! Next stop was at a Kiwi farm. I love those little fruits packed with goodness. We had an impromptu lecture on how they were cultivated. I never realised they are a bit like grapes and grown on vines that can be about 5ft off the ground so come harvest time workers walk under them and grab the fruit. Does that mean all kiwi pickers are small in stature?

In the visitor centre shop we were offered samples of the two different coloured fruits - green and yellow. Something else I learned. I hadn't realised there are yellow kiwis. We were even encouraged the sample kiwi wine. Not for me but MR MM declared it "refreshing" but not until he had tried three cupfuls!

Then it was on to the park of Te Puia in Rotorua. We'd been advised to have something to eat and drink first because we would be taking part in a Maori welcoming ceremony later on and then taken on a trek to see the geysers. It just so happened there was a well-stocked and spotlessly clean cafe on hand. Once we had fed and watered we were gently herded to our meeting point with the Maori warriors by our tour driver/guide Jim. But before proceedings could get underway one of our group had to be appointed "leader". It had to be a man.

A medical doctor from Cape Town in South Africa "volunteered". He was led away by a dusky maiden towards a Maori meeting house where he came face-to-face with fearsome looking spear waving warriors making all sorts of weird noises and all had their tongues stuck out. Not a pretty sight I can tell you. I expect those early explorers came across similar looking frightening scenes. They must have been scared half to death. The doctor, to show he "came in peace", had to pick up a fern leaf the chief warrior had thrown on the ground.

It was all very serious stuff and we had been told not to laugh at any part of the procedure. We didn't dare disobey that command.

Once the warriors knew we had no evil intentions they led us in to the ornately decorated meeting house to give us a display of the Haka War Dance. But before that our hastily-appointed "chief", the doctor from Cape Town, had to rub noses with the chief warrior and the rest of his tribe which he duly did and then returned from the stage to sit with us. This was a good show and we enjoyed it but it could scare the living daylights out of young children.

Afterwards we went around the rest of the cultural centre and saw Maori weaving and carving. They have a school where people of Maori descent are taught traditional skills like wood carving for which the Maoris are famous. It can take up to five years - it's a sort of apprenticeship I suppose - to perfect the skills. The chief reason we were at Rotorua was to see the steaming geysers and the mud pools that produce what many think is the elixir of life (or youth) - mud, glorious mud for which some people are prepared to pay lots of dollars.

Again Jim Archer, who is of Maori descent, guided us around the geysers. There's nothing like having a local with the knowledge.

Jim reckoned he knew when we would see the best geyser gushers...and he was spot on. We didn't appear to miss any. There were so many mud pools all bubbling away, and Jim told us new ones kept on appearing. Jim suddenly pointed out an old geyser to my left. I spotted MR MM videoing and I said to Jim "don't call him that he will be offended!"

Just then the geyser blew its top - no, not MR MM but a big geyser close by. It was truly spectacular. By the time the steam landed on us it had cooled down, thankfully. One of the natural wonders of the world.

On our way to see the geysers we were taken into a darkened room and saw two flightless kiwis. We had just one more geyser to see - one called Rachel's Geyser in a town called Papamoa. There were some very nice pavilion-style properties that had, we were told, once been thermal spa houses.

In a nearby park there were lots of men dressed in whites and playing crown green bowls - very English. We drove back to the ship after a great day out with Jim. There was no rush for Queen Elizabeth to leave and we found we had time for an evening stroll along the boardwalk close to where we were tied up. It was all very civilised. Hundreds of locals by the water's edge enjoying the evening sunshine and soaking in the view of the majestic Queen Elizabeth. People of all ages were there, some having picnics others eating fish and chips out of newspaper (no health issues here with old newspapers).

Most were there to see Queen Elizabeth sail off into the sunset. And as sailaway time approached more joined them.

They should not have been disappointed. I wasn't. I went dancing to the live band on the back deck.

In New Zealand I met a guy
He kept giving me the eye
I know you like it hot and steamy, it will blow your mind
Rotorua was the place and I got very hot and wet
The geyser exploded and what a blow that was!
Look, said the man, we can have a hot bath.
What? In these shoes you're having a laugh!

AUCKLAND: It takes three hours to drive from Tauranga to Auckland; it's longer by sea. We arrived so early I missed the sail in. We'd been to Auckland last year (2013) but MR MM decided not to look up his former Yorkshire contacts again this time. Well, they are of a certain age and have busy lives and we know all too well about visitors getting in touch! It's all very nice to see people you like from your past but it can be tiring for the hosts when folk arrive on the doorstep. They feel obliged to become "tour guides" and show you around, and to entertain.

MR MM's friends had given us a "Rolls Royce" tour of Auckland 12 months before - we thought that was hospitality enough. So we went shopping instead - what else? I found blueberries and also some kiwi berries which I'd seen at the kiwi fruit farm. Until then I had never seen the kiwi berries, just the larger fruits. They're delicious, small and smooth-skinned and very sweet. I bought lots of punnets full to have with my breakfasts.

I tend to eat breakfast in the cabin, partly because MR MM (my butler) brings things down to me and I can add berries and the like that I have in the fridge. You can't get fresh berries in the Lido. They are available at breakfast in the dining room but I seldom go there because I can't do with people at the table always asking a thousand, often personal, questions that have all been asked before and so early in the day.

I know we could get a table for two (if we're lucky) but MR MM rarely eats breakfast so I'd need a table for one. Not much fun that. Auckland has a nice atmosphere. We wandered around the marina and came across the winning New Zealand America's Cup yachts tied up. One was being prepared to sail and give tourists the America's Cup experience. It looked exciting if you are into being thrown around from side to side. Not for me. Well, I couldn't dress up could I?

As we headed back to the ship we noticed a large banner slung across Queen Elizabeth from Mast to funnel. "Happy Mardi Gras" it read, All very colourful blowing in the wind. Five minutes later it was gone! It transpired it was a trial run for the big day in Sydney where Cunard planned to have a presence in the Gay Mardi Gras - a visitor attraction that lures people from across the globe, allegedly.

Not having been I couldn't testify to that but we will know soon enough because after New Zealand we are on our way to Sydney. Seeing the Mardi Gras banner, even if it was ever so briefly, had plenty of Friends of Dorothy on board Queen Elizabeth excited. I was already thinking I might wear my coloured wig and a few sparklers for the Sydney parade which we aimed to watch.

One of my gay friends on Queen Elizabeth told me some of his friends were getting off in Sydney but he was "going all the way! You know I like to go all the way", he said with a wink! Whooo he is a naughty one! I presumed he meant he was going all the way round the world on Queen Elizabeth!

One of our treats to ourselves when we visit Auckland is to go for cocktails in the harbour side bar and restaurant in the Ferry Building, an Edwardian Baroque structure that stands out from its "neighbours" on the largely grey waterfront. As its name suggests it is right at the heart of the ferry operation in the city and within falling distance of where Queen Elizabeth was tied up. Who says New Zealand is in a time warp where little changes? Changes there had been aplenty in the bar and restaurant since we were there only 12 months before. It had been renovated and was now quite Zen and sleek.

Its terrace is the place from which to watch the world sail by - you can either just have a drink or plonk yourself at one of the linen covered tables and enjoy the extensive fare on offer.

We opted for a cocktail or two. There were plenty of combinations and service was quick and very professional. And the encounter with the bartender/cocktail shaker that served us proved again it is a small world. His name was Harry and we discovered he hailed from the market town of Wetherby. For more than 20 years MR MM had a house in a village down the road from Wetherby, and we lived there for a while but we'd not come across Harry in Yorkshire only in Auckland on the other side of the world. Cheers! and thanks for the cocktails, Harry, they were delicious! That night at dinner yet another meeting of people from the past. We were on a table for eight next to the Captain's Table, second sitting.

We were listening to what others had done on their run ashore in Auckland when MR MM spotted two people he immediately recognised sitting at a table for two just feet away. They looked at him and he them. He stood, they stood and they all shook hands. They were Dave Oates and his sidekick, Mark. Dave is one of the top cruise consultants with Travel Masters who operate out of Nerang on Australia's Gold Coast. Dave handles the firm's top-drawer clients who insist on cruising with

Cunard. We've met these two characters before - on the circumnavigation of Australia on Queen Mary 2 in 2012. They are fun people who know how to look after their clients. They should, they've bags of travel experience.

They are also well-known to the movers and shakers in the Cunard fleet like hotel managers and pursers. We met up with them later. Business was brisk, said Dave. He was already working with clients who were booked on the 2015 world cruise on Queen Elizabeth, and others who have reserved places on voyages of the other two Cunard Queens. Looks like Dave and Mark will just have to Carry on Cruising.

BAY OF ISLAND - OUR FINAL PORT CALL IN NEW ZEALAND

Another stunning part of North Island and another mapped out by that intrepid explorer and navigator Capt James Cook who set off on his sea-faring adventures from Whitby in North Yorkshire. In fact Capt Cook named them on his round the world journey in 1769. He anchored off Roberton Island and met the local Maori people and immediately started trading with them.

In fact the Treaty of Waitangi, New Zealand's founding document which guaranteed Maori protection of their lands, fisheries and resources but has subsequently been interpreted by some as the Maori ceding sovereignty to the British Crown, was signed just a short walk from Paihia. This was a tender port which are often problematic when a liner carrying over 2,000 passengers and around 1,000 crew arrives. But here was no problem. Large craft that could take hundreds at a time arrived to supplement the ship's tenders.

We were off the ship in a jiffy and I don't mean in a padded bag! There was a shuttle bus that dropped off and picked up in Piahai town. But that was not our final destination for the day. We had decided, after doing our research, we would take the ferry across to Russell which was the first capital of New Zealand.

What we found was a quaint picture-postcard or chocolate box scene village. May be they call it a town I'm not sure. Whatever it's description it was twee, neat and tidy and the locals were extremely friendly. It looked as though residents had cut every blade of grass with a pair of nail clippers and tweaked out all the moss with eye brow tweezers! There was not a blade out of place. All the streets had grass verges and no pavement walkways. I saw one dog and he had been clipped with a number one sized clipper right down to the end of his tail.

The first hotel in NZ to have a liquor licence was in Russell only then the place was called Kororareka.

The licence had been issued by the Colonial Treasury to John Johnson for the Duke of Marlborough Hotel on October 30, 1840. The Duke still stands and proudly displays an A-board with its claim to fame.

There's another "first" in Russell - the petrol station claims that accolade (but it doesn't sell petrol at 1930 prices!). It's all very quaint with lots of B&Bs and some hotels. It suits both backpackers and those with a bigger disposable holiday budget.

I was to have another "small world" experience in Russell. As we waited for the ferry back I got chatting to a lady handing out leaflets for the ferry and for attractions on Russell. "Eee by gum lass, thee has a Yorkshire accent" I said. "How long have thee been here? Six years and she loved it, she told me . "Where's thee from in God's own county?", I enquired? Bradford she said but told people who asked she was from Halifax because it sounded better.

It turned out she went to the same school as my much younger brother... and remembered him. Small world!

Once back in Paihia we went to explore - it's a one street town with lots of craft shops, galleries and eating places with a smattering of B&Bs and hotels. We had a bit of lunch in a waterside bistro but we were down to our last NZ$35.

The food took NZ$25 which left us just NZ$10. What to buy with $10? Two Movenpick ice creams my favourite.

We walked all the way back to the pier where the ship's tenders were operating mostly to shed the calories from the ice creams. And we passed the carved images of those Maori who signed the Treaty of Waitangi. Another day of discovery was over.

G'DAY FROM DOWN UNDER

Yet again we arrived in Sydney in the pouring rain. Are we rainmakers or what? But according to MR MM's former colleague who lives and works in the city "it never rains in Sydney!" MR MM's retort is..."no, it never just rains in Sydney it pours!" The skies cleared though as we approached our berth for two days in Circular Quay - the beating heart of Sydney. The Costa Ship, Deliozia, had been following us around the world and she was already in Sydney but anchored rather than being tied up alongside a berth.

It puzzled me as to why she was not alongside in the Naval Base at Garden Island which does let cruise liners use its docking facilities? Her passengers had to use tenders to get to dry land.

My first job was to nip in to the up-market hair salon, Trumps, close to Circular Quay, to book a hair appointment. It's a salon I've used before. Not the cheapest place around but its stylists are great at their job - and I should know, I'm a hairdresser of 51 years standing! Mel, who hails from Birmingham, is my stylist.

I usually have my hair cut as it gets like a brillo pad by the time I've gone halfway round the world. It's the water on the ship that plays havoc with hair. Honest!

We just love to visit the iconic Queen Victoria Building (QVB to locals) when we're in Sydney. It's a masterpiece of design and construction that has been restored. It is a gem of a place.

It also has some of the classiest outlets seen anywhere. One of the good things about Sydney is that most of the pavements have shops with overhanging canopies so you can walk along and not get that wet.

Useful when you're in the city and it's sunshine and showers, more showers than sun on our visits! I was in search of colour for my hair - Trumps didn't have the one I needed in stock, I'd checked. I found a hair suppliers close to the QVB. It was like being in Heaven for me as an old crimper. I could have spent all day looking at all the wonderful lotions and potions that you do not see in the UK.

I got my purple hair colour and then went back to the ship to dump the goodies in our ever decreasing cabin space. Rain had stopped again and we went off to The Rocks. MR MM wanted to buy a fancy silk jacked he'd spotted earlier in a designer shop called JoeBananas that had just "popped up on The Rocks.

MR MM knew JoeBananas had at outlet in the classy QVB - he'd looked in when we were last in Sydney but didn't buy anything that visit. This time, though, he really was determined to make a purchase. He'd actually seen the jacket in the window on a model but the shop was closed at the time. When we got there it was open this time. MR MM was told by one of the company's owners that only three jackets had been made out of the same material (called Opal Strata) and no more would be - it was that exclusive.

The jacket fitted him so he bought it. Just like that -no ifs, no buts! He now owns a coat like Joseph's Amazing Technicoloured dream coat. I jokingly wondered if it had been designed on the one Jason Donovan wore? Shame MR MM doesn't look like Jason but I can always pretend he does. We had decided to go to Doyle's fish restaurant in Watson Bay.

However, as so often happens with us, we ran out of time....again. It was 2-0pm when I remembered there was a Doyle's at Circular Quay - Peter Doyle's at the Quay side.

This is the original restaurant and I first went there in 1989 when I had arrived in Sydney on Sea Princess. The restaurant has stunning views especially of the famous bridge. We got a table right away (it closed at 3pm) and we ordered the best dish in the house - the hot fish platter for two people.

It had Lobster, squid, king prawns, calamari, octopus, stuffed cuttle fish, oysters plus giant thick chips and a healthy salad.

You will know who ate what! And it was presented beautifully - in fact this fish sculpture put in front of us was almost too good to demolish. But we needed food. It was Absolutely Fabulous! We were stuffed at the end of it. Best fish meal all cruise. We'd planned a late lunch anyway because we were determined to go and watch the Gay Mardi Gras early evening.

My hair appointment with Mel was at 5-0pm; at 6 o'clock MR MM met me and we walked to the Mardi Gras. The thing was we only had a rough idea where it would take place. We soon found out...we followed the crowds and I mean crowds. We ended up in Hyde Park (not the one in London) and there the crowds were gathered big time. We got separated at one point but MR MM is very tall so I spotted him.

We went with the flow. People were in all sorts of "get ups" and states of undress; fancy dress and fancy head gear. I'd stuffed my head band with palm trees growing out of the top and a few flowers in my bag at the last minute. I wore them and I blended in. We walked for ages and the crowds were unbelievable! I can't recall ever been in such a crowd, ever - not even at the Rolling Stones Steel Wheels Concert at Shae Stadium in the late 80s.

313

It was an eye opener and a bit of an education as well. Seeing all these "Gay people" all in one place - plenty guys dressed as "hello" Sailor types.

There were lots of angel's wings attached to naked backs; glitter, glam, white stilettos, beehive hairdos, masks, sequins - it was all there, and this was just the men! The crowds were fifteen deep lining the streets as far as the eye could see.

When the parade got underway - miles from where we were standing the noise even around us was ear splitting. The music, the shouting, the cheering the blasting of horns - it was electric!

There were people selling the Aussie flag...in pink. They were selling plastic stools to stand on so people could see over the crowds. Someone made a few dollars.

These stools were going quicker than hotcakes! We were lucky enough to find an inch of space in front of a large TV screen. I could see glimpses of the parade on that, but nothing else. I spotted the floats for HIV and Aids awareness. The Gay Liberation float got the biggest roar from the crowds. We stayed with it for 90 minutes before deciding to pull out of the crowds which were getting very pushy.

We sort of barged our way through the crowds which had got to 20 deep around us. As we turned a corner into a side street a half naked guy wearing a gold mask grabbed me and said he loved my head dress. He had a mate with him and they would not let me go. MR MM filmed it all of course, and we had a laugh. Turned out they were from Ireland and travelled to Sydney - like many others from around the world - just for the Gay Mardi Gras.

We walked for over an hour and still couldn't see the ship or the hotels around Circular Quay - we were lost! We had a map and were studying it at some traffic lights when a friendly bus driver stopped and asked where we wanted to be. He said we were a long way off our destination but he pointed us in the right direction and we got there, eventually.

At Circular Quay MR MM was gagging for a drink (something stronger than water) - and so was I.

We went to The Fortune of War, Sydney's oldest pub, which was heaving but we were quickly served. Indeed, MR MM had two pints of the local ale before we got back on board Queen Elizabeth which looked fabulous all lit up. Cunard took part in the Mardi Gras parade.

Not that we saw it, but the ship had a cape banner that was hung on the top of the ship all day long fluttering in the wind. There was also a large silver stiletto aloft and a drag queen known as Vanity Fair came on the ship in the morning, allegedly. As passengers we were not told, and no one I met admitted to seeing her/him but there was a photo in the local newspaper next day so it must have happened.

Some passengers thought it was a tacky idea - I didn't mind in the slightest but I wished we had been told. The so-called pink pound is worth a lot and Cunard obviously realised that hence their involvement with the Gay Mardi Gras. The banner had "vanished" by next morning though.

Sundays when we are in port means we seek out a church and attend a service to thank God for our good fortune at being able to travel so extensively. Our second day in Sydney was a Sunday and we decided to go to the 8-30am service at St Andrew's Cathedral, an impressive looking building close to the QVB but it doesn't have the WOW! factor of The Grace Cathedral in San Francisco.

The vicar made a special announcement to the congregation regarding Easter Sunday - two special guest would be attending - The Duke and Duchess of Cambridge.
The preacher said regular worshippers would get priority seat allocations and urged them to put their names down with church officials as soon as possible.
They run an after service "breakfast" - coffee, tea and toast. We joined in. Many of the 50 or so present for the service expressed their excitement at the news of the Royal visitors - so nationalism isn't that evident among the congregation of St Andrew's!

After the service we'd arranged to meet MR MM's former colleague who has lived and worked in Sydney now for more than a quarter of a century. David and his wife, Fiona, took us to The Glenmore Hotel - a popular local old pub in The Rocks area. It was quaint and quirky, with great food and good views over the harbour. At first the sun shone then the heavens opened. We sat under our umbrellas. Fortunately we had finished out meal.

David quipped: "But it never rains in Sydney!" No, only when we visit! The sailaway was the best I've experienced from Sydney and I've done a few over the years. Queen Elizabeth backed out and went right up to Sydney Harbour Bridge (it looked for a few moments as though she was going under the bridge) before heading out to The Heads and on towards Brisbane our next port of call. We stayed on deck until the lights of Sydney were no longer visible. There was music and dancing and dancing and music. A great sailaway from one of the greatest cities on earth.

Then in Sydney I met a man
He says, let's climb the harbour bridge
I know you would love the view
Not In these shoes", I might scuff the heels!

Brisbane - we'd been here every year for the past four and done the sights like the HO HO buses and been driven down the Gold Coast, but we'd not done a Brisbane River cruise. This was our opportunity. We took the shuttle bus into the city a journey of around three quarters of an hour. On previous ship's visits to Brissy, passengers on the shuttle buses had been dropped outside what was the old Treasury Building (now a casino) but not this time.

However, it was central and as we alighted a young lady was handing out flyers for a city tour river cruise - just what we wanted although our original intention had been to take one of the CAT's we'd noticed on previous visits. The river cruise went from the South Bank which was a bit of a walk away. Crossing one of the bridges to get there reminded me of London's South Bank because there was a Millennium Wheel, a museum and theatres close by.

We wanted to catch the next tour and had 30 minutes to get to the pier. We made it but it took a brisk walk through the Queen's Mall. I had all on to restrain myself from window shopping, or shopping! I had no time to glance even, thinking how pleased MR MM would be of me showing such will power, such restraint. At the boat we paid, got a seat right at the front and then we were offered a free coffee or tea and a scone which had a huge dollop of fresh cream, strawberry jam and a fresh strawberry on top.

I had been avoiding such temptation all cruise at the white glove afternoon teas so thought just this once! It was delicious.

The scenery from the river was fascinating. Brisbane has a futuristic city skyline and there are some fabulous looking apartments right by the water. We passed old wool stores that had been converted in to posh pads. Lots of boats were tied up at the bottom of the gardens on private moorings.

A good 2 hour tour to be recommend if you're ever in Brisbane with time on your hands. Back on dry land we went off in search of a local delicacy in these parts - Moreton Bay bugs. I first discovered them when we were on the Gold Coast 12 months ago in 2013. Now these are not the bugs you see people eating on that TV programme about the jungle Get me out of here! These bugs are a type of lobster. But where to find them?

We went into the casino in the Old Treasury Building thinking they may have them on their menu. No luck! But a security guard pointed us in the right direction - the Queen's Mall. Not quite up to the standard of the ones I had on the Gold Coast but good nevertheless.

Another good shore experience in Brisbane. Now we had the Whitsundays to look forward to where we planned to fly high!

At our Sydney port call there had been a huge turnover of passengers boarding and alighting - over 1,000 or almost half the ship.

Lots of Japanese came onboard; they're good ballroom dancers and they dress well - they look glamorous in their kimonos. A strange thing happened a few nights ago.

The dress code said formal on our list; then some bright spark on the ship's staff declared informal. Confusion reigned. Those of us who do dress up made noises about the formal becoming informal.

To clear matters an announcement was made over the public address system (a rare event on Cunard who don't do a roll call of events as a matter of routine line some cruise lines) telling passengers the dress code was informal but passengers could be "formal if they wished". In other words dress as you like.

There were an awful lot who did go the whole hog and dressed formally. Sort of giving a two-fingered "salute" to those ship's officers who decide these things and who couldn't on this occasion make up their minds - formal or informal.

*Gossip from the laundry. A friend of mine was very upset going to the launderette only to find the door locked but people talking inside. She knocked a few times and the door opened. Two women were inside. One of them admitted she'd locked the doors so no one else could enter. She wanted the laundry more or less to herself.

My friend told her she was very selfish to which she replied: "Yes I am but I don't care". How rude is that?

*Gossip from the dance floor. We have had three broken wrists on the cruise since Southampton. One in the rush to get to the chocolate buffet and two on the dance floor at a dance class. I am staying away!

As we headed for Japan we were on the "downward" journey and more than half way round the world on our 118-day voyage but still having a great time. In fact it got better. We'd had some interesting speakers or lecturers as some describe themselves.

I include Lord Michael Howard although MR MM disagrees. MR MM reckons that the former Tory Party leader should manage quite well on £300 a day plus expenses he draws for being a member of the Upper Chamber of the British Parliament without having to cadge a free cruise for he and his missus. In fact MR MM flatly refused to go to listen to Michael Howard talking about Sir Winston Churchill - saying he, Howard, wasn't fit to fasten the bootstraps of the British wartime leader. It's a point of view not shared by everyone.

I went and enjoyed his talk. His wife, Sandra, was also billed as a guest lecturer. She was dreadful, in my opinion. She spoke of her life as a model in the 1960s. In her talk she reminisced but mostly name-dropped. That was her "offering". Pretty boring stuff and as they say if you remember the 60s you weren't there!

*ALL DRESSED UP! One reason we cruise is to dress up. When you are retired, and when you spend most of your time in a hot climate, the opportunities to get out your "Sunday best" are few. But on a cruise, well you can dress in several outfits a day. I do! I was passing one of the shops on board Queen Elizabeth when the shop manageress spotted me "window shopping". Yes, for once I was not inside. She recognised me from our world cruises on Queen Mary 2 in 2009 and 2012. She came out and said "Maggie, just the girl, Will you model one of our dresses in a fashion show? How could I refuse? On Queen Mary 2 I'd modelled for the shops including the world famous jeweller H Stern.

Excuse me if I am in repeat mode, but when I worked on the SS Rotterdam, MRS STERN was a regular passenger and came to me for her hair doing. Small world! Back to this fashion parade on Queen Elizabeth.

The manageress wanted me to wear one of the classy dresses on sale from the Joseph Ribkoff label.

Now I had purchased just such a Ribkoff dress from the ship's shop earlier in the cruise but hadn't worn it. Well, didn't want to clash with any other passenger who may have bought the same number at a cocktail party did I?

It was agreed I could wear my own Ribkoff for the fashion parade. On the day of the show I did my hair and found a fabulous pair of shoes out of my large collection to match my dress, and stuck one of my signature flowers in my hair. Well, you have got to make the effort.

I was the second model on the catwalk and when I strutted my stuff I heard a huge cheer from the upper level of the Queen's Room - it was the "in crowd" encouraging me. All the passengers who took part looked "the bees' knees" and we were all given a round of applause. We all had escorts to walk us around. Mine was a handsome young thing with blond hair and worked in the shops on board, He made a wonderful escort.

CUNARD WHITE STAR SERVICE:

It's a service of which Cunard is rightly proud...most of the time. One such event is the after afternoon tea served on all three Cunard liners wherever they are in the world at 3-30 pm. local time.

The waiters and waitresses wear white gloves and serve an assortment of dainty sandwiches all washed down with a variety of different teas - my favourite is Earl Grey. I'd made a few visits to the Queen's Room to meet a lady friend for a cup of tea and a gossip. We don't eat the delicious looking pastries and scones

323

as we work out in the gym and are keep fit girls. Up each morning working our butts off as discipline is needed here and we have it.

No way will we undo the hard labour and torture we go through for the sake of vanity in a morning. So afternoon tea it is a time to catch up. My friend's husband went on the overland tour to China. It was a Cunard tour but she didn't want to go. Overland tours are popular on world voyages, they can be tiring but worth the effort as it is often a once in a lifetime experience to visit such wonderful places.

I also go to afternoon tea on my own just for a nice cuppa served in a very civilised manner. I enjoy the musicians that play there usually it's the resident string quartet, or maybe the harpist.

I love the way they dress in formal gowns although it is only mid afternoon. Being a dressing up kind of gal I appreciate this more than the pastries and scones.

Afternoon tea is so popular on Cunard that the queue to get in starts around 30 minutes before kick-off. I find this fascinating as many people have barely recovered from lunch. 4-0pm is the time I go when the crowds have died down. Afternoon tea is also served in the self service buffet The Lido. It doesn't have the same appeal as going to the Queen's Room for me, though.

WE'RE GOING TO A WEDDING....

Getting hitched at sea has become more popular apparently in recent years. In fact it was the reason given by Cunard to shift the registry of their three liners from Southampton to Hamilton in Bermuda so captains could more easily marry people on the High Seas. Liz & Richard (not their real names) were the only two to get married at sea on the 2014 world voyage of Queen Elizabeth. Now they nearly matched the Burtons in the wedding stakes if you get my drift! They had arranged to get married before joining the world cruise, but no family were with them so the "in crowd" became their adopted family for the day. And what a day it was!

It started as normal for me - gym, walk, talk. The wedding was at 3-30pm so plenty of time to get ready. Some of us had been given jobs to perform before, during and after the ceremony. MR MM volunteered to video the event, two other members of the crowd were witnesses. I was the ring bearer. One of the characters on the ship, Daisy, was flower girl. (I did Daisy's hair and added some flowers). She was a lady of a certain age and at times forgetful. She told me she didn't know what the flowers she was to carry were for. I told her they were NOT for her hair but for the bride).

After my walk and talk session, we went as usual into what I call God's waiting room - the section of The Garden Lounge reserved exclusively for world cruise passengers. It's not a place to linger unless you want peace and quiet; are into needle point or crosswords. Around 11-0am the bride to-be entered along with MR Right. Both colour co-ordinated in black and red. They're a charming couple and so loved up they dressed in the same colours - a good move for when they get sozzled they can recognise each other.

The bride-to-be had planned on having a hen party a few nights before her big day. Unfortunately (or may be fortunately) she was having such fun in the Golden Lion pub on board she forgot to turn up!

To make up for her "no show" she held an impromptu hen "do" in a section of the Garden Lounge where any passengers can congregate. Her husband-to-be disappeared to the Golden Lion with instruction that all male members of the "crowd" join him. As this was a spur of the moment event with no official invitations someone turned up in her bikini and sundress; I was in my workout gear from the gym, and another "hen" turned up in gym outfit. The bride to be looked fabulous in her black and red chiffon number. I must say we did look a motley crew. But who cared?

We were seeing the soon to be bride off in good old girlie fashion. There were though no T-shirts with our names on, or cowboy hats to identify members of the party.

Well, we weren't going to get drunk (not at 11am) and we couldn't get lost because we were at sea and none of us could walk on water.

Our small but perfectly formed group did liven up the normally sedate Garden Lounge with our merriment. Not sure what kind of drink was consumed but as I don't drink wine I had the cocktail of the day whatever it was. We were very noisy and we laughed 'till we cried.

She who was to marry did a dance with another lady and then the band struck up. It was their lunchtime spot at 12-30. We were singing and carrying on and we could see people thinking this could not possibly be happening on Cunard. When the bottles of booze were empty we went off to join the boys in the Golden Lion pub.

It was the same in there - laughter galore. In fact a crowd gathered thinking there was a darts match on! But time marched on and the bewitching hour approached but no one wanted to make a move away from the Golden Lion bar.

Eventually I escaped and went to get ready and then went to do flower power girl Daisy's gorgeous long hair before heading to the bride's cabin to help her. She already had "company", two ladies helping her drink yet another bottle of vino.

The Bride did look stunning in her long red gown with red and black accessories. That's her "look" and she carried it off amazingly!

The nuptials were being carried out in the small Admiral's Lounge. You can hardly swing a cat round in the place, but it is very special. This couple being jolly, friendly souls and well-known around the ship meant far more passengers wanted to see the ceremony than could be accommodated.

Those who couldn't squeeze in had to wait in the adjacent Commodore Club to congratulate the happy couple. The Captain (Alistair Clark) conducted the service and some taped romantic music was played. Champagne was served in the Commodore Club and after a while the mandatory wedding group photograph had to be taken.

It had been decided the best place was under the big clock on the steps outside the Golden Lion pub. We all adjourned there. To the clock not the pub!

A Japanese guy (not in the wedding party) stood behind the ship's photographer taking the shots. MR Japan decided to clown around taking his own photos of the wedding party.

He jumped up and down like a monkey trying to distract us all by pulling faces and making gestures. Then it happened - he dropped his expensive looking video camera. Smash, bang, wallop! Oh, what a picture what a photograph! He snuck off with his tail between his legs and his camera in pieces.

I often wonder why the Japanese sell us all tiny hand held cameras and they themselves have HUGE ones with lots of extensions and big zooms. Maybe it's a little man complex. I've gotta big one!
Not the end of a perfect day for MR Japan but for the happy couple and we "hangers on" or "invited guests" it certainly was a highlight of our voyage so far.

UP AND AWAY IN THE WHITSUNDAYS

The Whitsundays are another piece of paradise on earth...and again discovered by Captain James Cook who named them as such because he believed it was Whit Sunday when he came across them. There is some discussion still about that! Another place MR MM and I have visited before (lucky us). Airlie Beach is where cruise ships anchor and passengers are tendered in. It can be a fairly long job getting upwards of 2,000 people from ship to shore. But when Queen Elizabeth called there was no problem - whether by accident or design - big catamarans that could carry hundreds came alongside and transported us to shore.

On our previous visit we have just wandered around Airlie Beach and its surrounding area. It's all very scenic and spotlessly clean. This time, though, MR MM - who has no head for heights - wanted to see The Great Barrier Reef...from the air. The alternative's a ship's tour on a boat. Places on them are often limited as they take you to a pontoon on the Reef where only 200 people are allowed to stand at any given time. This is where you snorkel and have a lunch - or both. It takes almost three hours to get there by catamaran and more often than not the seas are rough making it a very bumpy ride.

On previous cruises lots of passengers complained when they got back they'd been sea sick, and others hadn't realised it took so long to get to the pontoon. Snorkelers generally love the adventure, others who've made the trip often wished they hadn't bothered. So by air it was. MR MM contacted GSL Aviation by email months before we even set sail.

He liked what he heard from them and the service they offered. He wanted to take the noon flight reasoning that the sun would be at its highest in the sky and so there should be little or no shadow. All looked set fair until the question of booking arose. MR MM found out that he had to pay in advance (not something he likes doing and especially where there is a chance the waters around Airlie are too rough for ship's tenders).

It has been known for this port call to be abandoned because of the weather. So MR MM thanked the lady at GSL Aviation for her time and effort and explained the reason he was not booking ahead of time. Well, it was going to cost around A$400 and that's a lot of money to lose if we couldn't go ashore. OK you could try and reclaim it from the insurance company but I wouldn't hold my breath! MR MM did, however, promise he'd make contact before Queen Elizabeth's arrival in the Whitsundays to see if places were still available.

He knew there was no guarantee but it was worth a shot. And so it proved!

The day before our arrival MR MM had checked the weather forecast. It looked good; every chance Queen Elizabeth would be anchored off. True to his words he phoned the airline.

When he gave his name they remembered him and the reason he hadn't booked five months before. Had they got two places on the noon flight the day of our visit? Would you believe it - they had just two!

Our luck was in. Once ashore we had an hour to kill before our scheduled pick up by GSL Aviation's transport. We "people watched". There is something very different when you arrive by sea in the Whitsundays. Villagers, all volunteers, don identical "uniforms" - well the men wear trousers and not skirts. They have sashes identifying themselves as "Whitsunday Ambassadors". And what good ambassadors they are. A tremendous "advert" for the Whitsundays and they all look to be "over a certain age".

No question or request seemed to stump them. And all were so cheerful. Well, who wouldn't be living in such an idyllic setting? I'd offer to be a volunteer ambassador too if I lived there.

Bang on time the GSL minivan arrived to take us to the village's airstrip. Not Heathrow, not even Leeds/Bradford….more Sutton Bank in North Yorkshire. The airport building was neat and tidy and airy. There was a small cafe off the main lounge. We were already checked in - that had been done on the way to the airport in the minivan. A young man appeared. He introduced himself as Josh, our pilot. After filling the plane with fuel, Josh got us all on the tarmac by the plane and we had our safety briefing after which we were ready to board. But there was no scramble to get the best seats. Josh called out our names and we were given our seat location.

When he booked MR MM had to give our weight so before we even got to the airport it had been calculated who would sit where so the plane would be balanced when it was in the air.

I do believe this used to be common practice in the early days of flying to get the weight distribution right. No room on this flight for some of the "heavy weight" passengers on Queen Elizabeth. They wouldn't have fitted in to the plane to start with! Take off was a rather bumpy affair but as we climbed it soon levelled out and it was a smooth ride for most of the hour long flight. We were all hooked up to the intercom system and heard the pilot give and receive instructions from the ground. We were around 1500 ft for a lot of the flight out to the reef. We passed over numerous of the 74 islands that make up the Whitsundays including Hamilton Island with its azure waters and its powder white sandy beaches.

Other islands we flew over included Hayman, Hook and Hazlewood to name but a few. The scenery was breathtaking.

Josh pointed out landmarks on these islands including spa resorts. We passed over two helicopters on Hamilton Beach.

They'd landed so their passengers could have a picnic. Nice one! You know when you reach the reef - you can see all sorts of weird and wonderful shapes below the waterline. Josh radioed to the control tower he was dropping to 80ft. What a view we had from that height. It was stunning. None of us had seen anything like it before and probably wouldn't again unless of course we returned and took another flight. We circled the famous Heart Reef which, as its name suggests, is shaped like a heart. Spectacular it was! Getting good photos from the cramped plane was difficult. The best pictures are in my head and will stay there for a long time.

After flying over Bart Reef, Hook Reef, Hardy Reef and Line Reef we turned and headed for the airport but not before passing over the pontoon used by the ship's tours. We climbed back to 1500 ft and Josh came on intercom and asked if any of us were passengers on Queen Elizabeth. Three of us were so he "buzzed" the ship. Another few minutes and the flight was over. We landed at the Whitsundays Airport and were then driven back into the centre of the village.

That flight was just tremendous; out of this world. Worth every dollar it cost. In Airlie we then got "shipwrecked". Well, we went to the Shipwrecked Restaurant for a drink and a bite to eat. To burn off some calories we walked back to our tender pick up point in the harbour.

Big queues of passengers waiting to get back on board Queen Elizabeth but the tendering operation was efficient and the wait didn't seem long at all. We'd had a day trip of a lifetime.

Back on the ship we heard tales of woe from some who'd gone to the Great Barrier Reef by boat - many had been sick on both legs of the voyage, others had missed out on getting to stand on the pontoon because there were so many people out there it broke the 200 person limit. I think we did the right thing to see the Great Barrier Reef from the air. True, we saw no fish but we did see the reef in all its glory. We were happy.

In Whitsundays I met a man he said
Come with me and we'll fly
To the great Barrier Reef
and swim under the sea
I said "In these shoes?" "I can't get them wet!

RABAUL, PAPUA NEW GUINEA

Not the most pleasant of port calls. It's a wake-up call; wake up to poverty! Ships call here because of its role in the Second World War. It was occupied by the Japanese who built submarine pens and establish a huge military presence with the aim of overrunning Australia. On January, 23, 1942, the Japanese assault began on Rabaul and it became the forward base for the Japanese campaigns on mainland New Guinea.

It was strategically important because it was a huge landmass immediately north of Australia and the Japanese built major air, land and naval bases.

It's what's left of these that is interesting to some who sail these waters. But it's not our thing. We've been here before. We just wandered around the settlement then and repeated it this time. On this occasion, though, we were greeted by a group of lady Gospel Singers all nicely dressed. And their songs were tuneful. Many of us showed our appreciation by making a donation.

Rabaul's main, if only, attraction is its active volcano just out of town. It always seems to be blowing its top but nothing serious - just spewing out smoke and ash. It was on our visit.

Rabaul is normally a dusty, dirty place and the people look poor, very poor, but they do make some really nice handicrafts like colourful shoulder bags - I bought one on our first visit here in 2012 and I got another this time. We were knee deep in volcanic ash in 2012 but in the run up to this visit it had rained for days so everywhere was clean and green for a change.

But the people still looked poor. Cunard laid plastic covering over all stairs leading to the gangway and all elevators were covered ready for the muddy feet to return. It wasn't to be - the day was very hot and humid and no volcanic ash stuck to our shoes.

In fact the heat got unbearable after a couple of hours and we returned to the ship but not before I'd "spent" US$100 - no I hadn't bought the place, just given money to the barefooted children and there were lots of them. They were cute. They'll pose for photographs for a dollar or so. I went prepared with lots of one dollar bills.

On my first visit to New Guinea in 1980. I went to Port Lae. I was working at sea and the ship was on a world cruise. I escorted a tour to the botanical gardens. All the time we were there I noticed a lady following us around. And as we were about to leave she pushed a new born baby in my arms, begged me to take it and scarpered.

I was left holding the baby! Not a good idea for me as I am not child friendly! The police arrived and took the child.

I often wonder what happened to that baby - can't remember if it was a boy or a girl. Didn't have hold of it long enough to find out.

On this visit there were dozens of new born babies in their mother's arms being breast fed while their parents tried to sell their wares - beads and bags in various shapes and sizes. Paper and notebooks, pens and pencils are good items to take ashore to give to the locals for their pupils are often without such things that school children in the developed world take for granted. We had a good sail away but there was no dancing - it was far too hot. The band again played Bob Marley reggae and the like. I just wished they could have played some different tunes because I was not the only one to be Bob Marleyed out. I don't want to hear "No Woman no Cry" again if I can help it. I've got earworm from it!

TURNING JAPANESE, I REALLY THINK SO

First port of call KAGOSHIMA.: This was a maiden port of call for Queen Elizabeth. We arrived to a great welcome from the locals. A large band, made up of local school children, serenaded us in and they were excellent. We had booked a ships tour to see an active volcano for Japan is a country with many volcanoes. We chose the volcano tour as it seemed the most interesting and we wanted to see more than just shops.

Yes, really, I was beginning to get "shopped out"! Japan being very built up and overcrowded a trip to the volcano and some peaceful gardens appealed. I wanted to see cherry blossom.

Our tour was for five hours. We were driven by coach to join a ferry to take us across to the other side of Kagoshima - a 15 minute crossing. Japanese cities love their Ferris wheels Kagoshima was no different (the wheels are a focal point and illuminated at night). The crossing was quick and I was entertained watching two young mothers with five kids having a hairdressing session.

Everything in Japan is very organised and extremely clean. There was an area on the ferry with a padded floor for the kids to play on which was where the two women were brushing and combing the young girls' hair into different styles.

Not sure what it was all about but they did a good job of creating up-styles. I was intrigued being an old hairdresser myself. The bus by the way travelled with us on the ferry. We got off and went out on deck for the journey over the water and got back on the bus as the ferry came in to dock. It was a roll on roll off type ferry.

First stop was to the mountain/volcano. Very quiet on this side of the water and lovely views. We could just see Queen Elizabeth in the distance. The coach climbed up a mountain road and stopped at an observation point so we could view the "live" volcano which we were told had erupted 58 times already in 2014. The last devastating eruption though had been 100 years ago but our guide said they are expecting another big one "any time". The volcano is monitored and all citizens have evacuation practice regularly. There were shelters everywhere.

There was free time to explore and we did. After about ten minutes (as if by order) the volcano erupted very fiercely and it was amazing watching the lava and ash rise and then fall. We were all soon covered in grey ash. Then another eruption and more ash came down on us. It looked like we were covered in snow. Problem was it got on our chests and made others wheezy.

It brought on my asthma. Despite that it was a spectacular sight. After this we went back to the ferry for the return to the other side of the water. Here we were taken to beautiful SENGANEN GARDENS and the SHOKO SHUSEIKAN museum. There were shops selling expensive souvenirs; also plenty of food vendors selling strange combinations like green tea and sweet potato ice cream. It was all very nicely done and not tacky in any way, but I always struggle to find something worth buying in Japan.

When I do I seem to go through money very quickly - everything seemed to be 6000 yen, which is around US$60. I managed to buy some chop stick type things with silk flowers like locals wear in their hair for around that price. I shall wear them for the Madam Butterfly ball. The gardens were lovely and the tour was relaxing and peaceful. We returned to the ship where there were hundreds of locals swarming around along with lots of local dancers and entertainers and ladies dressed in the most colourful kimonos and all with beautiful hair decorations.

The locals were fantastic and as we walked through the door towards the ship two Japanese men took your photo and then printed it off and handed it to you. Must have cost those two guys a fortune in ink alone. There were huge crowds gathered by the time it came to sailaway. The band played and many in the crowd waved orange flags. In fact it was a sea of orange.

341

They cheered when Queen Elizabeth cast off. We've been to Japan before, not this port, and have always found the locals give an enthusiastic welcome to cruise ships, at least the ones we have been on both of which happened to be owned by Cunard.

The Japanese we've met have all been very polite, very well mannered and very well dressed.

Their country is spotlessly clean; not a cigarette butt in sight, nor a scrap of rubbish and no graffiti, and no chewing gum on the pavements.

The young people love to practice their English. This cruise was port intensive in Japan, one reason we picked it. Helpfully, Cunard handed out a list of phrases and also instructions on how to use a Japanese loo. Yes, really!

In Japan there are two types of public toilets - squat, and western-style. The western style come with accessories, and you need to be a techie to use them. The seats have a console like a large remote for a TV attached to the side. This has buttons -one plays music as ladies in Japan do not like to hear any noise from the cubical next door.

There is a water splash button that washes your bits and bobs afterwards and also a dryer that blows hot air up your bum! In some the toilet roll is heated so the paper is warm! You can press a button to clean the seat and also some loos have weighing scales inside attached to the wall and even a contraption that's like a high chair for baby to sit in whilst an adult does her biz.

It is a work of art trying to figure what to press for a flush and waving my arm at all the settings that had a green button did not seem to work in one public loo. You also find there is a mini men's urinal in the ladies - for little boys - and changing facilities.

One thing that is missing is soap to wash your hands and often there's no hand drier, so Japanese ladies carry lovely looking handkerchiefs that are double sided - one being made of towelling. They use these to dry their hands and place them back in their handbags in a fancy matching pouch.

YOKOHAMA was another Japanese maiden call for Queen Elizabeth. Big welcome once more. Thousands standing 10 deep waiting for our the arrival at one hour before midnight! Many of them had night lights and waved them madly as if they were at a Barry Manilow concert! A fantastic welcoming sight. Next day the crowds were still around the cruise terminal; they stayed until sailaway.

Two Japanese ladies came on board and played instruments. It was a great cultural show. So what did we do with our long day in YOKOHAMA?

We took an all day Cunard tour to Tokyo. A long drive in heavy traffic.

343

Places like Tokyo you need a ship's tour because it can be difficult getting around. We did the city tour; visited the Imperial Palace, and the SENSO-JI Buddhist TEMPLE in ASAKUSA.

We had a Japanese lunch at the Grand Prince Hotel. The lunch was cooked in front of us on a stainless steel tabletop(the centre was the hot plate). We sat at a table for four. When the chef arrived he cooked vegetables and steak on the steel heated part. The steak was very marbled and tasted delicious!

Beef in Japan is reared by hand and the cattle have massages and their coats anointed to help produce good meat. So they say!

After lunch we went on to visit more temples and had some shopping time. There are lots of imported designer goods. Not sure who buys all this as the regular lady is very drab in the dress stakes although the young girls do have fabulous kimonos. Back at the ship we found the whole area awash with people. We had to push our way through the crowds they were so large.

Lots had children and little dogs, often designer type dogs wearing coats and some looked to be wearing dresses with little bows! One little pooch was being wheeled around in dog pram and quite a few wore nappies or diapers for my American friends! On our tour our guide explained that some Japanese families employ dog walkers and we did see a few men with may be 10 canines on leads.

We had a giggle when our guide got her words mixed up. She explained the government only had ERECTIONS every six years!

In the cruise terminal a local artist had set up shop and started to paint Queen Elizabeth on canvas soon after we had docked. It was a huge canvas. He seemed to be painting from memory - I couldn't see any photographs of Queen Elizabeth anywhere near him. I was fascinated with it. When we got back to the ship there were crowds of passengers around the artist and he'd got a long way to painting the liner but he still had some way to go before it was finished. We went for drinks in a cabin with a balcony that was occupied by some friends - they didn't have the same amount of luggage as us - only nine cases - so their cabin was not crowded like ours.

I decided to nip down to the terminal after we'd eaten on the balcony courtesy of room service, to see if the painting was finished. It was very quiet; most passengers were back on board because our departure time loomed. I had to be quick. I dashed to the spot where the painting was and I was blown away by what I saw. It was amazing - so good and colourful. The artist was there. He spoke English (I had not mastered any Japanese despite all the Japanese on board!). He told me about the painting.

He was pleased I had recognised him and he asked to have a photo taken with me, not the other way round!

Someone took the photo and then they found a large card and he wrote a message to me and signed it. I was so happy. I wondered if anyone from Cunard saw the end result? They should have snapped it up. It was great.

We passengers were treated to a quite extraordinary sailaway of flashing lights, cheering, waving and shouting crowds who had again turned out in their droves to see Queen Elizabeth leave their city.

It was made extra special as the skyline was all lit up and the Ferris wheel was a blaze of changing colours. All the local boats coming and going were decorated in illuminated colours. A terrific send off - the best we'd seen on this cruise so far.

But some of us wondered if the huge crowd were really there to see if we got safely under a bridge? There was, we had been told, only a maximum of 6ft clearance for a liner the size of Queen Elizabeth even when the tide was right! We made it under without incident. Phew! But it looked less - more like 3ft! Another good day in Japan.

Another day, another Japanese port. This time Kobe which is around the corner almost from Osaka. Kyoto was the destination for a lot of passengers but MR MM and I wanted to ride the Bullet Train. We had been to Osaka and Kyoto on Queen Mary 2 in 2012. I'd researched and knew we could get to HIROSHIMA on our own from

Kobe. There was a trip from the ship on the Bullet Train only this included a visit to the atomic bomb museum.

We'd been to the atomic bomb museum in Nagasaki. That was enough - very explicit, very, very disturbing. We wanted to be independent travellers and were going alone but the newlyweds asked to join us. Queen Elizabeth was greeted by another band playing on the quay and again hundreds of people waved us in. This was also a maiden port of call - our third in Japan.

From the cruise terminal we took a driverless train in to town, got off and went into the underground metro system - we were going against the rush hour commuters (and there were thousands) so no rush or crush for us. I've never seen cleaner trains. This underground journey took all of four minutes. We were then at the Shin Kobe - a Bullet Train station.

My research told me I needed to book the Nozomi 700 series which can reach speeds up to 185 mph. It's also the express. We'd all decided that we would travel first class one way and back in cattle (or steerage) just to see the difference.

You can buy returns but as we didn't know what time we would be travelling back we bought one way only.

The first class section was empty but for us. The seats were plush and wide with big footrests and our carriage had a carpeted floor.

We were given a cold towel and then the trolley dollies Japanese style arrived with refreshments.

The ticket collector came and punched the tickets and as he left the carriage he bowed to us all! How amazing is that? Can you see that happening on the Great Western?

Our train took off and I mean took off. It was fast, like being in an aeroplane. It was quiet and smooth and you did not feel to be moving. It was exciting and one hour 10 minutes later we were in Hiroshima having sped past villages, towns and open countryside. An amazing experience at such speed. We took a streetcar (tram) to the Atomic Bomb gardens where we and the newlyweds parted company.

We arranged to rendezvous at the train station at 4pm. MR MM and I walked around the peace gardens. They were really lovely but we did not venture into the Atomic Bomb Museum. Once was enough. We felt their pain. We'd just left the gardens and were walking across a bridge to head back to the tram stop when we saw a group of young ladies dressed in beautiful kimonos. We asked if we could take their pictures. They were very keen but wanted me in the photograph, too.

But then they started shouting to MR MM, "Papa, Papa" and beckoned him to join us. A passerby took a picture on my camera. I thought calling MR MM Papa was so funny - he'd not been to Hiroshima before so a case of mistaken identity perhaps!

We had a healthy Japanese lunch before heading to the train station. There was a queue for tickets for the Bullet Train but we were waiting no more than 10 minutes until we reached the front. The counter clerks were all very efficient and polite.

Travelling with the masses on the return journey was another experience. The seats were a lot narrower than in first class; there was no carpet on the floor but there was plenty of leg room for tall people like MR MM and the bridegroom who is also over 6ft.

Again the carriage was spotlessly clean. The trolley dollies came with their cart ladened with food and drink. They bowed as they left the carriage as did the ticket collector. The cost? Out first class was 26,860 yen and the return standard ticket was 19,880 each.

Was it worth it? You bet! We loved the whole experience. MR MM put this down as the second best thing on his WOW! list on the cruise so far - the other being the flight over The Great Barrier Reef. Don't be afraid to have a go and do the Bullet Train as independent travellers.

If you get stuck there are information kiosks in the stations staffed by helpful people; fellow travellers are also very willing to assist, especially the young people - teens, 20s and thirty somethings. The Japanese are a very courteous race. Local dignitaries came on board to honour Queen Elizabeth and her crew on this maiden call. They also rolled out the barrels of, er, sake.

But there's always a catch - we had to listen to speeches from the half dozen VIPs in the line-up and watch some fearsome entertainers wielding dangerous looking objects.

There was no shortage of sake which was served in wooden bowls inscribed with the words Kobe, Maiden Call Queen Elizabeth and the date. I took a bowl from one of the ship's waiters just to be polite. I dipped my finger in and smelt it - whisky, I thought. Not for me. It went down the sink in ladies toilet. It was a nice gesture by the people in power in Kobe. I had a good Sushi supper afterwards without the sake.

We had the Madam Butterfly themed ball in the Queen's Room. I wore my kimono and it was well admired so I had a photo taken by the ship's photographers. I will never wear it again so I had the photos for the record, and lots of Japanese were coming up and saying lovely comments and wanting my photo with them.

It was an amazing sight of East meets West. I was late arriving in the dining room because of all the attention, but it was OK. Our head waiter, Shetty, was standing at the entrance waiting to walk me to my table, as unusual.

He stopped on the staircase and stood with me for probably a minute 'till all the cameras stopped clicking.

No! I was not at the Oscars but could have been as many people clicked away. It was very funny. I love to dress up for a giggle.

We managed to get out of dinner quicker but not before MR MM had a word with the maitre 'd. MR MM had previously suggested to the lead waiter at our table he should "smarten up his act" after getting the orders wrong so often and being so slow. He did for a while but slipped back in to his old, bad, ways.

Being out of the main dining room by 10pm meant we could go to the ball! A bit like Cinderella!

The Madam Butterfly Ball was well attended with many people in Kimonos. Not just the Japanese but passengers like myself who like to dress on the themed nights. If you are dressed in the theme of things, the cruise director does a walk around the ballroom where all participants show off their costumes. Afterwards they usually have a progressive dance where you all dance a few steps then move on to the next person.

I went to join the dancers. We had a progressive waltz. I got a Japanese man to dance with. He was a brilliant dancer. Thing was he didn't realise we were only meant to go around the floor once. So after three rounds my head was spinning as he was whirling me around like a rag doll. I thought I was about to take off and go into orbit! The one word of Japanese I could remember was Arigato!

(Thank you). I looked up at him with a smile and I shouted ARIGATO! He stopped. Wow!

He was a fast mover and it was more of a fast quick step than a waltz. The next partner was a friend of the bridegroom so we had a more British type shuffle before the music finally stopped.

There is another lady I meet at formal nights who has the most amazing costumes. She makes them all herself and they are very good. She is a sewer, and the detail she creates is quite amazing. Her kimono was stunning! She got a lot of attention and photos taken and like me she says she does it for fun and she cannot understand why anyone would not want to join in. My Kimono was bought from my favourite designer store - Ebay.com - and cost next to nothing.

Nagasaki was the next port of call and our last in Japan. Another maiden port call for Queen Elizabeth. We were in Nagasaki on the maiden visit on QM2 and received a huge welcome, including a performance of Madam Butterfly in the theatre. I was hoping this would happen again but sadly the ship's plaque receiving ceremony was at 11-0am when most of us were off the ship, so no Madam Butterfly this year. We did a full day tour two years ago taking in all the main sites, including the Atomic Bomb Museum and the Peace Gardens. This year we decided to explore the city on our own.

We took a number of street cars doing different routes and hopped on and off as we pleased. It is a very good way to see Nagasaki and inexpensive using a day pass. Nagasaki is also easy to navigate - and the walking is easy, too. We hopped off one tram near a shrine, and another time we got off at the main railway station where a group of musicians were entertaining in the open air. There was also a huge shopping mall on the station complex with a supermarket - more blueberries for the cabin fridge.

In another part of town in yet another shopping arcade Nagasaki's cultural side was on display - people painting pottery and others creating paintings on canvas and on board.

A group of young men and women from the city's music centre were part of the exhibition. They were dressed in medieval style outfits. As we walked by one lady took my arm and said "Will you dance with us"? I was taken aback; I didn't know what to say - just agreed not wanting to be disrespectful. They all formed a group and gave me the hand of the young man in white tie and tails. A kind of a young Fred Astaire!

We did a sort of practice dance then the music was turned on and it was like chamber music. I began to wonder if I was being auditioned for Strictly Ballroom Japanese style! I felt I wasn't dressed for the part in my European winter clothes but they didn't mind. I soon got into the rhythm of it all and after around five minutes I thought that must be the end but no, the music continued and once again I found myself going round in circles Eventually the music stopped. We all bowed to each other.

One lady spoke a little English. She told me she'd been to London and Bath. The Japanese sure love to dance.

A crowd had congregated close to our berth come sailaway but nowhere near the numbers that came to wave off Queen Mary 2 in 2012. A school band played and 14 young girls danced a bit like you see before big American sporting events.

It was a very happy sailaway. The girls all shouted bye bye see you again! The music played on 'till we were well away from our berth.

Our Japanese ports of call had been fantastic. I liked the country, it's clean and the people are organised, friendly, polite and exceptionally well mannered. Everyone, everywhere made us very welcome but it did not have the WOW factor for me. I felt it a bit flat and too organised to the point where you dare not lose a hair from your head for fear it landed on the floor. I saw only one cigarette butt all the time we were in Japan.

I can't imagine any of the Japanese having a real good laugh. It would have to be an organised tummy rumbler!

Their attention detail is wonderful. Buy something and the shop assistant will gift wrap it for you. I made a purchase in Nagasaki and it was wrapped to perfection and then I was handed a free gift, perfectly wrapped - it was a reusable folding shopping bag.

I am glad I've seen the important parts of the country. I don't feel the need to go back a third time. It did not give me a "buzz" but we had a fabulous time.

In Japan I met a man who liked to stand on his head
He told me he had a big water bed
Come let me lay beside you he said
What in these shoes"? It 'll spring a leak!

A DAY OUT IN SOUTH KOREA

This country is never far from the world's news headlines given the unpredictability of the leader of the communist North and his threats against South Korea. In fact the two countries are still technically "at war" - but it's been more a war of words in recent years. The border between North and South Korea is a long way from - Busan - the port where Queen Elizabeth docked on its maiden call. Busan, though, has had a name change - it used to be called Pusan. Like our ship, MR MM and I had not been to South Korea before and was one of the reasons we booked this particular world voyage because of the number of "new-to-us" ports of call.

We'd booked a ship's tour because if anything did hinder our transport we knew Queen Elizabeth wouldn't leave us behind. We had no idea what to expect of South Korea. We knew about the DMZ (or demilitarized zone).

It had been in the news a lot since the death of Kim Jong-il in 2011. But that was a long way off and no tours were offered to that area (sadly in MR MM's eyes. He'd have loved to have got a glimpse). The ship's tour took us first to a heritage site where there were golden

Buddhas. They were in the most stunning location on cliffs by the edge of the ocean.

This was Haedong Yonggungsa Temple around a 40 minute drive from the ship's berth. On the drive we saw a skyline of high-rise buildings a lot like you see in many cities around the world these days. The buildings were all much of a muchness. We past construction sites where new homes were being built, then suddenly we were at the temple. A site of breathtaking beauty. We were greeted with the sounds and smells, Buddhist chimes and bell tinkering and Zen-type music came from inside stone sculptures. We'd been in cooler climates for a couple of weeks so it was a bit of a shock to step out into the heat again.

This tour was not for those "walking wounded" or people with limited mobility. There was a lot of walking, and lots of steps, involved if you wanted to get the real value of seeing all the sprawling site had to offer. I suppose you could always just sit in the coach and gaze but that would be a real shame for this was a temple site like no other we'd seen on our voyage. At the approach to the site there were traders either side of the road selling their wares, unfamiliar to us.

There were old ladies, many dressed in black, crouched on the road surrounded by things they had for sale.

They didn't like to be photographed. Must have been a culture shock for them seeing 150 white people many dressed in cropped trousers and T-shirts descending. As we got closer to the temple proper we past stone statues on either side of the road - these turned out to be signs of the Zodiac, or Chinese year signs. They were all there including rat, dragon and dog.

I had to have a photograph with the rat - my year sign in the Chinese calendar. Now the real test of stamina - we were faced with 180 steps. OK these were down the hillside but they had to be climbed on the way back.

This was where I got my first WOW! factor feeling. Straight ahead was the ocean with a large golden Buddha sitting on top of a cliff. What a sight! We walked close to him.

Further along there were yet more golden Buddhas of all shapes and sizes. The temple had lots of lovely decorative art work.

Some reconstruction was taking place, like many temples we've seen on this trip. In China, Japan and South Korea they are keen to restore temples. Many of the original structures were made of wood and have been destroyed by fire (is there any wonder given the amount of incense that's always burned on a daily basis?).

After the "ancient" it was on to the modern - the futuristic part of Busan with its glitzy skyscrapers many of them on the banks of the Gwangan River. Our coaches stopped and we walked through gardens where the street lamps were in the shape of trees with green "leaves" sprouting out and powered by solar energy.

So green energy is alive and well in South Korea, too. We went to the space-age Apec Conference Centre, set in parkland and with absolutely stunning views all around especially over the water. This really was a bit of a different land and waterscape to what we had seen in other cities on our voyage so far.

We stopped and gazed in amazement at the buildings all around as we returned to board our coach. It was a bit like the Embankment in London, but only a bit.

Next it was lunch. I have never seen so much food laid out in my life. We were in a hotel complex. It made the "trough" also known as the Lido dining area on Queen Elizabeth look like a soup kitchen! There were dishes from around the world - Chinese, Japanese, Italian, Indian, a steak bar, a bakery, fresh fruit on a turntable with mainly Lychees and dragon fruit. It was self service. You took what you liked and went back for more - if you had room! One guy at our table was annoyed that we did not have time for him to try out the lot. That was just being greedy.

After lunch we were taken to the JAGALCHI fish market - the biggest fish market in Korea. I love to eat fish - all kinds fish. This was a real eye opener - enough fish for me to live off for life!

Fish in tanks, fish on slabs, fish, fish everywhere and so many different kinds it blew the mind.

I have never seen so much fish in one place. It made you wonder if there were any fish left in the sea to catch!

It seemed a bit cruel in some ways as the fish in the tanks were still alive but no room to swim. The place itself was not too smelly, but wet underfoot. There's was an indoor section and an outdoor one that was if anything even bigger than the covered part.

There were crowds but then the fish market is one of the major attractions in Busan for locals as well as visitors.

The locals buy - the visitors look. We had one hour of free time after the fish market stop. Not a problem. There were stalls everywhere some selling replica watches or pretend famous brand sun glasses while others offered fast food Korean style.

Didn't see any of the usual fast food chains. It was busy, busy, noisy, and smelly at times with the aromas of the different foods being freshly cooked.

There was lots of loud music. This was big city life Korean style. They looked a happy bunch of people and were extremely polite. People from our coach went off in separate directions. It was a bit of a nightmare getting everybody back in the right spot at the right time such were the crowds. But "Big Jade" - that was the name of our Korean guide - had a "secret weapon" - Little Jade, a doll type figure on the end of a long pole which Big Jade held up.

You really couldn't miss Little Jade, or big Jade for that matter. We mustered outside a pet shop.

Now the Koreans are known to favour dog as a dish. This pet shop, and there were others close by, had the most adorable puppies, all very tiny and fluffy and mainly the Maltese breed.

Some passengers on our bus thought these were for the pot but that wasn't the case. Shops that sell dog to eat are specially licensed and this was not one of them. It was what it said a pet shop. I think most people on the tour wanted to take a puppy back with them.

There was a musical sailaway from Busan. An attractive, leggy young lady sang Korean songs wearing micro mini hot pants with a short coat over her top and wore five inch heels on two inch platforms. Talk about sex on legs! She was accompanied on stage by a group of ladies dressed more conservatively - in national costume. A port and a country definitely worth another visit.

I met a man in South Korea
He asked what ya doing here?
Let's dance gangnan style
I said "what in these shoes?" I 'll probably break a leg!

THEME NIGHTS: There are plenty of these on this world voyage on Queen Elizabeth and lots of passengers get into the spirit of the themes. Being in the Far East you would have thought one of the formal nights would have a Chinese flavour about it.

But you'd be wrong. They put on a masquerade ball. A pity really but it didn't stop me wearing a Chinese silk dress I'd had made three years ago. Well, some gowns have to be seen more than once. I didn't bother going to the Queen's Room for the masquerade ball. Well, I wasn't dressed for it and anyway there was little room on the dance floor which had been "commandeered" by the Japanese by day and by night who'd turned it into a Japanese "Mecca Locarno".

The Japanese love their dancing. I've spotted them practicing their steps outside on Deck 9 soon after dawn. Some passengers said they gave up on the beginners' daily dance classes because the Japanese came en mass and took over the floor.

Many were not beginners but already good dancers. The sauna room was also a popular hunting spot for the Japanese. It was often packed out. I saw one Japanese lady had her wet washing with her.

She said she'd washed it in her bathroom and took it to the sauna changing rooms to spin dry it in the dryer provided for swimsuits! Unbelievable but true. In the gym they stand on their heads for about 30 minutes followed by the lotus position for another 30 minutes 'till the exercise class begins.

I get so chilled out watching them. I am in my own state of Feng sui, Funk chewy, chop suey and who flung dung to know if I am on my head or my heels!

SHANGHAI REVISITED.

Hard to believe Shanghai, not that long ago, was a city few Westerners visited or wanted to visit. How times have changed. Gone is its sleazy past. Shanghai could be testament to all that is good in capitalism but instead it's a showpiece of what some brands of Communism can achieve. We did a big tour in Shanghai two years ago so this time we decided to take the shuttle bus into the city and do our own thing.

It is always at least an hour to get into Shanghai from the docks. Cunard on this visit arranged for the shuttle bus just to drop passengers off at the silk museum and factory.

On our previous visit the drop off was also in the Bund, a popular part of downtown Shanghai near most of the attractions.

This caused a lot of dissent among passengers who hadn't been to Shanghai before and among some of those who had because the silk museum and factory is in an out-of-the-way part of docklands. It was a long walk to The Bund that's if you could find your way there. We got to a main road and hailed a taxi because we wanted to ride on the fastest train in the world, the Maglev.

363

It was a white-knuckle ride to another part of the sprawling city but once at the Maglev terminus it was easy finding our way in.

Buying tickets was simple. Helpful girls in the ticket desk spoke perfect English. We paid by plastic and set off to the Maglev platform. We bought VIP tickets so we could travel in what you'd describe as Communist First Class. We wanted to compare the facilities on the Maglev with those on Japan's Bullet Train where again we had paid the extra to travel "first". This time it cost us 160 Yuan each for a round trip.

The Maglev doesn't go far at the moment - just from Shanghai central to Pudong International Airport. It runs on magnetic levitation and travels at speeds up to 400 km per hour but it reaches that speed in the rush hour only. Our journey was not in the rush hour so it was a more "sedate" speed of 301 km per hour. Inside our carriage was a clock which showed the Maglev's speed. It went from 0 to 301 km in two minutes.

It was very fast and smooth and the train tilted when it went around a bend. So life in the fast lane once again and MR MM was as happy as Larry. Another "first" for us that came with a buzz factor. After we'd returned, (we didn't leave the train at the airport terminal) we caught the underground metro to get to LUJIAZUL where all the fantastic modern high rise buildings are located like the Oriental Pearl TV Tower, and the JINMAO TOWER.

We walked and explored the Super Bowl Mall then crossed under the Huangpu River in the Bund Sightseeing Tour tunnel. This is a pod-like train carriage that carries around 20 people. The tunnel is all psychedelic laser lights whirling around and other images appear on the walls of the tunnel as you travel through. Not good if you have epilepsy.

The BUND is where most of the action takes place and it is a good spot to people watch and take snaps of the business district skyline across the river. We ended up in the classy Waldorf Astoria right in the heart of The Bund. It was built in 1808 as a gentleman's club for the British and its appearance, outside at least, has changed little. It is one of the very old buildings on The Bund.

Inside it retains most of its original features but beyond the original building line there's a swish modern extension as good as any in the world. It screams quality and class.

We went to the Waldorf Astoria because I was getting thirsty and hungry around mid-afternoon and it was the closest hotel or restaurant to where we were walking at the time. But what a find.

The entrance door from The Bund was up 14 steps. When we were half way up the double glass panelled oak doors were opened by two young ladies in livery. Very classy! We were then in an ornate grand hall with Corinthian columns.

It was in fact a central atrium that went up two floors. Lots of carved wood (oak or mahogany I couldn't decide) in the original building.

We went to the grand ballroom with is chandeliers, old Masters and an ancient oil painting of that part of The Bund.

It was still recognisable today. Leaving the original building line of the old part we entered the chic, modern part of the Waldorf Astoria. Very classy, futuristic with its own brand of elegance.

It was after three in the afternoon so food options were limited (we were too late for lunch and too early for dinner). But a snack was all we really wanted along with a cold drink.

We chose a smoked salmon combination and from the table where we sat we had a good view of an impressive water feature. The food was delicious. All the food is cooked in view of diners; no expense looked to have been spared on the furnishings and fittings (including huge modern chandeliers) and the loos were among the best we have ever used. The staff were exceptionally friendly and very professional. There is a second entrance out of the Waldorf from the modern part of the complex but we decided we'd leave the same way as we had arrived - by the steps down to The Bund.

We passed a massive oak table straining under a huge floral decoration when I spotted the sign for the bar.

This was not any bar, this was the Waldorf's Long Bar. No, Raffles in Singapore doesn't have exclusive rights to such a bar!

This one, I learned, was opened in 1911. Lots of carved wood, just like in the ballroom and the games room and much of the rest of the original building. Glasses sparkled in the half light; oysters were laid out on a bed of ice and the champagne was chilled. All was set for the evening. Such a pity we didn't find the bar before we went to the restaurant. Still there is always next time. So how long is the Long Bar in Shanghai's Waldorf Astoria? How does 35 metres grab you? Cheers!

We had been to Shanghai before and thought we knew our way around but we have missed this hidden gem! May be locals don't like to advertise its existence preferring to keep it to themselves. The secret's out now though. Our next Chinese port of call was Xiamen pronounced "Shaman" and another maiden port of call for Queen Elizabeth. There were no crowds of locals to greet us as most ports in China are out of reach of Joe and Josephine Public.

We arrived in port late because our progress had been slowed by thick fog for over 24 hours. No professional guides in China, but we had students keen to learn and ours was nervous but he did well!

We went to more temples and shrines and by now we really were getting "templed out" - one temple had a giant Buddha dedicated to some medical man from days gone by and the statue was on a plinth at the top of 800 steps. But some fit people did climb the staircase, that looked as though it went to Heaven, despite the heat of the day. I just gave him three bows from afar. After our four hour tour we took a shuttle bus to town for a look around. Not very impressive but extremely busy with both traffic and people. There was one main street which was supposed to be traffic free only you had to watch out for cars!

Lots of narrow alleyways led off this main street but they were dark, spooky and I wouldn't have felt safe venturing down them.

Goods in the shops looked cheap enough but the handbags and shoes were 100 per cent plastic on inspection. Queen Elizabeth didn't sail until one minute to midnight but we had no thoughts of staying in town until the last minute - it was not a welcoming place after dark we thought. For me, Shanghai has the WOW! factor; it's one of my favourite cities in the world. Xiamen was a pleasant surprise and many told me about lovely gardens on an Island cross the water which could be reached by ferry. Someone said it was beautiful rather like Torquay and someone else said it was tatty and dirty like Blackpool. Funny neither of them mentioned it being Chinese.

In Shanghai I meet two men
Both wanted to sell me silk for my bed
You can slip and slide and slither around
Well, In these shoes what more can a girl want?

QUEEN ELIZABETH IN HONG KONG

Continuing our epic voyage around the world, Queen Elizabeth arrived in Hong Kong shrouded in a haze, or was it pollution? We had been sailing at a snail's pace for 24 hours because visibility was so bad. The ship's fog horn sounding all the time. This was a two-day port call and we docked right in the heart of Hong Kong by one of the Star Ferry terminals.

Weather can be problematic - good or very bad. If it rains it can rain for days without let up. The sun never appeared at all on our first day. The atmosphere was sticky, humid and it was very warm. The haze, mist, fog - call it what you will - blanked out most of the stunning high rise buildings so the light show that takes place most evenings was not to be on our first night. Fortunately for us we have been to Hong Kong a few times over the years. the last time being in 2012 on Queen Mary 2 when we had magnificent weather and we able to see the lights come on the high rises that front the harbour from our vantage point which was Felix's Restaurant on the 28th floor of the swish Peninsular Hotel - a favourite "watering hole and eaterie" for lots of old Colonials.

This time while in Hong Kong we decided we'd visit the former Portuguese colony of Macau which, like Hong Kong, has been handed back to the Commies of mainland China. MR MM had been to Macau before - 38 years ago. He wanted to see if he still recognised the place. It was a place I had always wanted to see but never got the chance on previous sailings in to Hong Kong. There was a ship's tour but we looked at the itinerary and it included a lunch in the Sky Tower, and a museum visit - neither which appealed. These lunches on tours take a good hour or more out of your day, and as we were over fed and overweight the last thing we wanted was more food.

We worked out it was very easy to "do Macau" on our own. MR MM had been on the Internet and researched it all. We had to take our passports because we were technically leaving one country and going to another and then returning to our first country which was Hong Kong of course.

We had to retrieve the passports which were held for most of the voyage in the Purser's office. Passports in hand, off we trotted. We were berthed at Ocean Terminal, Kowloon, right next to the Star Ferry terminal. Within a few minutes we were at the terminal buying our tickets to cross over to Hong Kong Island, a journey that takes about 7 minutes.

We knew the system - as seniors we get concessionary rates - HK $1- 40 cents to cross. Once on the other side we walked to the Macau ferry terminal - it took around 15 minutes.

Inside it was all hustle and bustle; manic. We had to get to the third level but where to buy tickets?

In all the mayhem a guy shouted "here" and pointed to a desk selling tickets that wasn't an official looking one - the official windows had lines at each one. We could have been queuing all day. It turned out the man who'd shouted was an agent. He was very helpful and he rushed us towards the departure gate. We had about five minutes to catch the 10-30am ferry.

It was all rushing and pushing but you have to go through passport control because, technically you are leaving one country for another. It sounds crazy when both are Chinese satellites. But that's communism for you - no logic!

It was extremely busy and I thought we are not going to make the 10-30 then I spotted a sign above one check-in desk which read "Seniors over 65 and disabled queue here!" Being a "young-looking 65" we both joined this queue which had only four others waiting in line. Of course I wasn't queue-jumping because my date of birth is on my passport.

I really must stop using the Cliff Richard eye cream that has kept me looking youthful all these years!

Once through passport control it was on to the embarkation desk. We were going to travel on the Turbot Jet - a hydrofoil. I saw a sign to "embark here", and one for "standby" A guy, seeing us holding tickets for the journey, waved us over but to the standby desk. Once he waved "over here" to those standing in the standby line, a rush of little people came pushing and elbowing me out of the way, shouting:" Who wa chu wah cin chew woo ee" Translated means get out the way, I am coming through!

To which I replied: "who wa doa wa you a finka you wa r an u effee chew ee Off"! Bet you never realised I spoke Chinese! It is similar to Yorkshire but less refined. Once on board our flying ferry we settled into our seats and looked around and noticed we were the only Europeans travelling. Not that it mattered or bothered either of us. We knew where we were going!

The TV was on in front of the cabin and I wondered why, where ever you are in the world, they always show cookery programmes first thing in the morning? All the same format - a man and woman chatting away and chucking food in a frying pan and chopping things up at a rate of knots. Not been a domestic Goddess it puzzles me as who would want to see fish been gutted when you have just got out of bed? Anyhow I digress, back to Macau. The journey took one hour.

We arrived in what was another airport style terminal and to the sight of spectacular buildings - all of them casinos.

Macao is the Las Vegas of Asia! In fact it allegedly does more business and has more punters than the American gambling city in the desert.

After disembarking the next question was how to get to the heart of town without spending a penny or a cent? No problem there were lines of good looking girls smartly attired all trying to entice passengers towards their mini vans. We got a map from a guide but MR MM had his own notes on how to get to where we wanted to. These beautiful looking ladies were all dressed in lovely uniforms and holding placards.

They were the hostesses from the Casinos and they were giving out vouchers to the different gaming joints. We spotted a line of buses - each casino has its own shuttle service to take you to their palaces so you can part with your hard earned cash.

MR MM knew we needed to take the bus to the Grand Lisboa Casino. So we did. By the way our return ferry tickets to Macau cost us £30 each. A fast 10 minute drive and we were at the centre of the action in downtown Macau. What an impressive building we saw in front of us from the bus it was WOW!-Big time WOW! It was all gold with a few colours of red and green interspersed. It was breathtaking and that's only the outside of the building which seemed to disappear in the haze. We never saw the summit.

This was our drop off - not outside but in the underground car park. Clever move! That way you can't just take the free bus ride and then walk away to another casino or none at all. You have to navigate, and I mean navigate, a number of elevators to get to ground level and then it was no easy job getting out of the building. But we did of course The Grand Lisboa is a hotel and casino and it's HUGE! The building is shaped like a lily - Macau's emblem.

Inside the casino it was all glitz; chandeliers and crystal beads hanging from the ceilings. And the noise was deafening.

Slot machine galore and tables for every card game going. We went up to the next floor, and the next, and the next and it was just a maze of gaming tables. Watching them play roulette was a new experience as they do not place chips on a table.

Each player had an Ipad type screen that they touched with a stylus to place their bets. For me that takes away the "fun" of being able to place your own bets with your own chips. Not that I'm a gambler but I do sometimes have a flutter in the ship's casino when I'm cruising. Most of the games being played we had never seen before so could not understand them. Plus everything was in Chinese. Not many people spoke English in Macau. And every floor of the casino - I think we passed through seven before reaching street level - was packed with punters, mostly Chinese but a smattering of other nationalities.

Not being serious gamblers (we'd done bingo only once!) we watched a while then continued to try to find our way out in to the daylight.

We eventually ended up in the Grand Lobby of the Hotel and what a sight that was! All over the top, glitz and glam, and quite breathtaking. Lots of designer jewellery for sale and the usual expensive hotel shops. Still if you had a win on the tables what's money!

We walked around the outside of this palace to greed, or good fortune depending on your point of view, and knew we were in the centre of Macau. Stunning buildings and water features. The Sky Tower, where the ship's tour had gone for lunch, was shrouded in mist so from the top nothing of the city would be seen. We continued walking and headed up the main shopping street. It was then I got a real buzz. We were in Lisbon - we weren't but could have been!

Macau used to be Portuguese, I knew that, but I never expected it to look like Portugal. The buildings and the architecture and those lovely fancy balconies. The pavements, well, I was blown away.

We could have been in Punta Delgado, Salvador, Brazil or Lisbon itself. Not China! It was fabulous and I loved it right away. We walked all day long and didn't get lost. Macau is quite small and compact - perfectly formed you might say! We saw all the sites MR MM had on his list. Most of the centre is pedestrianised making shopping easy.

We visited the ruins of St Paul's. All that's left is the huge facade of the church that was destroyed by fire in the 1800s. On our walkabout we also called into the Cathedral. There was a notice board just inside the door which read "NO TOURISTS TO ENTER". We found this rather off-putting. Wasn't Jesus a traveller /tourist when He was spreading His teachings in The Holy Land? We went to the fort and then stopped and bought one of those custard tarts just like the ones you buy in Lisbon. Delicious. Could have eaten two. Macau was very, very, busy, the narrow steep streets teeming with tourists.

We had a fabulous day out in Macau and we didn't win, or lose, any money. We just weren't tempted to the tables or the slot machines. We were so glad we had made the journey though.

MR MM didn't recognise the Macau he'd visited 38 years ago. But he didn't expect to really. St Paul's was the same; the fort was there; the narrow streets but how the skyline had changed was his parting observation.

The journey back was uneventful until we reached passport control where there was no over 65 exclusive line so we had to wait ages only to get to the desk to be told we needed to fill in an immigration form.

This caught us, and many other passengers off the ferry, out. We thought having filled in an immigration form on the ship to enter Hong Kong we were already "checked in" so-to-speak. Wrong!

However, the kind immigration officer let us back into the front of the queue when we had filled out the necessary paper work.

A ride on a Star Ferry and we were back at the ship. By now it was 7 o'clock and getting dark. We decided not to go off again. We were tired. A snack and early night called.

That's the problem with being a senior you get tired after a long day but on the plus side you get cheap travel in many countries around the world. Another good reason for taking a world cruise - do it while you're still fit enough.

I met a guy from Macau who spoke Portuguese.
He said I know you like a good jump
so come and bungee with me
From Macau Tower we can bump the bump
I said "In these shoes". I'd rather go to the casino!

Talking of been fit and well.

There have been so many people on this world cruise with chest infections. I know you get this a lot but this time they seems to have hung around for weeks. I got one after we'd been in Hawaii and it took three weeks to clear. Some people were quite poorly. In fact I had three days in bed because I had a fever as well.

Some passengers are thoughtless or selfish - or both. On a tour in Xiamen there was a guy sat opposite us on the bus who was obviously in a bad way.

377

He coughed and coughed and sneezed all the time. His wife (American) said to the tour guide her husband was "very sick but getting better".

He really should not have been on the tour and he certainly should have worn a mask like many of the locals. I don't wonder we get infected with people like that around. Selfish I'd call it but then he probably didn't want to lose the money he'd spend on the tour tickets.

DAY TWO IN HONG KONG

We woke to rain and thunder so there was no rush to get off the ship. But it was a busy day on Queen Elizabeth with those leaving and those joining at this popular stop.

It was not just passengers but crew coming and going too. Most if not all of the Japanese left so there should be vacant pilates mats from now on. I've loved the Asian food we had whilst the Japanese were on board. I hope it continues to be served.

The food on Queen Elizabeth has been really good so far and the alternative dining restaurants are very popular. However, the Lido is not my favourite place to eat but I have eaten there a few times at night if we have missed dinner. I have to admit they have had some very tasty dishes on the menu in the Lido especially when we have had such a mix of passengers onboard.

From our dock in the Ocean Terminal it was no more than a 30 second walk (if that) to the huge shopping mall - Harbour City.

It has every designer shop you can name and a few others beside. Plus there are also three Marco Polo Hotels, and lots of eating places. No one can accuse me of not liking shopping - but this was overkill just like in Dubai and Singapore. You need to be a multi millionaire - or be married to one (and MR MM certainly isn't) - to enjoy these places. It is just too much even for a shopaholic like me.

Because of the weather we had little other option than to seek refuge in Harbour City and I ended up in the Vivienne Westwood outlet buying a handbag and three pairs of shoes. I like her quirky things so that was my best buy in Hong Kong.

The skies cleared for sailaway and the much hyped Hong Kong laser light show was eagerly awaited. It was like the weather had been - a damp squib.

All it consisted of were a series of beams of light that MR MM's camcorder hardly picked up. The unofficial light spectacular - when the skyscrapers are all lit up at dusk - is far more impressive. Hong Kong is a magical place at night especially from the deck of a ship. Sydney and Hong Kong have the best skylines for night time sailaways of all the ones that I've seen.

Lots of passengers skipped dinner to stay on deck and witness the sailaway. We've been lucky enough to see it many times but it is always different and never boring. It's something not worth missing just to eat when on liners like Queen Elizabeth food is available in one form or another 24 hours a day. Next day I did my welcome on board meet and greet for Cruise Critic members who had joined in Hong Kong. But other members of the forum who had been on board for a while also joined in. It was my sixth meet and greet since leaving Southampton.

Before the 12-15 pm meet and greet (timed as such to avoid clashing with the Captain's midday broadcast) I'd been to the gym and surprise, surprise, it was still busy with Japanese standing on their heads! Perhaps some of them were on for the rest of the world!

We never really expected to be making the two calls into Egypt because of all the unrest and political upheaval, and leaving Hong Kong we finally got confirmation the Egyptian port calls had been cancelled. The alternative? Two days in Haifa, Israel. Most passengers seemed happy but MR MM was among those who were less keen because of the way the Israelis have for seven years blockaded the Gaza strip basically making the 1.6 million Palestinians live in an open air prison, their movements severely restricted along with the goods that are allowed through the blockade which is total - by land, air and sea.

GOOD MORNING VIETNAM

Ha Long Bay, is a UNESCO World Heritage site famous for its limestone mountains and stunning beauty and was our first port of call in Vietnam. We arrived early in the morning picking our way through the maze of limestone mountains shrouded in a heavy mist. Quite an eerie sight.

We have experienced scenery something like it before in Thailand when we took a trip to James Bond Island. Here we'd booked an 11 hour ship's tour to Hanoi. Immigration officials boarded but despite the ship's itinerary and tours being given in advance to the authorities they suddenly "became concerned" about the three and a half hours it would take the coaches to reach the capital. Really! We were held up for one and a half hours before the Immigration officials gave the green light for the Hanoi coaches to proceed. MR MM was not alone in thinking this was a long time to negotiate a bribe! It's a practice well known in the Far East , Asia and the Middle East - but they don't cross palms with silver any more. Paper money, preferably US dollars is the "currency" of choice.

We' d deliberately chosen to see Hanoi - we'd been to Ho Chi Minh City (formerly Saigon) - and were not fazed by the three and a half hour bus ride.

The journey from the ship to Saigon was three and a half hours but we got to see some of the countryside, the villages and the people going about their daily toil.

The Northern part of the country is very flat and full of paddy fields; farming being the mainstay of this area.

Oxen and water buffalo were being used to pull the wooden work tools. Vietnam is still very much a Third World country and the poverty is very visible -people live in shacks surrounded by rubbish and rubble. A few have gardens; many side roads looked to be just dirt tracks and the pavements just dust and earth.

But the road we were on had a good surface most of the way to Hanoi. We had one "comfort stop" - at a workplace where women were doing needle point type embroidery, and where other girls and ladies were making high end accessories like Kiplin Handbags and Cath Kitson handbags. Because of our late departure thanks to the immigration fiasco, it was lunchtime when we arrived in Hanoi.

We pulled up outside a classy looking building in the French Quarter - our eaterie. The food was great but because we were running late it was a bit of a rushed affair - we were in and out of the restaurant in under an hour.

Not all food on ship's tours turns out to be first class but I've found Cunard researchers are pretty good at sorting out the wheat from the chaff so-to-speak. Passengers expect standards to be high and the place be up to the class of what one would expect from the cruise line. At this Hanoi restaurant good Vietnam style food was served.

Afterwards we went on a quick fire tour of the City. We had just three hours to do the main sites in Hanoi. We hot-footed it to yet another temple in a beautiful park and we walked the streets of the old city which were noisy and smelly but full of life and a hive of activity. I saw lots of shops selling branded goods. Some were called "Made in Vietnam" but no time to look at these places, sadly. A friend spotted "Mulberry" bags. We had no time to look at those either.

On we marched to the next stop on the tour - the Garden and The Temple of Literature. The day we were there a group of students had graduated and had gone to the temple to thank the Buddha.

The last place we visited was the mausoleum of Ho Chi Minh. Our guide was very informative and we learned a lot about the cultures of the country - and the Vietnam war! The journey back was mostly in darkness. There were few street lights and the houses looked to be dimly lit. No one had curtains at their windows and all the homes were tall and very narrow. May be 3 metres wide four story high and 10 metres deep.

The Vietnamese look to be a nation of shopkeepers. They all appeared to live over the shop. Most families we spotted were sat in the half light on the floor either watching huge TV screens or eating sat in a circle at a low table or on the floor. There are millions of scooters and bikes in Vietnam and the people ride them with up to five on - two adults and three children.

They carry everything from beds to heaps of parcels and furniture on their backs. Many seemed to park their scooters inside the living room!

We arrived back at the port very late but the ship waited. A good reason to take a ship's tour in places like this. If you're late the ship always waits. One couple just made it back by the skin of their teeth after doing a private tour with a local guide.

Heading back to the ship they hit a traffic jam caused by a bad road accident which blocked the road they were on.

They ended up having to do a 20 mile detour. Ha Long Bay for us was a tender port. The tender ride to the ship was about 15 minutes.

We were on the last tender but there was a hold up with the tender in front. We bobbed around on the water for a while, eventually getting back onboard around 30 minutes after we'd boarded the tender.

In Vietnam I met a man
He said I'll give you the ride of your life.
Get your leg over the back of my moped
and we'll go for a spin
I said "In these shoes ?" You'll be dead!

Next day our port call was in Chan May, Central Vietnam. We were due to arrive around 10am but the captain made a public announcement that we would not reach Chan May until around 12-30pm; the reason given? Queen Elizabeth had had a "technical problem" the night before which had delayed our departure from Ha Long Bay. No explanation of "the technical problem", but many of us had heard a lot of hammering before we got underway from Ha Long Bay. All became clear or clearer when a lady and her husband who had a cabin four away from ours asked me if I'd heard the noise and commotion? I said I had.

The lady then told me what had caused the last tender to have to bob around in the water the evening before. She explained she and her husband were on the penultimate tender from shore to ship (we were on the last tender).

Their tender reached the pontoon and the driver of the tender crashed into the pontoon not just once but twice! This collision by tender and pontoon caused not only damage but distress to some passengers who were frightened as it all happened in total darkness.

385

And that story was confirmed by a lady from Arizona I knew who was travelling in The Grills and whose suite was directly above the damaged pontoon. So the pontoon was not a technical problem but the result of the crashed tender.

The ship couldn't move because the pontoon couldn't be retracted. Hence all the hammering to get it to close which it eventually did but hours later.

What a pity Captain Clark and his team chose not to tell us the truth and instead decided to spin a yarn; a fabrication. Shame on him and the rest of his officers!

Strangely enough we had a similar incident of a tender smashing into Queen Mary 2 on our world cruise in 2012. It happened in the Indian Ocean. We had just dropped (the late) Sir David Frost (who had been a ship's lecturer) off on the island of Mauritius. The returning tender (Number 16) crashed into the pontoon twice causing damage to the tender to the extent that it was taken off in Fremantle and was never returned during that world voyage.

Because of our late arrival following the "technical problem" it meant we had a late start to our HIGHLIGHTS OF IMPERIAL HUE tour. Hue became the first UNESCO site in Vietnam and was where a lot of fighting in the Vietnam war took place.

Over 4,000 were killed and the place reduced to rubble. Much of the original ancient architecture is under restoration.

To get to Hue we had a one and half hour drive and a guide who was informative but hard to follow because he spoke so fast and kept saying: "Do you get it?" No, we did not but we never told him.

He talked non-stop (and I know all about how to do that!). It was a hair-raising ride on our coach. The driver must have been a top gun pilot in the war as he took off like a Bat out of Hell as they say.

I know we were running late because of tender crashing in to the ship's pontoon the previous evening but gosh the bus driver was fast and furious! The scenery was completely different in this part of Vietnam to that we saw on our journey to Hanoi. Mountains rose high in the sky and they were covered in forest and lush vegetation. There were paddy fields and farms. We past many rivers and lots of villages in a dreary state.

Arriving at our destination once more food was part of the tour. We could have missed lunch but it was all arranged so we went to a hotel where once again we had wonderful things to eat from the buffet.

Plus we were entertainment by locals as we dined. One hour on and we were on the road again. First stop the Imperial Citadel. Built between 1804 and 1835 by Gia Long the first emperor of the Nguyen dynasty who is credited with unifying what is now modern Vietnam in 1802. The Citadel is modelled on the Forbidden City in Beijing. This was a massive place and most of it was under restoration (some had been completed but a lot more needed to be done). We visited an Opera theatre that had been restored.

I had a photo taken behind a seat that looks rather like the one I have in the Leeds City Varieties Music Hall in Yorkshire. Seat M13 has my name on it if you ever visit The City Varieties.

The next stop - another Buddhist shrine - THIEN MU Pagoda. Here we were on the banks of the Perfumed River.

Many locals were worshiping. They had lit small fires and were throwing lighted paper in to the water. This was one of the most fascinating things we'd witnessed and all in a very picturesque setting. More walking through the hustle and bustle of the crowded streets trying to avoid the scooters. On to another Imperial site - The PALACE OF SUPREME HARMONY. Dedicated to supreme Emperors. It was so peaceful it was spooky! It was around 5-30pm and getting dusk. The buildings dated back to God knows when. The guide did not seem to be worried we had to catch a ship.

He rambled on and on about an Emperor who had been a serial adulterer; who'd had mumps and was sterile,(allegedly!). He'd built a pavilion and took ladies into it and wrote poems to them! OH! Yes, I bet he did! I bet he did more than write poems According to the guide, the Emperor had many ladies.

WOW! Scandal!

We had to climb steps as it got darker and darker to visit the main attraction - A TOMB of an Emperor. Gripping stuff!

I expected any minute a ghost to whiz by in white shrouds with ghost busters following on behind. I could hear, Who you gonna call? GHOST BUSTERS in my ear.

It felt very weird as darkness fell. The guide rambled on and on about the Dynasty and the Queen of Dynasty and I had a vision of Joan Collins floating by the lotus pond in a floaty chiffon number with big shoulder pads and a big wig. By now it was so dark. I think I began to hallucinate!

We managed to leave the site just as another of our tour buses full of passengers arrived to view the same lot in the total darkness. Anyhow, being good Cunarders they carried on regardless. Back on the bus, a pit stop to a hat factory had to be scrapped because it had closed. Undeterred, our guide stopped the bus at the next door shop so we had the opportunity to buy tat in the dark.

This was also our "happy stop" before the long journey back to the ship. Locals at the shop - which seemed to double as their home - were sitting around eating their evening meal They all jumped to attention as our bus pulled up in pitch darkness. Our guide spoke to them and the next moment torches appeared those who wanted to use the loo were led down some steps to two outside toilets. No mains electric lights so the torches were placed on the toilet cistern.

No hand washing facilities but I was prepared with my packet of anti-viral wipes and a few pieces of toilet tissue I carry for such emergencies. One has to have an open mind about these things when in such parts of the world. I was the second in line because most people stopped and looked at the handicrafts and clothing that was for sale. I didn't see any sales made and if there weren't any that's a pity. I felt bad afterwards as we never got chance to leave some dollars for use of the loo as we were quickly whisked back on the bus.

We'd had a chance to shop for tat from street vendors at the pagoda shrine. They were so aggressive; wouldn't take "no" for an answer. They didn't come near the buses though, they stood on the side lines waving pashmina scarves and hats. One lady vendor threw a pashmina over my shoulder and would not take it back. She wanted US$20 then $10 then $5 and then $4. I gave her five to get rid of her. I did not want the $1 change. I also gave dollars to the kids after they'd posed for photographs.

In Hanoi I was accosted by a trader as we went into a temple. She was selling T-shirts for US$2. I said "no" but she insisted then she saw the police and ran off with me holding the T-shirt for which I hadn't paid. When we came out of the temple she was waiting for me.

I had US $2 ready in my hand and she indicated she had been crying because she didn't think I would turn up.

I gave her a further US$2 dollars ending up with two unwanted T-shirts which I donated to the Charity collection on the ship. They were quite nice but not me. At least I may have helped the poor lady put some food on her table.

I also bought some bookmarks to fend off three lady street hawkers. I guess if you had lots of time you could find nice things to buy. We actually bought a lacquered Charger in the lacquer factory in HO Chi Minh two years ago. It was expensive - around £260 - but is very unusual and the colours are stunning.

Vietnam, a fascinating, diverse, atmospheric country with colourful people. For me seeing HO Chi Minh City was our best run ashore in Vietnam. We saw the water puppets there and visited the lacquer factory where men worked with their bare feet in water polishing the wood with wet and dry sand paper. A back breaking job.

The Vietnamese people appeared to be workaholics and the country should become a so-called Tiger economy before too long. I think Vietnam could be a fabulous place for a longer chill out holiday, but apart from Ha Long Bay we saw no nice hotels to stay in. Ha Lang Bay is more equipped for tourism and has quite a few high end hotels. The rest of the country probably suits backpackers, and there were plenty around. For me it's Goodbye Vietnam - I've seen enough love you but have no plans to come back again in the near future.

*Royal Ascot is one of The Queen's favourite engagements in the year. Her Majesty and a good number of Royals head for the Berkshire racecourse each June. The Royal Party are driven in open landaus down the track. Men have to wear morning dress while the women put on their best frocks and fancy hats.

Among the females it's something of a hat stakes - who can wear the most eye catching, outrageous creation.

A little bit of this Royal ritual came to Queen Elizabeth, the Cunard liner, as she sailed the waters towards Singapore in the shape of a Royal Ascot Ball. I wore a new dress I had designed myself and had made up last year out of fabric I had bought in Thailand on the QM2 world cruise in 2012.There was some left-over fabric so been artistic I made myself a hat for the races. Something over the top, naturally! It turned out well and I turned a few heads and I had people admiring it all night. MR MM had his morning suit and his top hat for the occasion - the "uniform" he had when he went to Buckingham Palace in 2004 to be Invested with his MBE by Her Majesty. Two other gents had morning rig - the rest had DJs. I love Cunard themed dress nights they are such good fun. It is always nice to see people make the effort and it doesn't have to break the bank - just takes a little imagination.

ON A LITTLE STREET IN SINGAPORE

On a little street in Singapore! I arrived in Singapore singing the Manhattan Transfer song. I like Singapore and have been many times over the years. It changes each time; always a new building to see. One of the latest is the new cruise terminal, The Marina Bay. I was told by our taxi driver it opened last year (2013) We were not impressed! It was so high security I doubt I will want to bother going on a cruise to Singapore in the future if we have to endure such slow immigration procedures. For the first time on any of our visits we had to undergo a face-to-face immigration inspection like you get at airports. In fact the place looks like an airport.

We didn't object. No point but this took forever, and at one stage they were going to fingerprint us - all 2016 passengers. The immigration inspectors were very slow and looked at every page in our passports in a jobsworth sort of way. When that was done we had another passport check and then a long walk to a room again like you see in airports. Here we had to queue for ages to go through customs.

We had nothing to declare so went green. We all had to take off our shoes, belts and hand over cameras and mobile phones yet we were all in transit. Baffling!

We then queued for over 40 minutes for a shuttle bus. Couldn't see any taxis. Fred Olsen's Black Watch was berthed next to us and what an old lady she looked. Her passengers were going through the same hoops and we were all sharing the shuttle buses. All morning was spent getting off the ship. It was almost one o'clock by the time we reached our drop off point not far from Sun Tec City - about two minutes from the Fountain of Wealth. The drop off point was actually at the Millenia Walk Mall.

Given the hassle getting in to Singapore it was just as well we had no set plans. We were in port for two days, thankfully. We always like to pop in to Raffles. I know it is overrated but still is a magnet for old colonials like us.

The free wi-fi I'd hoped for didn't materialise. I did buy eight batik napkins in the gift shop though. Then the heavens opened with thunder and lightning and torrential rain. It was sticky, hot and humid.

We dashed across the road to a Mall we'd visited before. On the ground floor there's a shop called The Toast Box, a cafe which serves the most fantastic coffee and toast. Memorable!

I popped up to level three to good old M&S. No designer shopping for me here. What I needed was a few new pairs of

"KNICKERS" Yes, you heard correctly - all I bought in Singapore were M&S knickers! I'd had to throw so many pairs away after washing them on the ship in my silk wash.

The water is chemically treated on board and they'd turned grey. Now I don't mind 50 shades of grey if it's like the book, but grey undies are not me. My mother would have said "you can't wear them.

" What if you get run over?" I never really knew which run over she meant - was it to be a bus or a man?

So it was with my late dear mother's warnings ringing in my ears I shot to this branch of M&S. MR MM waited outside and before he could shout "get yer knickers off" I was back with three pairs of white, Bridget Jones style. I'm not into buying the teeny weeny, with a thong in my heart type.

I was amazed they only cost $35 HK as opposed for US$35 a pair in Bravissimo. Not as good but will suffice.

Waitrose called. We needed tonic water for my vodka. Five bottles was all MR MM could manage. It was the slim line with a twist and hey was on offer. We took a cab back to the ship, very cheap - $7-50 HK from Raffles. Sod the expense and the shuttle bus.

Again we had to run the gauntlet of passport control not once but twice before being searched and scanned and no one smiled. They were all stony-faced. It made American immigration officers seem like your best friends! We called it day. We'd "commence" our Singapore visit the next day.

Day two in Singapore: We were greeted with booming claps of thunder and pouring rain. Things could only improve and they did...eventually. Pity the 1200 poor souls who were departing Queen Elizabeth that day - not a brilliant start for them either!

Our intention was to go to Changi early morning to see the prison but we changed our minds, not for the first time on this voyage and I am sure it won't be the last.

We managed to get through the performance with immigration with not too much of a delay. May be somebody had had a "word", or slipped some brown envelopes.

We took the shuttle bus to Millenia Walk and headed for the MTR, the underground - a brilliant people-mover that's clean, efficient and cheap to ride. Our revised destination was Chinatown as opposed to Changi.

The stop is at Chinatown Point -another shopping Mall. We walked to the SRI MARIAMMAN TEMPLE. Yes, yet another temple. Never been in so many and probably never will again. This claims to be the first Hindu temple in Singapore. There was an Indian wedding taking place.

This temple sits right next to Pagoda Street where all the Chinese and Indian tat is sold. So another sightseeing tour of tat. Then we walked through the Hawker Markets and the food markets and the Chinese health shops selling herbal medicines and all sorts of lotions and potions including some rather big looking horns - for horny men! I noticed MR MM didn't bothered to look at these. We saw some nice old building downtown but curtailed our sightseeing because it continued to rain.

On the way back into the Chinatown Point Mall to get to the MRT we a spotted a Toast Box café - this looked more upmarket than the one we'd used before but it still had the 60s theme in a sort of shabby, chic meets rustic French sort of way. It was enough to attract us. We ordered a toasted ham & cheese sandwich which was not anything worth writing home about but at least it filled a void. The coffee though was a good as ever.

The shuttle bus pick up/drop off was convenient for a shopping Mall. I'd been in it before and this time I nipped in and scooped up a few items including some eye pad things.

They come with match sticks to keep your eyes open after a late night so I bought the shop full! Would you credit it, when I went outside to catch the shuttle back to the ship the sun was shining just as we were about to leave Singapore. Hey well, you can't win 'em all!

MALAYSIA.

There is still an international passenger line-up on Queen Elizabeth which makes for an excellent cultural mix. Alas, most of the Australians have now left and so too most of the Japanese. A pity really. I like both nationalities for different reason. The Aussie free-style of thinking and behaving is a breath of fresh air in a world often dominated by the politically-correct brigade. The Aussie's don't seem to suffer from that "species".

As for the Japanese, they're graceful, elegant, move fast and talk fast. They're like birds fluttering around all chirpy and nice even though they move around in packs.

I will miss their presence especially early morning in the gym where part of their routine is to stand on their heads for half a hour.

Can't see many of the new Brits who've boarded doing that at six in the morning. But I'm always open to being proved wrong.

We have Asians and Chinese passengers in good numbers. The Indian ladies in their saris are really colourful, gentle people and courteous too. There are more than 80 German world cruisers along with a bunch of Americans who board Queen Mary 2 in Southampton for the journey to New York.

A list of world cruise passengers nationalists circulated the other day - some are from Kazakhstan, Taiwan, Iceland and Chile. For me that's what makes a cruise - a good mix of nationalities. Sorry, but a ship full of Brits fills me with dread.

KL ON YOUR OWN: Kuala Lumpur (or KL as seasoned travellers call it). One of Asia's great destinations. We just had to visit. But how to do it on your own from Port Kelang (pronounced Klang) -one of the busiest ports in the world we heard. The sail in reminded us of parts of the Panama Canal - lush rain forests on either side before opening out into the port which seemed to go on forever. Large cranes and ships everywhere. Once we docked we were alongside a nice terminal building which looked a bit colonial to me, but it also looked new and had a long pier that would not have been out of place in Southport it was so long.

Cunard offered a DIY package - they'd provide the transport and a guide and you did your own thing in KL for a number of hours. We went for that option, and it proved a good move. Traffic can be horrific in Malaysia but luckily we were in the country on a Sunday so less cars, vans, buses and bikes around. The journey we were informed could take 90 minutes - but we did it fast, in just 60.

Doris was our guide and escort and what a lovely lady she was - informative, courteous and helpful giving us her take on the good, the bad and the ugly in KL.

She couldn't stress enough for us to be careful with our belongings because pickpockets and bag snatcher were plentiful. It's something you have to watch out for anywhere, sadly, these day and KL was probably no more dangerous than most of the other cities we'd already visited. Anyway, I always use my Pac Safe bag when out and about. It's slash proof and you can fasten it to a chair without fear of it being snatched.

Doris gave us a map and had circled the places she considered important. We had five hours in KL. MR MM and I were prepared to make the most of our one and only visit. MR MM had been in the ship's library and done some research.

He'd worked out what he thought we should see in the time we had. Doris told us about the pink buses that do a tour around the city and they were free. MR MM is not keen on pink as a colour so we skipped the free pink ride and opted for the monorail. We'd done the one in Sydney (before they dismantled it of course) and enjoyed the sights we saw then.

Now we were about to try the KL monorail. He mentioned to Doris what we planned to do but she did her best to try and dissuade him. She said it was not easy to find or get to - what a monorail? MR MM was having none of that, he was a man on a mission so the monorail it was.

Our coach dropped us off at the iconic PETRONAS TWIN TOWERS. Breathtaking! All glass and stainless steel, glimmering in the sunshine. It was a hot, humid day probably 33C not really the sort of day in which to do too much walking.

Just a few yards from our drop-off point was a shopping mall. Yes, another one only this was part of the towers complex. Doris said: "follow me". We knew why, of course, because she'd tell us where we should muster five hours hence for our return to the ship. Of course there are always one or two who don't get it. Our spot was on the lower ground floor and we checked our watches to make sure we were all on the same time zone.

Doris was the official guide on our KL trip but we also had on board Kevin, the ship's port lecturer from Manchester who doubled up in the ship's tour office at sea. Our first task was to find a money exchange. No problem, there were plenty in this mall. Then a "happy stop" at the luxurious loos in this mall. Relieved, we went on our journey of discovery. We had to find the subway that would take us to a train that would take us to a monorail station. Not difficult. Signs from the mall pointed to the underground.

The next exercise in this Krypton factor adventure was to figure out how to buy a ticket. We had the local currency but how to get the ticket machine to accept it and spew out tickets was another matter. The station was teaming with people, most getting off underground trains to go into the mall. Everybody rushing no time for them to stop and explain. After a while we sussed out that the local notes we were using were too large a denomination for the machines to accept. MR MM approached a lady behind a ticket window who gave him smaller value notes.

Bingo, we had our tickets. Escalators took us deep underground to catch a subway train.

We'd been on plenty of subways already on this world cruise. Just like the underground in Singapore, the carriages in KL were clean despite being very busy.

Two stops and we got off and re-entered the living world above ground level and found our way to the monorail. We had to walk across a road and cross an overpass bridge to reach the monorail station. Was this what Doris had meant about being difficult to find? It was easy peasy! At the monorail station the ticket machines were not easy to fathom out but we did get the knack. The monorail platform in the direction we were travelling was empty when we got there but filled up quickly. When the train arrived (just two carriages) and the doors opened we were faced by a carriage full of people packed like sardines in a tin. We pushed our way forward (we had no option because people were pushing us from behind) and managed to grab hold of a strap and cling on. We were in the first carriage.

MR MM had gone ahead and I could not get to him. No problem as he always tells people we are not joined at the hip! At least we were on the monorail and had got there without much difficulty.

Not a chance of a window seat never mind seeing the view outside. We stayed put but after two stops lots of passengers got off so there was space and even a window seat. WOW! I had great views of the city in front and below - there were temples, mosques, flashy buildings, slums. All life seemed to pass before my eyes.

MR MM knew from his research that not all the monorail stations connect to the subway trains we wanted to get us back to the twin towers mall. So we got off the monorail at one that did. We didn't quite know where it was only somewhere in downtown KL. It certainly wasn't in the wealth belt. There were high rise buildings standing next to ones that looked like slums and others in need of major repairs. There were temples, too.

The one we discovered was in the shadow of the monorail station where we had arrived. This temple had a mosque in front of it and a slum next door. Good markers we thought if we got lost!

Temple elders beckoned us in, We had a good look around, made a donation and left to further investigate our surroundings. But we had landed in an untidy, down-trodden part of KL that didn't actually have a very nice "feel" about it. Not that we felt unsafe but decided to head back to the Twin Towers.

On the return journey we went wrong somewhere and got off the subway train at a different station but in a shopping mall. We soon realised our mistake but it took some time to find our way up to ground level. Be warned some of these shopping malls seem to go on forever and are often linked to other buildings. Anyhow, we made it out and we actually found ourselves at the main entrance to the twin towers (more by good luck than map reading).

Before going back inside we walked around the area and looked at the stunning buildings that make the KL cityscape so futuristic, and iconic.

We had to take some photos to remind us of what we'd seen. Not easy when the Twin Towers seem to reach into the clouds.

MR MM got down on his knees and I thought my God! he'll never get back up without something to hold onto. I can't remember him even getting down on his knees for a proposal, never mind to take photographs!

Anyhow, he made it back up, just as well as I was halfway down the road pretending not to have noticed. We still had a couple of hours to kill before meeting up with Doris and the gang from Queen Elizabeth. We'd decided in advance we'd go to Traders Hotel and have refreshments in its Sky Bar - it was easy to get to just a walk through the mall up one floor and out through glass doors on to a giant patio with a water feature.

By sheer fluke we were passing when the water feature came to "life" with "dancing waters" a lot like the one in front of the Burj Khalifa in Dubai.

And as in Dubai the mechanism is checked sometime during the day to make sure everything is working before the evening performance.

We stumbled on the testing in Dubai in 2012 by chance and now by chance we were in the right spot at the right time to see the KL waters dance. We preferred the dancing waters of Dubai! When the waters were still we set off for Traders Hotel and the sky bar on the 33rd floor.

MR MM has no head for heights and didn't want to go to the bridge that links the twin towers (there was no chance even if he had because places were limited and all had been sold for that day).

It's something many visitors to KL feel they "must do", go on the bridge and look down. Scary!

From Traders Sky Bar there are fantastic views of the whole area around the Petronas Towers.

We soaked up the views while having refreshing drinks followed by a lite bite, a Malay fish dish. Needless to say there were photo opportunities from the Sky Bar. We took advantage and helpfully the hotel runs a complimentary buggy service back to the Petronas

Towers. We took it because we had just 30 minutes before our rendezvous for the return coach journey to Queen Elizabeth.

I found our meeting point straight away but spotted a camera shop and I wandered off. I noticed it sold camcorder batteries, something MR MM needed but had not spotted so far on our voyage for his aged (2008) camcorder. And I'd been unhappy with the camera I bought in Singapore in 2012 - which was a replacement for one that got dropped in Japan that year. I'd thoughts of getting a new Nikon and I saw just the model. So in five minutes we'd bought a new camcorder battery and a new Nikon camera. We made it to the meeting point with three minutes to spare.

But some didn't. Doris herded us out of the mall towards our waiting coach fully intent on leaving the stragglers behind. Well, time is time is time! Luckily for them they saw our group and rejoined us. It could have been a very different story for them - a long walk back to the ship, or an expensive taxi ride!

Doris made no comment when MR MM told her we had found the monorail and ridden it - the only difficulty being with the ticket machines.

DAY TWO IN MALAYSIA....GEORGE TOWN, PENANG.

Another "first" for us, George Town in Penang named after Britain's King George 111. From the ship it looked nice enough. Not many high rise buildings and certainly no skyscrapers to be seen.

It was seriously hot. Probably high 30s or low 40sC. We got off around 9-30am.

I'd put on my cool long batik dress and I took my big sunhat with a large flower on the side - looking more local than a local.

Again MR MM had researched the place. We wanted to do something "local" so we decided we'd hire a trishaw and "driver" for a few hours because it was "different" and none of the ship's tours took our fancy.

It was just a short walk from the ship to the terminal exit and we were greeted by six or more trishaws and their peddlers waiting for business. The trishaws were all decorated with flowers and all matched my hat! We negotiated a price (US$20 an hour for three hours) and told our man where we wanted to go - no shopping malls just a ride around down town George Town. Our trishaw owner whose name sounded like Primark spoke English and understood perfectly.

Getting on the thing was not an easy in my long dress with the two front slits. I quickly realised I was wearing the wrong thing.

MR MM is tall and he sat next to me and we suddenly became joined at the hip - almost welded - something he likes to say we are NOT! Well, there wasn't a lot of seat. To say it was a tight squeeze is an understatement.

Goodness knows how some of the "fatties" from the ship would have managed. They would have had to take two - Hers and His!

I wondered how Primark, who was very slim (almost skinny) would manage with 20 plus stone of combined weight to pedal around and in the heat? He did exceptionally well. Off we went along the main drag out of the port - a very busy road but trishaws seemed to defy any highway code, and other road uses gave them a wide berth.

Sitting there I visualized myself as some famous lady from a bygone age, or Dorothy Lamour In Road to Singapore, pedalled about in a chariot surrounded by orchids and frangipani and the smell of Shalimar!

Then a car sounded its horn and woke me from my dream. We were riding down the centre white line in the middle of the road surrounded by bikes and cars. The flowers I was dreaming about turned out to be silk and the smell was petrol fumes! This was getting exciting! Primark steered us over to a village built on stilts called Chew Jetty. Disembarking the trishaw was not easy on my modesty, and my dress was becoming a problem.

When I tried to get off the seat, I was stuck with the heat and my dress was so far up my legs I was doing my best not to flash my new M&S white undies.

We walked around Chew Jetty - it reminded us of a similar place we visited in Thailand on our way from James Bond Island.

There were also fishing boats and nets that reminded us of Cochin in India. There were little stalls selling the usual tat and guess what - yes another Temple. We didn't linger and once back at our trishaw I asked Primark to take us back to the ship.

I needed a change of clothes if nothing else to spare my modesty. It wasn't a long ride back to Queen Elizabeth, around seven minutes. When I returned to the trishaw I'd changed into trousers and a long-sleeved top as we were in direct sunlight.

Our journey continued. We stopped at Fort Cornwallis built on the orders of Captain Francis Light a trader for the British East India Company who had founded George Town in August 1786. We passed the impressive Town Hall and the Parliament and court buildings - all pristine white. We went into the Anglican Church and chatted to the warden. We were given a book for Easter week.

Back on with the journey and Primark, who probably weighed 8 stone wet through, pedaled away at an even pace. He gave us commentary as we past the sites he thought would be of interest - they were. In the middle of the old town the traffic was busy. He weaved in and out between buses, bikes, cars and scooters.

The drivers all seemed to be careful of the trishaws so we did not feel in any danger. We saw a Batik museum but we did not have time to go in. I would have like to have seen inside being a fan of Batik but our three hours was shooting by.

We were, however, ready to get walking again instead of being ridden around. MR MM was so hot his cotton shirt stuck to the seat.

We were ready for a cold shower and a long cold drink. Primark dropped us back at the terminal. We paid him and gave him a decent tip because he had worked hard. After getting off the trishaw he smiled for the first time especially when we gave him extra cash. I was shocked to see he only had three teeth. Bless him! On the walk back to the ship MR MM found some more local currency in his pockets and went chasing off to find MR Primark.

He'd left the spot where we picked him up but after a search MR MM found him around a corner.

He handed over all the local currency we had left. Well, it was of no use to us we were about to leave Malaysia. That brought an even broader smile to Primark. He'd had a good day and so had we. If you want to do something other than sit on a coach in George Town, I'd recommend a trishaw ride - it's different, informative and dare I say entertaining in a strange sort of way.

I liked Penang a lot. It had a feel of how Singapore used to be when I first went there 30 odd years ago. There was a decent sailaway party where I danced, danced and danced along with others who liked to jig.

CEYLON THAT WAS

It's called Sri Lanka nowadays but in Colonial times it was known as Ceylon. As a kid growing up in Bradford I knew about it because that's where all the tea we drank came from - Ceylon.

Never dreamt of course that I would ever get to visit Ceylon. But I have several times. This was my latest trip, and what an adventure it turned out to be. The place is quiet now the war with the Tamil Tigers has ended. There is peace, we were assured, but it was obvious the authorities still take the security of visitors very, very seriously. We docked in Colombo. Now this is the sort of place you don't attempt to do independent tours - I'm not sure even if they are available.

When I was booking ship's tours I decided I'd get on the one going to Kandy. MR MM didn't disagree. I'd been to Kandy before - it was once famous for the elephants that wandered around the city's streets. But no longer. It was a marathon tour - 12 hours.

The last time I was in Sri Lanka was 33 years ago and I had vivid memories of abject poverty; where there were many maimed people who had suffered from leprosy. I can see them now as though it was only yesterday - they were all lined up outside the main buildings begging. Men with no limbs and no sight either.

It was a desperate place. But Sri Lanka has been at peace for the past three years, said our guide after welcoming us on to the coach.

He was pleased, he said, our ship had called. He said the clouds had been "grey for years" but now they were there to spread gold dust on the people and they were "so happy".

It was an interesting comment and I hope it is fulfilled. There may be peace but the authorities were taking no chances. Police motorcycle outriders appeared as if from nowhere their blue lights flashing and sirens wailing. They took up their positions - one ahead of the lead coach (there were four buses for this Highlights of Colombo tour) and the other at the rear behind the last coach.

The signal was given to move - and we did. The sirens on the police motorcycles clearly audible. It was like that for much of the journey. Apart from providing security these police motorcycle riders were pathfinders and carved a way through a solid wall of traffic. We squeezed through gaps so small you'd have thought the buses would have collided with other trucks or cars or motorbikes, and we ran red traffic lights - all without incident.

The road was jam-packed for much of the journey to Kandy. In fact if we hadn't have had those police outriders I reckon it would have taken us at least seven hours just to reach Kandy. It still took us three hours even with our police outriders to do the 120 miles.

The guide explained our visit just so happened to be taking place the day before the island celebrated New Year and the roads were extra busy because most islanders were on the move going to visit friends and family. After the hustle and bustle of the capital, Colombo, the traffic did eventually thin out which meant our police escorts turned off their sirens and then the pillion police officer just pointed a white baton at oncoming drivers warning them to get out of the way. I didn't see anyone disobey! Passing through the countryside reminded me of Vietnam. It was very similar. Our guide was chatty and told us stories about the conflict with the Tamils and how the British had built the road on which we were travelling.

The British left their mark on the architecture, too. We sped through village after village. They all looked very poor and each village had its own cottage type industry. One did pottery, another basket work, and another sold pineapples. One sold nothing but plastic blow up toys (not the ones you buy in Ann Summers!) but the type you see at any seaside shop or beach shop.

Plastic rings and lilos and the like. That village was known as the plastic village which seemed about right. It got its supplies from the nearby plastic factory. They were probably "seconds".

We passed paddy fields and lots of farmland. The whole place looked about five notches down the scale from Vietnam - poor infrastructure and rubble everywhere! Poor housing, although I have to say there were a few decent ones in and amongst the rubble. Speeding along with the aid of the police escorts clearing our path we kept to time and we arrived at a rest stop (a comfort stop as our American cousins describe them but in Asia they're often referred to a "happy stops"!). Our "happy stop" was at a Government Guest House. The loos were clean and food was being prepared (but not for us). We had just 25 minutes to do whatever and then had to be back on the buses to continue our white-knuckle ride edging ever nearer to Kandy.

This cruise is truly multi-cultural and that's also reflected on ship's tours. And how the "foreigners" loved to shop. Many packed into the tiny shop at this Government Guest House and looked to be grabbing anything that looked like batik. It reminded me a bit like a Harrod's sale on a reduced scale of course. Perhaps because we had police escorts passengers decided they really had to get back on their bus on time. Well, you know there is often one if not two who are "late" and use the excuse they had to "queue for the loo!"

We were still over one and a half hours drive away from Kandy. When I first visited Kandy it was to see the Elephants. They used to wander freely but now I was told they are all in an orphanage. There was a ship's tour to that orphanage - just enough to fill one coach for that, I heard.

As we got closer to Kandy the scenery became spectacular! The island was very lush everywhere even in the busy towns and villages. There were tropical forests and everything was very green. The road wound its way up a very steep mountain side with sheer drops either side. This road was constructed by the British in Colonial times.

We had a scheduled stop at the Botanical gardens in one of the suburbs of Kandy. Magnificent!

It had species planted by British Royals. Indeed, Prince Charles had visited in recent times and taken tea in a pavilion that our guide pointed out.

MR MM asked the guide if the Prince of Wales had "hugged" any of the trees or talked to the plants on his visit. He didn't get an answer although the guide understood the question he just grinned.

We saw the bungalow used by Lord Louis Mountbatten when he was Vice-Roy of India; I went in to the orchid house which was stunning. The gardens were in remarkably good shape - a credit to those who look after them. When we left to return to our coaches we had to run the gauntlet of local traders selling "genuine" spices.

By now it was time for a "hunger stop" - lunch at a swish hotel by a lake. It was in what I called the "Pimlico" of Kandy. No shacks around here just palatial villas with stunning views over water and the Temple where a tooth from the Lord Buddha is kept in a locked wooden casket. The hotel's grounds were manicured; there was not a single piece of litter anywhere.

The buffet lunch tables were ladened with every type of food imaginable. It was delicious. So good some "did an Oliver Twist" and went back for more!

The let down was the shop. It was small and sold what was "rubbish" in my book. However, it didn't stop a group of French passengers raving over "genuine" copies of Lacoste T-shirts for which they wanted US$30 a piece. Silly money! They were buying lots of them and I dare not tell them they'd been 4 for US$10 In Vietnam.

Lunch over it was time to head to the Buddhist Temple where the tooth was kept. It was just across the other side of the man-made lake from the hotel.

I always thought there was one of the Lord Buddha's teeth in Singapore as well. It would appear his teeth may be spread around the world. But are they all "genuine"?

Temples have various dress codes we'd discovered. Some are strict about exposed flesh others not so bothered. At this temple they were extra strict. It was flagged up ahead of the tour that you had to be covered up to gain entry. Some missed reading it while others like MR MM weren't bothered about going in anyway.

MR MM was wearing shorts that came just to the knee. A no-no. They had to be below the knee to be acceptable.

Two friends of ours from Barcelona were wearing shorts that looked to be the same length and went below the knee. Not in the eyes of the fashion police at the temple gate. Tony was told his shorts were too short he wouldn't be allowed in while his partner Kim was waved through. Tony protested that both sets of shorts met the dress code - but he wasted his breath. So he went and paid US$5 for a sarong to cover up his exposed flesh. He was then allowed to proceed.

Quite a few ladies were caught short, too, because their shoulders weren't covered. The sarong sellers did good business on this day! I must confess I did not see mention of the dress code before we set off but as I always tend to dress as a local I was fine. I wore a long wrap sarong skirt and long sleeved top.

The dress code bit appeared to be a right scam really but the real rip-off came at the end of the visit when passengers were leaving the temple grounds.

Uniformed guards on the exit gate "demanded" the sarongs visitors bought for US$5 at the beginning of the tour be handed back with NO refund! It happened to Tony. He was told to hand his sarong back. He told the guard in his best Anglo/Saxon what he could do - and it wasn't "have a nice day"! Approaching the temple you had to remove your shoes. Now this caused me and many others concern as the shoe rack was many yards away from the temple entrance.

417

The footpath to the entrance was so hot you couldn't put your feet down without feeling a burning pain. I made a mad dash for the entrance. I could have been an Olympic long jumper! Men kept their socks on and some ladies had brought a pair with them. I never thought to do that, but it's worth remembering for future reference, not that I will be visiting this temple or any other again anytime soon. We are "templed out".

I must say of all the temples we have visited on his journey so far this was the best. I was given a dish of lotus flowers to offer to the Buddha. I had to give a donation to him on the way out. I only had US dollars but that was OK, Buddha had no preference as long as it was money, money, money! The walk around the temple was very peaceful even though there were many worshipers in the place. I saw wonderful marble statues of Buddha in different positions.

I met up with MR MM outside the temple grounds by The Queen's Hotel - a colonial style building at a busy intersection where hundreds of people and hundreds of Tut-Tuts tried to avoid each other. MR MM had seen an Anglican church among the buildings around the outside of the temple site and went in there to say a prayer. It was Maundy Thursday. He left a donation, too, the amount it would have cost him to enter the temple.

Our police outriders were relaxing close to where we were waiting for our buses. They were happy to pose for pictures. I had mine taken with them.

Once we'd all been counted in, our convoy set off on yet another three hour mad dash out of Kandy, down the mountain and through the villages we'd seen earlier in the day. It was rush hour Sri Lankan-style with thousands of scooters, hundreds of large truck, scores of buses used by the masses (packed to the gunwales and with no air conditioning) and cars galore on the one main road.

I had an aisle seat and could see the action in front when we went around the many bends - the policeman riding pillion wore white gloves and carried a white baton. He was "conducting" the traffic as if he was conducting an orchestra! It was stylish and fascinating to watch. His left arm pointed upwards and his right he waved frantically as if his hand signals were a warning to other drivers to slow down, slow down, move over, get out of the way!

It was like the story in The Bible of Moses parting The Red Sea to let the chosen few through.

We were those "chosen few" on this day in Sri Lanka and our "Red Sea" was the main road between Colombo to Kandy! Traffic came to a standstill either side of the road; locals poured out of their shops and homes to see what the commotion was all about.

The locals waved and watched in disbelief. They must have thought we were royalty!

This slowing down the traffic and the acrobatic behaviour from the police went on for a full one and a half hours 'till we reached our "happy stop", same place as on the way out. Just 15 minutes though this time. Moving again, the police performed minor miracles; they were incredible. What was more incredible was the way the drivers of cars, trucks, Tut Tuts and buses just did as they were meant to do, slow down or stop as we sped through. Few times was it necessary for our drivers to stop completely.

In fact they said without the police escort we would still have been on the road in a week's time. A bit of an exaggeration - but only a bit! Our convoy pressed on.

There appeared to be some mobile phone calls between the drivers of the four buses. It reminded me of the days of truckers in the UK talking on their CB radios.

"Ah, breaker one-nine, this here's the Rubber Duck.

You gotta copy on me, Big Ben, 10-4

Pig Pen for sure.

'Cause we got a little ol' convoy

Rockin' through the night.

Yeah, we got a little ol' convoy,

Ain't she a beautiful sight?

Come on and join our convoy

Ain't nothin' gonna get in our way.

We gonna roll this truckin' convoy

To Colombo all the way.

Convoy!

And so we rolled on down the road 'till we got back to the ship in exactly three and a half hours. Brilliant driving and brilliant police work! It made my day just watching them. They performed how police used to when they conducted traffic at junctions in days gone by. The same hand signals but these cops were on a moving motor bike that was travelling at speed. An amazing sight! An unforgettable experience!

PIRATES OF THE INDIAN OCEAN…

The waters in the Indian Ocean and the Red Sea along with parts
of the Suez Canal are considered by the international community to
be pirate infested. So at least one "pirate drill" is usually carried out
on ships sailing in these parts. We had picked up three "security
guards" - they came on board without fuss or drama unlike the time
we were on Queen Mary 2 in 2012 when they arrived to great fanfare
in a sleek speed boat which was more James Bond-style. To prepare
for a potential pirate attack , passengers are briefed and then an
attack is simulated. Those with inside cabins stay in their
accommodation; those with balconies, suites or ocean views go and
sit/stand in the corridor while the all clear is given. It took about 15
minutes to complete our practice pirate drill. Then it was all over.
These three "characters" - most of us thought of them as mercenaries
- patrolled the ship at night. The outer decks were closed after dark to
ALL passengers and the back of 3 deck and several yards down
either side on the approach to the stern were off limits for all the time
the mercenaries were on board. Some anti-pirate gear had been
rigged up.

We were told we could approach the guards if we saw them about the ship and we were told we could identify them by their clothing - their dark tops all had the same wording. They were all, apparently, ex-British forces. May be SAS, may be SBS, may be Royal Marines. They had "served" but were no longer on Her Majesty's Service, instead taking the dollar of cruise lines to make ends meet! We've been through these pirate waters several times in recent years - when we were on Queen Mary 2 in 2012 the Royal Australian Navy guided missile frigate Melbourne came in close and gave us a display of her captain's seafaring skills and her helicopter pilot's flying ability. It was good fun. Broke up an otherwise boring sea day. MR MM is nearly always seen with his camcorder during the day. He got some excellent film of the Melbourne. She sailed first down the starboard side and then portside so everyone on Queen Mary 2 could get more than just a quick glimpse of her - everybody that wanted had plenty of time to catch all her sophisticated "features".

She did the same sort of speed at QM2 for about an hour. Her helicopter circled overhead and had a cameraman on board who could be seen taking pictures of his war ship and of Queen Mary 2. We heard later that this footage had been shown on Australian TV.

Well, a few weeks before QM2 had made her first circumnavigation of Australia and it had been a rip-roaring success.

At every port she had been greeted like a true Royal. People turned out in their thousands to see her.

Captain Kevin Oprey was Master of QM2 at this point on the voyage, and the bridge must have been in touch by radio with the Melbourne's commanders for Capt Oprey told us over the PA system when Melbourne was about to resume her anti-pirate duties and he gave three blasts of Queen Mary 2's whistle.

Within a minute of that announcement you could see the frigate had picked up speed and her steel hull was cutting through the water like a knife cuts through butter. We waited, alas in vain, for her to respond with her guns! That transit of these waters is hard to beat. There was nothing of shimmering magnitude on Queen Elizabeth's sailing though. All MR MM saw were flying fish!

INDIA THE REAL MUMBAI.

This bustling metropolis was not somewhere MR MM had wanted to visit. He'd made that quite clear long before we joined the ship. But as it was a port of call he had to join in with what I arranged. And it actually worked out fine. He even expressed his delight. Most uncharacteristic! I spent hours researching on the internet (isn't it a wonderful invention?) to get an idea what to do. I had been there but 30 years before. All the signals pointed to a company called Grand Mumbai Tours. It scored highly with people who'd taken its tours in Mumbai. But I needed 10 to make it worthwhile cost-wise. So I put out "feelers" on the Cruise Critic website and soon had the numbers.

For several months before we set off on our world voyage the owner of Grand Mumbai Tours, a gent called Pranav (no not satnav!) was in touch by email. He seemed good fun. All was booked. Everything on the day worked like clockwork, and Pranav turned out to be a really fun character from beginning to end.

Here is where Pranav took us:

1. Gateway Of India - This is where it all began and ended. The most important British Heritage Monument.

2. Taj Mahal Palace Hotel - The most beautiful hotel in India, and the most photographed hotel in Asia.

3. Mumbai University - One of the biggest universities in India which imparts education through colleges affiliated to it.

4. Rajabai Clock Tower - The "Big Ben" of India which plays chimes every fifteen minutes and we heard about its history.

5. Bombay High Court Building - A British heritage monument and the oldest court in Mumbai.

6. Oval Cricket Ground - A public cricket ground where over 200 cricket games take place on Sundays, and also a place from where you can see Mumbai University, Bombay High Court, Rajabai Clock Tower all in one line for a good photo. On Sundays,(which is when we were there,) this place was "overrun" with hundreds playing cricket.

7. Victoria Terminus Railway Station & Municipality Building - The grandest and the most beautiful station in the whole world. Victoria Terminus is now known as Chatrapati Shivaji Terminus and is a World Heritage Site. There were thousands of people rushing (yes, even on a Sunday) to make it to their train on time. This station featured in the hit movie, Slumdog Millionaire. It was also attacked by Pakistani terrorists the other year.

8. The Hanging Gardens - another of the "wonders of Mumbai".

9. Kamla Nehru Park - which has the huge old woman's shoe - and from where there are good views of the beautiful skyline of Mumbai city.

10. Dhobi Ghat - This is the biggest open air laundry in the world. And yes, they do wash their dirty linen in public! A sight to behold.

11. ISCKON Temple of Hare Rama Hare Krishna - Explore the beautiful, rich and modern temple of Hare Rama Hare Krishna's.

12. Marine Drive and Chowpatty Beach - Marine Drive is also known as the Queen's necklace, and Girgaum Chowpatty is the famous beach in South Mumbai where huge idols of Lord Ganesha are immersed into the water on the last day of the Ganesha festival.

13. Drove past British heritage buildings like Prince of Wales Museum, Maharashtra Police Headquarters, Flora Fountain & Hutatma Chowk, the Telegraph Office, India Post Office Building, Kala Ghoda Area, David Sassoon's Library, National Gallery of Modern Art, Flora Fountain & Hutatma Chowk.

14. Crawford Market - The biggest and the oldest market in India. Fruit, vegetables, spices, pet cats and dogs, fish, confectionary, perfumes, dry fruits all sold under one roof in a market covering 24,000 square feet.

15. Banaganga Water Tank - A mythological water tank, sacred to Hindus. The water in this water body is considered holy just like the water of the Ganges.

Many Hindus do lots of religious rituals on the banks and on the steps of this beautiful and peaceful water body, including immersing the ashes of the dead. This place is surrounded by many temples. Ducks and huge catfish flourish. This place is in an area where you see contrasting lifestyles. Hindus who can't afford to go to the Ganges use this water tank as a substitute.

16. Khau Galli - The famous street food lane of Mumbai where working class people eat street food during their lunch break. We tucked in to freshly made Paav Bhaji allegedly "specially prepared" for us. It was delicious I must say.

We had an action-packed tour with Pranav and it was a fascinating experience. Even MR MM said so. I went to Bombay, as it was known, in 1980. It was a filthy, dirty place but with fabulous buildings and some very shabby shanty towns. There were many beggars and people with missing limbs. Then it was a city of great extremes - wealth and poverty - little appears to have changed only the rich have got richer and the poor got poorer!

There were, and still are, sacred cows to be seen, but on our visit we spotted only three. The streets are a lot cleaner now, and there appeared to be fewer stray dogs. There is still a lot of rubbish, and people still live on the street or in flimsy, filthy shacks.

The beggers are still there, probably in even greater numbers and it was disturbing to see so many children begging for money to buy

428

food. At least that's what they said. It made me weep. However, all spoke excellent English so the education system must be working!

If you have read Slumdog Millionaire (the book is more realistic than the movie) you will have a good insight to what Bombay was like when I went before. It was the only place in the world at that time that had left an impression on my brain.

My verdict on our tour? Of all the places we were taken in Mumbai by Pranav, I loved the ISCKON Temple of Hare Krishna the best.

I expected George Harrison to pop up any minute. Hare Krishna the song made popular by the Beatles was being played in the temple. This temple was so different to the numerous other temples we'd visited in the past six weeks.

We had to take our shoes off and leave them in a shoe, but I was worried because I was wearing my newly acquired Vivienne Westwood comfy shoes I'd got in Hong Kong. (well I have to keep appearances even in the slums). I was imagining the shoes going missing and some young beggar selling them on as the young boy does in Slumdog Millionaire. My worries were unfounded of course. The shoes BTW are washable so after a visit through the filth and grime of the markets I washed them in the ladies toilet in the Temple that was our only comfort stop. Another strange thing about the shoes which are green with silver bows on the front. A teenager beggar with one hand was wanting money.

Nobody gave him any but I felt so sad I did and he blew me a kiss with his one and only hand and pointed to the shoes then he bent down and kissed them.

I was so cut up and so were the others he ended up with more money (and a banana) from our group.

The Temple was packed with worshipers. It was paid for by an American, we were told, and one of his American disciples was talking to the 2,000 plus crowd who were all seated. Children were being shown how to make sandalwood paste which they use to mark their foreheads.

While I thought this temple was just outstanding, it didn't mean we didn't see other interesting sights and sounds in Mumbai.

At the Oval cricket ground there were hundreds and hundreds of kids playing cricket on its 24 acres. Victoria train station could have been Paddington before it was revamped. Inside we saw the platform where they filmed the dancing in the Slumdog Millionaire film. Pranav our guide confessed he wanted to be an actor - I hope he makes it. He's a good man with a good attitude and bags of fun.

At the Banaganga Water Tank we saw lots of rituals taking place including a young girl having her head shaved meaning one of her parents had died.

At the market apart from the exotic fruit and veg, there were lots of song birds in cages (of the feathered kind and not the ones that used to be in cages in the red light district). Puppy dogs, too, were caged. The man selling them handled them very roughly in my opinion. It all seemed a bit cruel.

Eating Pav Bhaji from a street vendor was an experience and we lived to tell the tale! Time to say our farewells to Pranav - a young man full of life and an excellent tour guide.

I thought Mumbai was a really good port of call. You must go with an open mind because their lifestyle is not our lifestyle and their standards are not always our standards. I loved the day we had there.

We followed it the next night with a Night of the Raj Ball on board Queen Elizabeth. Lots dressed up in Indian outfits including some men who wore Maharaja hats.

There was the man in Mumbai
He said come and see Hari Krishna hari hari
Take off your shoes and sit on the floor
I said ,"in these shoes?"
I'd rather keep them on and listen to George Harrison!

MEDICAL EMERGENCIES...

These happen quite frequently on world cruises. There is usually at least one death on board during a world voyage and some passengers have to be medi-vaced to get treatment ashore. I know. It happened to me in Punta Arenas, Chile, on the 2013 world voyage aboard Arcadia.

Queen Elizabeth made an emergency stop at Muscat so two very sick people could get emergency treatment - one was a member of the Spa staff and the other an elderly gent who was a passenger.

A day or so before an urgent broadcast had been made on the PA system calling for blood donors to contact the medical centre. There was no shortage of volunteers willing to give their blood when it matched that of the very poorly passenger. At the time of the call for blood the ship had left India and would have been off its coast or that of Pakistan en route for Abu Dhabi.

Someone on board took the decision to order the engine room to go full steam ahead to Muscat (a retired American Admiral on board suggested to MR MM we'd travelled at 26 knots for 12 hours or more according to his calculations). Why head for Muscat, capital of Oman?

Well, the Sultan of Oman is one of the richest men in the world and he has provided the kingdom with world-class medical facilities.

Queen Elizabeth went in close to Muscat - a city we visited on our 2012 voyage on Queen Mary 2.

In fact we wished we had gone in to harbour and been allowed to go ashore. Instead Queen Elizabeth stayed just outside the harbour entrance so a launch could come alongside and take off the two patients. But what sickened me (excuse the pun) were those passengers intent on filming the evacuation of the two sick people.

MR MM had shut down his camcorder for the evacuation out of respect.

Some passengers though lent over the side straining to get snaps of them being taken off. Is there no respect anymore?

I know how traumatic it is having to be medi-vaced from a ship without people watching as if it were part of the cruise ship fun.

Sadly the elderly gentleman didn't make it. He died in hospital in Muscat, we were told later.

His wife was said to have carried on with the cruise (they were doing the world apparently) to Southampton then went to Muscat to repatriate his body.

AN ILL WIND....

The medical evacuation and the dash to the Oman meant Queen Elizabeth was ahead of time by 12 hours reaching Abu Dhabi - a bonus for instead of arriving at 6am we berthed at six o'clock the previous evening. Not that it was a problem.

The port authorities, and Cunard's agent, were on the ball. It meant we had chance to go downtown on the hastily arranged shuttle service.

Abu Dhabi is the richest of the Emirates but only now is it really trying to make something of tourism we were told. The shuttle bus dropped us off at, yes, a shopping mall. But we wanted to have a wander outside. Not the best idea.

By this time it was dark and as usual in the Middle East the streets were almost deserted of people. No one walks, they all ride around in limos - well gas is cheap! And it's still roasting even after dark.

It wasn't long before we returned to the shopping mall where we had been dropped off by our transport. It was surprising quiet. There were shoppers but not droves of them.

In fact passengers from Queen Elizabeth who, like us, had decided to venture downtown were almost a majority.

We discovered we had a slight cash-flow problem after we decided we'd dine in a restaurant...one of my credit cards didn't work in the ATM machine. I only tried it once fearing if I tried again it may gobble it up and then we would have been stuffed.

I phoned the card company who already knew I was travelling because I'd flagged it up to them before we set off in January. They had a list of all our ports of call, too. I went through all the rigmarole of security questions and just as the guy in the Indian call centre was about to tell me whether the card worked or not we got cut off. Typical!

So I decided not to try to use the ATM again that day. However, wandering around the mall I spotted some colourful bikinis - just what I wanted. But I only had the one credit card with me at the time and that didn't work in the ATM. Would it work in a shop till? I was about to find out.

I made my purchase, offered my card (the one the ATM had rejected). Bingo! It worked. May be it was the ATM which had the problem and not my credit card.

It's always good to have a few credit cards when you travel a lot as you just never know when something might happen and one doesn't work for some unknown reason.

OUT AND ABOUT IN ABU DHABI.

We had a four hour ship's tour booked for our day in this desert kingdom because we knew it would be hot, hot, hot!

Abu Dhabi is very new. Well the whole of the Emirates are new. They were little more than desert until around 50 years ago. The only industry they had 'till the late 1930's was pearling.

I remember going to a conference from Cyprus to Abu Dhabi in 1994. I stayed a week in a fab hotel. There was not such a lot of new build at that time, only the old city and the souks. Now all the old had gone and now it's all new build or looks that way.

Our guide confirmed it. He said all buildings that were over 30 years old had been pulled down and replaced with glitzy high rises and fancy structures. That was stating the obvious looking at the cityscape. Abu Dhabi is the richest of all the seven Emirates and is the capital of the UAE. It has most of the oil and the gas.

It was Abu Dhabi, of course, that bailed out its more famous neighbour Dubai the other year. Dubai, run by the racehorse loving Al Maktoums, ran out of money building the Burj Khalifa Tower - the tallest building in the world in 2014. The Ruler of Abu Dhabi stepped in with his abundance of petro dollars so the job could be completed,

436

but on one condition, apparently. It had to contain his name. Hence Khalifa.

I digress. Back to our trip. First stop was the Sheikh Zayed Grand Mosque - the largest mosque in the UAE which opened in 2008 and must be clearly visible from the moon even on a cloudy night. It can hold up to 40,000 worshippers, yes 40,000.

It has giant chandeliers made out of Swarovski crystals. It's out of this world to look at. I have never seen such opulence but it's beautiful in every way. It's built of white marble and inside it's covered in a hand woven carpet that was made in Iran but stitched together in Abu Dhabi and is said to be the largest carpet anywhere in the world.

I'd go as far as to say this mosque is more beautiful than even the Taj Mahal. After putting our shoes back on our next stop was a museum and heritage village. It showed how these people of the desert had gone from living in tents and riding camels to owning palaces and driving Mercs, Rollers and Porsches.

Camel rides were offered at US$5 - or if you couldn't afford that you could trade in your wife and get the camel to take home!

MR MM rushed to book a camel and trade me in but discovered they smelt awful and were nowhere near as fragrant as me, so changed his mind.

Our drive around Abu Dhabi was an eye-opener. We saw huge villas set in massive grounds; skyscrapers galore and everything was clean; no graffiti, no litter.

I expect you would be severely punished for such offences. I liked the country and I enjoyed our day there, but it didn't have the WOW! factor of Dubai. I think Abu Dhabi has lost its charm and that old Arabic feel it had when I when I went there 20 years ago. Shame really. But there's not room for two "Dubais" next door to each other!

In Abu Dhabi I met a handsome Sheik
Salam! he says and I say Hi as I only speak
Yorkshire!
Come with me into the desert
We can make love under the stars
Come to my Bedouin tent and relax on my silk carpet
What says I "Not in these shoes". I can't get sand in my feet!

DUBAI

We could have rowed from Abu Dhabi to Dubai the distance is so small - something like 80 nautical miles. We didn't of course, we let Queen Elizabeth take us there is the style to which we had now become accustomed for our two-day stop over.

Both MR MM and I have been blessed - we have been to Dubai many times in recent years. I never tire of looking at the souks, especially those that sell "sparklers".

I'm not a fan of brassy yellow gold but I find nice white gold and diamonds hard to resist especially if the stones are set in the white gold!

We just happened to be in Dubai on Good Friday and, yes, most of the classy shops - like my favourite, Sky Jewellers - were closed until late in the day. I said "most" but not all. I found one that had great pieces at excellent prices but I had to haggle.

Dubai is one of those places where you can buy almost everything. It is known for traders who try and flog you "genuine" fake Rolex watches or "genuine" fake designer handbags.

We had time on our hands, excuse the pun, so I decide to check out these "genuine" fakes.

We were taken to a room at the back of the shop (away from prying eyes) and out came the genuine bling that made our eyes water. All supposedly Rolex. I wouldn't have known not being a fan because they are big, bulky and not feminine enough for me. I don't do big and bold even if they were on offer for the equivalent of £90 sterling.

It was the same with the "genuine" fake designer handbags - big, bulky things that are not "me". I was glad to get out of the shop and into the souk. I would rather buy an ordinary bag or a genuine designer one if I needed one. I love my little Vivienne Westwood bag I got in Hong Kong. I don't need cheap imitations.

So back to the jewellers where I ended up with a pair of diamond and amethyst earrings. I thought they would be nice with my dress for that evening - the night of the World Cruise dinner. It was a major operation getting ready for this big dinner - an event all world cruise passengers on Cunard liners are given as a sort of "thank you".

They are stunning occasions, amazing events not to be missed. I'd done "maintenance" the day before (we women need high maintenance as we get older). I had been pampered into looking half decent, buffing, scrubbing, polishing, painting (no I had not become domesticated and this was not my new cleaning job as a stewardess on the ship). This buffing, scrubbing etc was all in the name of beauty!

Nails polished, legs buffed and hair fluffed I was ready for action. We were taken to the JUMERAH MADINAT a venue next to the Al Arab hotel (the one that looks like a sail). I have been before for a world cruise dinner and knew what to expect. I was not disappointed. It was as good as ever. If anything better than the last one I attended in 2012.

These are very formal affairs dress-wise. We were all in the proper rig and greeted by the Captain and some of his senior officers after we'd got off our coaches. Then the belly dancers appeared. Waiters served drinks galore; there was music and dancing and falcons on the arms of handsome Arab men. There were even Bedouin tents to relax in and this was before dinner! The wine flowed but as I don't drink vino I was persuaded to have a few vodkas and slim line tonics before going in for the meal and the entertainment. Most people looked "well oiled" before the dinner started such was the generosity of our hosts, Cunard. Of course there are always the odd ones who make themselves ill by their greed for a free drink.

Everyone had been allocated seats at numbered tables. Our table number was 23. We had no idea who was hosting the table until we made our way to it.

We then discovered we were in exalted company - our host was Queen Elizabeth's Hotel Manager, David Hamilton, a very important member of the ship's company. We felt flattered.

It was a great night. The food was excellent, the drink plentiful and the company outstanding. The entertainment was just fantastic and so different. Couldn't have been better and we had a prime table location right on the edge of the dance floor.

Seeing the cabaret acts was not a problem. On the buses going to the dinner everyone had been quiet and reserved.

A much different story, of course, on the journey back to the ship. Passengers were laughing and singing and occasionally losing their footing! Some German guests on our coach started a sing song singing the chorus of "It's a long way to Tipperary" and they even knew the words to "My Bonnie lies over the Ocean". Don't ask me how they knew the words to these songs.

Cunard is generous with its hospitality to those passengers doing the full world by staging such memorable events as black tie World Cruise Dinners. I did, though, hear three people moan and grumble but couldn't be bothered to listen to their reasons why.

There was nothing that I spotted anyone could complain about. Well, may be one - there was no Loyal Toast. Mind you if they had been on P&O's Arcadia cruise in 2013 like we were they would have had good reason to be unhappy.

What we got then were invitations to a couple of luncheons on the ship (there was no special menu); an invite to a coffee morning, again on the ship, where the coffee was clap cold and biscuits were served in paper napkins. That's P&O's style of "rewards" for world cruisers. What style? No style, certainly not Cunard style!

DUBAI DAY TWO

There's more to do than shop 'till you drop in Dubai believe me. We took a taxi to the Marina Mall at the far end of Dubai past the Al Arab Hotel - a journey that took more than half an hour and didn't cost an arm and a leg. I think it was US$30.

This Mall is very classy but outside by the water's edge it is even classier - with a wonderful promenade with cafes. Apparently no alcohol can be served in this area.

We'd decided to go to this part of Dubai and catch a ferry back into the centre.

One of our friends on the cruise had a companion with her who had lived and worked as a bean counter in Dubai. She "highly recommended" this ferry ride back to Dubai City.

It took one and a half hours and we saw all the wonderful buildings from the sea; we past the Jumerah Palm and the Al Arab and saluted the QE2 which is in a dock tucked away from Port Rashid. Cost of the ferry around £8 each. Excellent value.

I have to say after seeing all the skyscrapers in the leading cities around the world, Dubai is the best! Wonderful architecture that changes each year. Amazing buildings.

After leaving the ferry we took a taxi to the Burj Khalifa to see the water fountains. It was nearing 1-0pm and we knew they tested the dancing fountains at this time each day to make sure they are all working for the spectacular evening show.

We always find it exciting to walk around the Dubai Mall. The Aquarium is just awesome.

MR MM discovered a Waitrose. It's was a big Waitrose, the biggest he'd ever been in, and it had blueberries and Actimel!

We've been fortunate that around the world we've been able to find blueberries and Actimel in most ports of call. I never ran out. I walked behind MR MM in true Arab style as I don't do food shopping and I couldn't see a shoe department! There was a notice on a doorway that led to the pork butchers which read "Non Muslims only"!

Around 1,000 newbies joined Queen Elizabeth in Dubai - the last segment of the world cruise. I did another Cruise Critic meet & greet and I have welcomed on board over 200 members on this world cruise. They were mostly all great fun people. I was honoured to have met them all.

The past two nights MR MM and Hugh from North Carolina who, along with his wife Carole, have been long time tablemates have worn their Arabian outfits.

I dressed in style even though there was no theme night. We got some strange looks from some people but many thought we all looked great. And who cares what others think about dress? We don't!

A VICAR .....

Time was when vicars, priests and Rabbis were regular "features" on cruise ships but, alas, no more. While they may be thin on the ground most of the year at Easter and Christmas it is a different story.

They are very visible. We went to the Anglican Easter Day Service held in the Queen's Room. Normally the church services are held in the Royal Court Theatre which can accommodate well over 1,000.

This Easter it was decided by someone that the Roman Catholics should have the theatre and the Anglicans be accommodated in the Queen's Room. It turned out to be the wrong way round. There were around 500 packed in to the Queen's Room yet just dozens in the theatre.

Earlier, we got Easter eggs in our cabin. Our cabin boy had arranged them on the bed and created a "feature" using some flowers I wear in my hair. It was very artistic of him.

All AT SUEZ

One of the great waterways of the world has to be the Suez Canal. Built with sweat, blood and tears. This stretch of water which allows ships to leave Europe and enter the Red Sea without going around Cape of Good Hope is a God-send shipping tycoons.

It saves them time but it costs them too.

It opened in 1869 and took a decade to build. The water north of the Bitter Lakes flows north in the winter and south in the summer. It's all seawater. The Suez has no locks unlike the Panama.

Our transit began early, very early - 4-30am in fact. I was still in the Land of Nod and by the time I got up to go to the gym at 6-30am we were already well on our way north. A good job I have been lucky enough to go through the Suez several times or I would have been disappointed at missing the beginning.

It was not too hot, but was windy on the decks which made it feel cool.

Most people stood on the decks watching the ever changing scenery and taking loads of photographs. In my opinion for what it's worth I think there's more to see on the Suez than the Panama.

446

On the Suez there's lots of human life which adds to its fascination for me at least.

I dressed for the occasion in my Egyptian outfit the one I purchased a few years ago and I headed off to the Britannia restaurant for breakfast.

It was very quiet in there with most passengers soaking up the sights and sounds of the canal transit, and my butler MR MM was busy making movies on deck so unable to serve my breakfast in the cabin.

Once up and about I realised it was Sunday so went to the church service. The poor preacher was short on worshippers - most of his congregation were marvelling at God's wonders outside (with a little help from man) rather than giving thanks and praise to Him. After church I spotted "Ali Baba" and a few of his henchmen. Not the 40 thieves, just a handful of fellow Egyptians selling their wares on board Queen Elizabeth.

It seems to be something of a Cunard tradition when vessels transit the Suez Canal they allow a handful of traders to come on board and they depart on the pilot boat when the transit is completed.

We've seen it on the Queen Mary 2 on both our passages and now on Queen Elizabeth.

These traders sell mainly jewellery and kaftans and wooden boxes.

I'm nosey and like to have a look at what's on offer. There were a few passengers rummaging through the stuff and some said it was too expensive. I told them they needed to barter. I spotted a lady holding a dress like the one I was wearing.

I said to her "that's nice, I got mine for US$10 but also gave him two Cunard pens and a Queen Mary 2 postcard three years ago".

She told me the guy wanted US$25. How much? I took over the bartering for her and got it knocked down to US$15.

Then a passenger yelled at me "how much is this?" holding up another item of clothing.

I looked at him and I said I have no idea. "Why not?" he said you work here. Oh no I don't, I'm a passenger.

He looked closer at me and said "Ah! Yes, I see it's you Maggiemou" We laughed. I got them to barter and they bought the items and I'll bet that when they got them home wondered why on earth they'd bothered!

I've been mistaken for many people in the past but never an Egyptian.

I hadn't bought anything from the traders so I went to my cabin and got some Cunard postcards and two pens and went back to the bazaar they'd set up on board.

For US$10, three Cunard postcards and one Cunard pen (I feel a song coming on!) I got a fancy bracelet to wear with my Egyptian dress. The other cards and the pen I gave to another seller.

He was very happy especially after I rounded up more customers for him. It was all a bit of fun. I don't know why but in Egypt they love pens.

The night of the transit was meant to be a theme night, Egyptian of course, but it was scrapped because we were not stopping in Egypt.

Goodness knows why they cancelled it....we still sailed "past Egypt". Many passengers had brought Egyptian-style outfits with them, others had bought them on board, especially for this particular evening event. Another misjudgment by someone on the ship.

But it didn't stop me and many others dressing up Egyptian-style. To Hell with what the ship decided. Sometimes those in authority don't appear to think.

PETRA - THE ROSE CITY

One of the first ship's tours I booked after we decided to go on Queen Elizabeth's 2014 world voyage was to the ancient city of Petra in Jordan. I said to MR MM "that will sell out fast and so I'm going to get our places early so we will not be disappointed".

It seemed to him strange that so many months ahead of even setting off I was booking a ship's tour happening towards the end of our four month voyage on Queen Elizabeth.

But I knew from past experience the ship's Petra tours would be very, very popular partly because it is difficult, if not impossible, to do it on your own in the day from Aqaba - the distances are vast from the port to Petra and back and are mostly through desert.

Come the day I was not wrong. Over half the passengers and over half the crew went on tours to Petra. The days when the crew got free tours as they did when I worked at sea look to be long gone. They had to pay. All right not the same money as we passengers. Loads of busses lined up to take us all on the two hour drive to Petra.

To avoid congestion the times of the tours were staggered by one hour.

Our guide was very good and informative. The journey out was mainly through desert and not a lot to see apart from sand, sand and more sand, some Bedouin villages and camels and herds of goats and goat herders.

Wadi Mosi, the village drop off for the walk in to Petra is spectacular - its stunning mountains and wild terrain breathtaking. This is where in The Bible you read about Moses striking the rock with his stick to get water. The drive into Wadi Mosi is geared up to cater for tourists - its life blood. There are hotels aplenty including a Crowne Plaza, a Movenpick and a Hilton to name but three. They are all built in the tradition style of the country - low rise and sand or rustic coloured to match the surrounding landscape.

No concrete boxes looking like prison blocks you see in so many places. The authorities are to be congratulated for holding a tight rein on what's built.

Petra is known as the Rose City because the stone is all shades of pink and the sand is red. I even came across a dog whose coat was red!

I went to Petra in 1988 and a friend of mine in Yorkshire - a well-known classical pianist - played a concert there at the invitation of Queen Noor. I remember he had to get his Steinway piano into the Rose City. No mean feat but the piano made it in one piece.

451

The City of Petra is Jordan's most visited attraction and has been a UNESCO World Heritage site since 1985 but it was a "lost city" for a thousand years or more. It's easy to see why it was "lost" for so long - it's all carved out of the rugged rock formations - some of the most amazing shapes I have ever seen.

Petra is considered one of the seven wonders of the modern world. The locals use this title to call everything from hotels to local shops and stalls "The Wonder of the World" shop, hotel etc. They are very proud of their heritage and rightly so.

Jordanians are friendly people and at the time of our visit it was still a safe country for tourists given the turmoil in all its neighbours.

A visit to Petra is not for the faint hearted or the walking wounded although some less mobile passengers attempted it with their walking sticks. I didn't see anyone on a Zimmer, though. To see Petra properly you need several days but in four hours you can get a good feel of the place. It was hot, very hot, but we knew it would be before we went and so dressed for the occasion. We knew our tour was going to last four hours and we had to walk around four miles mostly under an unforgiving sun.

In his pre-tour talk the Cunard port lecture had warned of the heat and the walking and to attempt the tour passengers had to be fit!. I had to admire the people who went and made it back in one piece.

452

Two I knew fell down with the heat exhaustion and an ambulance had to be called. Most make the journey into Petra on foot but there are horses, ponies with buggy carts and camels to take you there and back...at a price! Petra, in case you didn't know, is where they filmed Indiana Jones, and judging by the speed the horses went I think all the drivers thought they were Harrison Ford!

The first part of the guided walk was downhill. We saw fabulous caves and heard about the people who had lived in them. We saw lots of tombs.

The guide was very good but the slow pace and the heat and standing made MR MM and I restless so we trotted off on our own. At the bottom of the hill we came to the entrance to what is called the SIQ. This is where you enter the city proper. A walk of 1200 metres into the Rose City, a chasm of winding paths, narrow at times, cut away by nature through sandstone cliffs of pink, purple and cream. Steep 100ft rock walls on each side. The colours were spectacular. The changing colours and patterns of the worn away stone formed pictures in our imaginations. It was cool in parts when the walls gave good shade from the baking sun.

As we reached the end of the SIQ we caught our first glimpse of why we there. I remembered the WOW! factor from my first visit all those years ago and I said to MR MM as we turned a corner "Be prepared we are nearly there". Then sure enough we were and

453

WOW! What an awesome sight. With the sun streaming through the narrow exit from the SIQ we caught our first glimpse of the best-known surviving monument in Petra - The Treasury Building. It took our breath away!

It's a fantastic sight and even having looked at pictures of it doesn't prepare you for its sheer magnificence when you've got it in your sights. It makes all the modern, glitzy, high-rises we've seen around the world fade into oblivion. And to think when the carvers of Petra were working creating these wonders they had no power tools.

In the main street there was an abundance of camels (people took short rides on their backs) and the usual array of locals selling junk - most of it so dirty from the dust and sand you could not make out what it was. The horse and camel owners did a good trade. I heard stories of people allegedly being ripped off price-wise. May be they were, may be they weren't. We stayed on two feet and declined offers of a "free ride" that was not free at all!

We walked around the site and got to the amphitheatre and I recalled that was where my friend played his piano all those years ago.

It was very hot and windy around 12-30pm and a bit of a sand storm whipped up. We thought we'd taken enough water with us but were running out so bought more. You need to stay hydrated in desert condition.

Some people though didn't drink enough liquids and collapsed. There's no air ambulance to come to the rescue in Petra remember! Around one o'clock we had seen enough and decided we needed to start to walk out of Petra and up the hill to the Crowne Plaza Hotel for our prearranged lunch, which was included in the tour price.

The climb out took us around an hour and although not difficult it was exhausting mostly because of the temperature. We began to feel hot, got thirsty and a little tired. We kept having water stops every 30 metres. We just made it out before we ran out of water again.

We did manage to beat the masses to the lunch. And a good lunch it was too. We were offered a Mediterranean/ Middle Eastern diet. Pitta bread and hummus was on the menu along with slow cooked lamb and rice, chicken and spicy roasted vegetables.

We had time for some "retail therapy". I was interested in buying Frankincense but they wanted US$20 for a gram! Wonder what Mary and Joseph would think of that?

We left Petra at four in the afternoon for the drive back to Queen Elizabeth; had two stops allegedly for "comfort breaks" but really about more shopping opportunities - as if we hadn't had enough of them already this day!

We arrived back in Aqaba, the port where we were docked, around seven. It had been a brilliant day out, full of mystique and adventure. Wonderful, one of the highlights of this world cruise.

TIME TO PACK!

Just before we entered the Suez Canal we asked our cabin steward if he would, at his convenience, start to retrieve the suitcases he had taken away when we joined Queen Elizabeth on January 10.

He brought them the day of the transit - all 14 of them. Only shouldn't there have been 15? MR MM and I couldn't agree.

He said 14, I said 15. The only way to check was to turn on the camera and bring up the picture of our luggage outside the Premier Inn in Harbour Parade, Southampton, as we waited to be transported to the ship.

The camera never lies and it didn't this time. After we had a count up sure enough there was one piece of luggage that wasn't with us. We were able to show the picture to our steward; point out the piece that was unaccounted for and he went hot-foot to look for it. He was successful. Now we had all 19 pieces in the cabin (we'd kept four with us all the time). Packing could commence.

We still had 12 days to go before hitting Southampton and the end of our world voyage but time just flies. I never leave the packing until the "last minute". It doesn't work and you can end up having major rows with your husband, partner, travelling companion. Not worth the hassle.

Packing has to be done sometime, the sooner the better when you are on the last leg of a world voyage. We've had a ball on this world cruise but time to go home soon. Packing reminds me of that.

We may have had 19 pieces of luggage but this was by no means the record. That was 29 pieces carried on by the couple, Glenn and Monika, who got married on the ship. They'd even more cases when they got off in Southampton.

HOLY LAND ISRAEL

An unexpected call to Israel. Egypt had been dropped because of all the unrest. At first most people thought it a good idea to have two days in The Holy Land but for some it turned sour mainly because of the attitude of officials especially at Haifa Port where Queen Elizabeth docked.

When the port changes were announced passengers were told the ship would hold on to their passports and these would be handed to Israeli immigration officers to be processed. This alarmed MR MM, and others, who didn't want an Israeli stamp in their passports because it can result in the holder being refused admission especially to some Middle Eastern countries.

So concerned was MR MM he wrote to the Purser. He got a reply which said the ship would be handing passports back to passengers and they would have to clear immigration themselves.

Fine, because that way the immigration officers could put an entry stamp on a plain piece of paper that was not part of the passport. It's a practice that has been around for years because of the animosity of many Arab countries to the behavior of the Israelis.

458

And this is just what happened. We were among the first off, just after 6am. In fact the immigration officers were unprepared.

We waited in line while they had a briefing from senior officials; then we were made to walk some stairs to another part of the rundown cruise terminal in Haifa to be cleared.

Cunard staff controlled the flow of passengers allowing only around 20 to leave the ship at a time to avoid long lines.

Only a proportion of the immigration desks were manned - seven I think it was - not enough to clear smoothly and efficiently the passengers and the crew. Yes, everyone - there were no exceptions - had to go to immigration whether they were getting off the ship or their duties meant they had to stay onboard.

We had a run-in with burly port security guards after we'd returned to the ship and then attempted to go ashore again. We'd been told by the ship we didn't need to take our passports proper after we'd been through immigration - that copies would be acceptable along with the stamped piece of paper. Wrong!

It was the attitude of this uniformed guard that got our backs up. He was officious; downright rude.

He showed all the signals that suggested he not only thought he was superior but he knew he was a superior being! We tried to reason with him but he just kept on raising his voice in a threatening and menacing manner.

He berated us for just having copies of our passports and told us we had to go back to the ship and return with our full passports (we always carry laminated copies for security reasons mainly because it's not unknown for passengers to have their passports stolen when ashore).

In fact this was only the second or third country that wouldn't accept copies of passports.

MR MM was so brassed off with this jobsworth's attitude he said he'd go back on the ship and stay there until we sailed (he actually never wanted to set foot in Israel in the first place).But I talked him round.

I've done the tourist bit several times. MR MM hadn't but had no desire to go to Jerusalem or Bethlehem or to any other Holy places although he is a Christian.

We decided as the train station was next to our berth we'd take one to Tel Aviv. We soon saw how high the security was in Haifa, indeed in the whole of Israel.

Soldiers, both men and women, looked to be10 a penny and many carried machine guns. Our bags and cameras were scanned when we entered the railway station and before we'd got to the ticket window.

We bought tickets for the express service to Tel Aviv which cost around £10 one way. Not bad as it took about one hour.

The service was efficient and it was a double decker train - we'd seen ones like it on German Railways when we were in Berlin a few years ago.

The train arrived on time and we went to the upper level. We had good views of the countryside and then of Tel Aviv when we reached it.

When we got off the train we followed the exit signs and they led us into a shopping Mall. Only this shopping mall was not one at the high end of the market. I saw no designer goods, more your everyday corner shopping mall with some familiar names like Mango and Accessorize and Forever 21 and the ubiquitous H&M.

Yes, in most of the countries we've visited on this cruise we have seen at least one H&M.

I didn't bother looking at the shops. MR MM asked if I was feeling unwell!

We took the escalator down to exit the building and as we left our bags were searched.

Out into the sunshine for a look around. We set off walking without a destination in mind. The streets were full of cars and the pavements bustling with people dashing and speaking on their cell phones. There we no signs we could see in English.

We wandered around aimlessly and after a while decided it was not for us and headed back to the train station to retrace our steps to

Haifa. Funnily enough I had spoken to a passenger on the ship who told me Tel Aviv was "just a rambling big City". I guess he was right. We stopped in the Crowne Plaza hotel to use their toilet facilities, and in a convenience store to buy dates.

We enjoyed the train journey but this was not one of our better days out on our own partly because of the attitude of that port security guard. We'd lost interest in Israel.

Talking to others back on the ship who had taken the train to Tel Aviv, they all said the same thing - they could not find anything worthwhile to see or visit and returned to the ship.

We had refreshments and then went walkabouts in Haifa to see how it had changed since I last visited in 1987.

In the 80s I used to visit Israel a lot. I had a friend who worked on the Sea Princess and I used to sail on that ship at least three times a year. The Eastern Med was a popular cruise destination in those days. It was from the Sea Princess that I went on a tour around Jerusalem and the Holy Land with my Yorkshire musician friend. He worked as a pianist on the ships. He would act as an escort while I was a passenger on the tour.

Mount Carmel was just a sparse covered mountain with a few buildings running up the hill. Nowadays the mountain is very built up with high rise apartment blocks.

Haifa is very steep - some of the street look as steep as those in San Francisco.

We headed towards the mountain to visit the most famous landmark in Haifa, the Baha'i Shrine and Gardens. The founder of the faith is buried there in the golden domed mausoleum set in beautiful manicured gardens.

We then headed for the area known as HADAR Carmel before going to the markets and downtown area. The shops in the Hadar area sold so much absolute junk - cheap looking, nasty, no style, clothes and shoes. It must have been bad because I didn't give even the shoes a second glance!

If they were giving them away I'd have had to pass on them; they were so tarty looking which made my tart's trotters look like Jimmy Choo's instead of Maggiemou's!

The shoes were definitely "follow me home to the bedroom shoes".

I've never seen so much junk in one street in my life, it made Vietnam look like 5th Avenue!

Not tempted into buying we carried on through the maze of uphill streets and eventually we were in a fruit/fish market. It was now gone 6-30pm. We began making tracks back to the ship because the sun was setting. We wandered down hill and ran out of road at one stage and ended up on a road under construction.

Cars zooming around and no walkway. We gritted our teeth and hung onto to a wall as we rounded a blind bend. We could see the ship in port and just kept her in our sights as we picked our way down roads and alleys to sea level. We made it back at 7-30pm by which time it was pitch black.

As we looked out over the city from the open decks we wondered what day two in Haifa had in store.

We ended up going on another train journey. This time in the opposite director from Tel Aviv. I'd remembered visiting Acre, or AKKO as it is in Hebrew, all those years ago when I was in Israel on Sea Princess.

We didn't experience the same verbal abuse from port guards on our second day - perhaps someone had been down from the charm school!

It was just a 30 minute train ride from the port to Acre - an hourly service and cost £3 each way. Good value we thought. The ship organised a tour but this is easily reached doing it on your own - and a cheaper option, and it's more fun exploring.

Acre is known as the City above and a City below.

In the days of The Crusades, Richard the Lionheart and the Crusaders were in Acre. Richard decamped to Cyprus where he married Berengaria in Kolossi Castle near Limassol.

The Crusaders lived in the tunnels underground. When I first went there were no touristy things. The place was very shabby and in need of restoration. The residents lived in little houses with corrugated roofs held down with rocks. Washing hung on the roof tops but every home seemed to have a television aerial.

Today it is a modern city with a beautiful promenade. Much of the old city has been restored. Although I'd been before that was on a ship's tour. I'd never been by train. Acre station was not in the middle of town. It was a walk and it took us the best part of an hour to pick our way through the streets basically following our noses yet again. Although we did tag on to a party of German visitors who we suspected were heading our way. They were.

The promenade was impressive with its pebbled walkway inlaid with nautical shapes.

We passed a monument to someone or something - a sculpture of a man holding another aloft on his hands. We didn't have a clue who, what or why but I did break into song with.."You Raise me up...." I have earworm because we've heard it so many times from singers on this cruise.

We walked across the moat and came to a restored building that was the HOSPITALLER FORTRESS. Hospitallers were a monastic military order established to treat the sick in the Holy Land. Later it was used as prison by the British during the Jewish uprisings.

There was lots to see. But there was a lot of noise from jet engines - military jets. It was constant. We spent most of the day looking around. We got in to the old city with its narrow streets. The sights and smells were intoxicating. I found the Templar Tunnels I'd visited years before but they were unrecognisable. All restored and nothing like I remember.

Now they have wooden walkways and fancy lighting and a sound system. One thing hadn't changed - you still had to crouch down. Heavyweights would get stuck like my Yorkshire friend did in the 80s.

We continued to wander down narrow streets, past stalls selling yet more poor quality items. One thing puzzled me on this cruise - why in so many countries were there T-shirts, hats, beach towels and the like with an image of Bob Marley on them? Why?

We passed a stall selling Falafel and I said to MR MM we should have one of those for lunch but it was still a bit early to be eating. When it was time we spent ages trying to find the stall again but we eventually did and were pleased we had taken the time and trouble.

It was the busiest food outlet around and we were the only Europeans. Most of the clientele looked to be local - always a good sign.

The Falafels came in different sizes - we ordered two large ones and two bottles of coke. We recognised some in a Cunard tour group who passed but they didn't spot us!

After that feast we were full to bursting but a brisk 30 minute walk to the train station worked off some of the calories. At least that's what we hoped.

This had been an excellent day out and it hadn't cost a lot to see so much.

Israel is the one place in the world where I have I never found anything to buy. I thought that would change if I went into the duty free shop in the port terminal.

One of the crew in the Golden Lion Pub had told MR MM things were inexpensive in the duty free. Sure enough that looked to be the case.

We had been in Israel two days and all the prices were in the local currency the shekel. So I assumed this would be the case in the duty free shop like it is in every other duty free I have ever been in. Not in Israel it's not. Everything was written in Hebrew - some squiggly writing with numbers after. Everyone took it for granted this was the price in the local currency. Wrong!

The prices were in US dollars yet there was no sign anywhere to tell you. I fell for it and so did lots of others including members of the ship's crew who aren't paid a fortune and could ill afford to be scammed in this way. In my view this was a complete rip-off; deceit of the worst kind. So remember if you visit a duty free in Israel you may not be getting the bargain you think you are.

I bought perfume and it turned out I could have bought it for the same price on the ship.

Don't say you haven't been warned. PS: Managed to pack three more suitcases today - only nine days left to finish the job.

MORE ON THE PACKING....

I've already spent one sea day packing our 19 pieces of luggage and as these are all in our modest cabin (we don't do Princess Grill or Queen's Grill which have suites) there is barely any room to move around.

We can get into the bed; access the bathroom and the wardrobes. This is how most of the world cruisers are or will be very soon as we get ever closer to Southampton.

But there's good news - we should go off the ship with less weight than when we boarded. How come? Well, I have donated some of my clothes to the crew, especially the female entertainment staff.

I've given them my dressing up things and some other items, and I have sent some items to the Country Fair which will take place before we reach journey's end. This is where all unwanted goods go to be sold and the proceeds given to the ship's favourite charities.

MR MM has given away a large amount of his shirts and other items to the crew and to our cabin steward. None had really been worn all that much but MR MM decided he didn't really need to have three dozen shirts (long and short sleeve) so he had a cull.

That will save him some weight in his suitcase! He didn't though give away any of the colourful ties and bows in his collection.

Our steward told us the crew really appreciated the donations we had made to them, especially the shirts which went mostly to people behind the scenes who are not paid a lot. Gratifying to know.

FRIENDS OF.......

On most if not all cruise ships there are various "friends" groups. There are Friends of Bill (alcoholics), Friends of Dorothy (gay, bisexual, cross gender and the like) but a new to us Friends group was Friends of Terry.

So who is Terry? Well, a Yorkshireman who hails from Castleford but who lives in Flamborough on the Yorkshire Coast.

His surname is Waite but he is NOT THAT Terry Waite the one who was held captive in the Middle East for around five years before being released.

This Terry Waite's claim to fame is as Founder of the Duckling Club - quack, quack! Now Terry has done several world cruises but our paths had not crossed before to the best of my knowledge.

We hadn't heard of The Duckling Club until one day when MR MM was having his usual one pint of Old Speckled Hen in the Golden Lion pub on board. Dorio, one of the top bartenders on board who comes from Moldova, happened to mention this Duckling business and said he could organise an invitation.

469

MR MM thought why not? Within the hour there was the invitation in the letter rack outside our cabin. Now I knew nothing about this of course. I don't go to the pub of a lunchtime. When I quizzed MR MM about it he was both "vague and vacant". I thought he must have had one Speckled Hen too many!

Anyway we decided to accept and attend. And we were glad we did for it turned out be a one of the more memorable get-togethers on the world cruise.

It was staged in the Yacht Club on Deck 10 close to the Commodore Club. We weren't the first to arrive. In fact there must have been more than 100 already in the place when we did put in an appearance. It was Roarin' 20s night and I had to dress for the occasion and went in my gear which made me look like a, er, flapper or maybe a slapper!

is the Duckling Wing Commander. The party kicked off with few words of welcome from him and then the youngest world cruise passenger, American Andrew Vogts who was just 13, set to work playing his fiddle. He really can fiddle can Andrew, and he wears some colourful, some would say outrageous, clothes and shoes.

After Andrew's first spot, it was time for fun and games. Terry walked across the Yacht Club and pulled me on to the dance floor to be "initiated" into The Duckling Club. Well, in for a penny in for a pound! I was game for a laugh even if it was on me.

I had to put a stuffed duck (a dead one of course) between my legs. It's a long time since I've had a large squashy thing there! Duck tucked in my thighs I went for it.

Of course the dance was the chicken dance. I was dressed in my twenties dress, hair all in a twenties style. Looking all glam with a stuffed toy up my skirt! The mind boggles! It was hilarious and we all had a good laugh - quack quack! I had to eventually drop the stuffed toy in a bucket but Terry kept kicking it away as I was about to let go of the duck but I made it eventually. I was actually well practiced at squatting down after going to the gym for four months, and visiting toilets in Arabia and other far flung places. Good job I had toned my thighs all this time in preparing for the duck.

After my "performance" there was more singing from passengers, a type of "Sing along with Joe" meets karaoke. The resident singer the on QE, Paul Ritchie, a Duckling Club member, did his stuff which made us realise how good he was and how awful our singing was! I sang back up with Amanda Reid the ship's entertainment officer. It was a hoot - no a quack, quack!

If you happen to come across Terry and get an invitation to attend his Duckling Club. Don't hesitate. It was good fun, honest!

Talking of Friends of Dorothy. On one cruise I heard of a passenger turn to another after reading the ship's daily programme, and say "Oh, Dorothy, your friends have organised a party for you tomorrow. How kind of them!" Of course they hadn't!

NO NEW JOKES

There was a time, not too long ago, when if you saw a comic more than once he or she would have some difference jokes to crack. Not nowadays. The same old jokes are recycled not only by one comic but by several.

Mike Doyle is a funny man we have seen several times before on cruise ships. He was funny. It's probably a couple of years since we last came across him and had no hesitation in going to see his second house show.

How disappointing. Not only did we both remember him telling the same jokes the last time, but we'd seen several other comics in the meantime and they, too, were telling the same old jokes.

Regular cruisers have heard the ones about the vacuum flushing system of the loos on cruise ships; stories about the self-service buffet and the one about the age of passengers on Saga cruise ships. We didn't bother staying more than fifteen minutes. Time to get some new material me thinks.

NAPOLI - GOOD, BAD AND UGLY

Naples has never been a favourite port of call of mine. I've always found it a bit scary and not a good place to wander around.

Garibaldi Railway Station is full of gypsies, tramps and thieves so a place to be avoided if you can. I'd no desire to go to Pompeii, Sorrento or even the Isle of Capri - been there and got the T-shirt. However, MR MM had not been to any of these places. Two passengers I'd become friendly with during the cruise, Dave and Dee (no relation to Beaky, Mick & Titch) who speak the lingo invited us to join them on a trip to HERCULANEUM to some old ruins from the time Mount Vesuvius erupted and covered the area in mud. Herculaneum survived better than it's more famous neighbour Pompeii because it was covered in mud, rather than the ash. It is much smaller than Pompeii and just a short distance from Naples Port where Queen Elizabeth docked.

This was our DIY excursion for the day.

It was a journey of discovery, disappointment, thrills and spills and more. We had not really decided how we'd get there by public transport- bus or by train.

Just off the dock there was an information desk so Dave, who speaks Italiano, approach the lady behind the counter.

She was pretty but all she wanted to do was talk to Dave in, er, English. Did she NOT understand Italian? Anyway she was not helpful. We didn't discover whether we could reach Herculaneum by bus so we decided the only option was to let the train take the strain. But first we had to get to the railway station.

We studied the route map at the tram stops by the harbour and found we could reach the Port railway station jumping on a Number One or Number four tram. We boarded a Number Four without realising you pay on the road side before you board.

It didn't seem to matter, no one asked us for a ticket. Still we like to pay and made sure we got it right on the return journey.

THE GOOD!

Once on the tram Dave got talking to a local guy. It transpired he lived in the next street to Herculaneum. Alfredo was his name and he spoke English but Dave wanted to speak Italian as there is not much call for it in the Cotswolds where he lives! So a bit of both took place.

It turned out Alfredo had worked on Princess cruises as a head waiter before he retired. So meeting Alfredo was a stroke of luck. We were confident it was all going to go well.

We got off the tram and Alfredo took us to the train station ticket office. We bought returns to Herculaneum. The cost of the ticket for four people return was just over Euro17.

Alfredo was very helpful. He led us into the Porta Napoli station which is one stop before the dreaded Garibaldi.

No matter how much you research a place before hand you never quite know if you will find the experience easy or a challenge, especially when you are in countries where there are no information desks or signs in English as we had discovered in Israel.

So Alfredo was a God-send. He sat with us on the train to Herculaneum and told of his years on Princess Cruises. An Interesting man. Alfredo put us off at the right stop - it had taken just 15 minutes from port to destination station. We said our goodbyes to Alfredo and set off to walk into Herculaneum.

At the site there was a short queue for tickets which cost €5 each although it was free for seniors so we didn't have to pay. We got a map of the site and a handbook that explained the building and other important features.

We spent over two hours wandering around. It was quite impressive and easier to navigate than Pompeii but it's smaller of course.

The weather was cloudy with intermittent sunshine so not too hot for walking. It kept looking like rain but it held off.

Around 12-30 we went in search of an Italian lunch. When in Naples the only thing to eat is Pizza. So that was the order of the day.

But before we could tuck in we visited a market where Dave and Dee bought two kilo of Mozzarella cheese for a neighbour back in England.

We came across a small pavement restaurant and relaxed there for a while and had our Pizzas. They were delicious!

We kept a weather eye on the sky and spotted storm clouds heading our way. We dashed back to the train station and arrived under the canopy just as the heavens opened.

At the station in Naples we had to get the tram back to the ship. So far all had gone well and we were having a good day. That's the good!

THE UGLY!

Whilst the men were buying the tram tickets (we were determined to pay this time) my lady friend Dee and I spotted a most unusual sight. I was gob-smacked and could not believe my eyes!

There was a lady who was gynormous, probably well over 30 stone. She was bent over a waste bin outside the station. She was naked from the waist down. Not a pretty sight!

She was huge and gross and was standing (wait for it!) pooing on the pavement!

It was horrendous! She was shouting in Italian. No one seemed to care. Then she leaned over the waste bin and pulled out paper to use as toilet paper. She then walked about with the paper hanging from her bum - an even worse sight.

Oh and all that cellulite. We tried to look away and pretend not to notice but it was impossible not to look as she was so close to us. Her ranting was unbelievable! I was very disturbed by it all.

The police were around but none went to her aid. We got the tickets and walked away to the tram stop. We could still see her.

She laid on the pavement wrapped in a sleeping bag and we could see she had bags with her.

This piece of pavement outside the station must have been her "home" and the waste bin her "bathroom". It was very upsetting. I had never seen anyone naked in a street like that, or anyone with as much cellulite in my life!

My friend Dee is a retired nurse. She was not as shocked as I was. "Seen it all before, darling" was her response! We just wondered where social services were, or if they had any? The lady needed someone to care for her. Shame on the Italian authorities is my view.

THE BAD!

The tram arrived and my friends got on in front of me. MR MM was behind. Suddenly all Hell broke out and I was in the middle of it. MR MM was behind and getting further away. Men pushing shouting and banging on the side of the tram. I was getting pushed around and saw MR MM was getting pushed as well. I grabbed him and pulled his arm before he got trapped in the tram door. I didn't want to lose him as he had the tickets that we had paid for. It all happened very fast. We got out of the scrum and the commotion and the shouting that had all come from nowhere and sat down. This is where nerves of steel kick in!

The people around us spoke in Italian and my friend Dave understood what they were saying. They had spotted someone they recognised as a pickpocket. He was trying to get off the tram and aiming to rob MR MM then run off into the back streets while the driver of the tram was trying to catch the pickpocket. Confusion reigned!

The people told Dave to carry his rucksack in front of his body. I had my Pac Safe bag and in all the hustle it never left my shoulder. I had my hand on it all the time. I was carrying the money and credit cards. MR MM only had a camera case in front of him hung around his neck. He had nothing in his pockets so had the pickpocket succeeded in getting in to MR MM's trouser pockets he would have been very disappointed.

We all gave a sigh of relief and carried on with our short tram ride to the pier. Dee was ready to whack any other pick pockets with her 2 kilos of mozzarella!

There was one more pickpocket on the tram the locals said, and they kept an eye on him. He stood at the back and no other locals went near him. They knew!

The cruise terminal's design, both inside and out is very nice. It has some classy shops with good (inexpensive) prices.

I found a pair of shoes as a girl can't visit Italy without buying shoes! I think that took my "count" of shoes to 44 pairs - I went on board with just 37 pairs!

All in all a very nice run ashore in good company. The Good, The Bad and The Ugly! Where was Clint Eastwood when we needed him? He never showed up in Carmel either if you remember. Ah! Well, that's Naples for you!

In Napoli. I meet a man
Ciao mia Bella bambina
Hi! says I, I love a man who speaks the love lingo!
Come with me to Herculaneum it will be a great place to see when it is finished
"What in these shoes?" Not in a million years!

VIVA ESPANA! PALMA MAJORCA

We had our penultimate port of call in Palma De Mallorca (Majorca to us Brits) in Spain.

A short stay for some reason known only to Cunard and the ship's senior officers. We were leaving at 4pm having arrived at 8 in the morning.

One wag reckoned Queen Elizabeth's captain, Alistair Clark, was so scared of being late for the rendezvous with the other two Cunard Queens off Lisbon he was taking no chances and ordered an early cast-off.

Rather a shame as Palma is a beautiful port of call. The sea front reminds me of Cannes.

It was a first visit for MR MM and he was not too bothered what we did.

We were all on wind down and had no more tours arranged and no particular plans other than to get packed up and ready for our arrival on Southampton on the 9th May.

Majorca has always been one of my favourite places. It was the second place I ever visited overseas as a teenager in the 1960s. The first place being the Spanish mainland and I went there as a 16 year with school friends. I remember it cost £65 all inclusive, and that was with a Dan Air flight as well! How times have changed.

I progressed to Majorca as it was also a cheap place to go in those days. I've been many times over the years.

In fact it was through going there I thought about buying a property abroad. I almost bought a place in Cala Vinas, Majorca, but then decided it may not be the right move. Well, we can all make mistakes1 Twenty years later I ended up in Cyprus! It was really nice to go back to Palma.

Since my last visit I could see how the marina had grown - hundreds of luxury yachts moored. From the ship on sail in we had spectacular views of the Cathedral - it changes colour as the light and sun shine on it. A landmark that to me IS Palma!

Off the ship we followed the rather long walk way to get out of the terminal. Our plan was to walk around the bay to the Cathedral and look around the old City.

The terminal was very quiet. Most passengers had gone in the opposite direction to board the shuttle buses.

We came to a glass panelled door in the terminal that had a big hole in it. The glass was shattered but being laminated safety glass it was still in place. (more about the glass later).

The walk along the promenade was very nice - pedestrianised with a good cycle lane but we had to watch out for bikers. They rode fast and furious.

The walk from the ship to the Cathedral was about 4km. We had a gentle stroll rather than a power walk because MR MM was filming all the time.

Once we reached the walled city we crossed the road and passed some lovely gardens and saw some war memorials. We visited the Cathedral but being a Sunday it was busy with worshippers and visitors. What a magnificent building.

Across the water from the Cathedral we came across The Palma Beer and Tapas festival. All beers brewed in the different villages on the island apparently. MR MM's mouth was watering and I knew any minute he would decide we needed to rest awhile.

Sure enough he had eyed a beer that he fancied. The sellers at the stalls did not take money we had to change Euros into plastic coins called fletch - not a currency traded on the world's money markets!

So Euro10 was changed to see how good the beer was.

I did not want anything but MR, greedy guts, had to try the local pies which he told me after were filled with pork.

Not being a beer drinker I went to the next outdoor café and had a delicious coffee for Euro 2-40.

I sat in the sun. It was very relaxing to watch the fountain that looks like the water being pumped from a fire tender when a ship makes a maiden port of call. Service was very slow and I guess it is all slowly slowly, manyana!

By the time I'd finished my coffee, MR MM had managed two beers (only small plastic cups) and two pies.

So the Euro10 had been spent as fletch was not convertible back to Euros. Well, that was his excuse! More walking about and we found our way to the main shopping street.

The trees were just stunning and all the central reservations had lovely urns filled with blooming Rhododendrons. Some lovely classy shops but also the ubiquitous Zara and the old faithful H&M.

I decided it was a good idea to eat tapas for lunch (not that MR MM would want lunch one would have thought after two pies and two beers), and found a nice looking tapas bar.

It was authentic and we noticed it was busy with locals. Always a good sign. The tables were all reserved inside. We sat at a table on the pavement.

We ordered a mixed Spanish platter of local dishes, and some Calamari just in case we did not like the local dishes.

It arrived and it was all very good. More people poured into the place and seemed to disappear. We realised later it had a cellar bar.

We also noted we were the only foreigners in the place. Sa Ronda was the name of the restaurant.

The meal was different although not sure what it all was. MR MM had a couple of glasses of red vino and I had Coke.

It was a pleasant lunch and afterwards we walked to burn off the calories....again!

We ambled through the quaint back streets that had some interesting architectural features and we eventually picked up the promenade near the ship.

We came across a name I recognised - TITO'S. This was a blast from the past. It was the nightclub that most tourists to Palma were taken to in the late 60s and through the 70s. Tours from our hotel took us there. We were served cheap sangria and watched a flamenco show. On the way home everyone (almost) would "chuck up" from the cheap booze! Not I, of course! I had memories of this earlier in this cruise when we went to the Luau in Hawaii.

Happy days eh!

We were back at the ship around 3-0pm an hour before sailaway. It was a short day in Palma and we weren't the only ones to think the ship could and should have stayed longer. But Captain Clark had other ideas and things on his mind like the rendezvous in Lisbon with Queen Mary 2 and Queen Victoria two days ahead.

We will be in port along with the two sister Cunard ships. Queen Victoria and Queen Mary 2.

Queen Victoria will lead us up the river into Lisbon, with Queen Elizabeth in the middle and QM2 behind.

We will be one mile apart from each other and then when docked we will be 40 metres apart.

This will be the first time all three ships have been berthed alongside together in port. We had, however, a sailaway party out of Palma and the entertainment staff were again there dancing in their black thick shirts and navy blue polo tops just like they had been around the world and no matter what the outside temperature. It's not a good look.

I think it's time Cunard brought some colour in to the entertainment staff dress code. I reckon it would give an altogether different impression of these young people who try so hard to make passengers' voyages enjoyable be it a segment or a full world cruise. Anyone listening in Harbour Parade, Southampton?

In the evening we had our last World Cruise cocktail party. We'd had one each segment and the champagne flowed as normal The food they serve at these parties is fantastic - on this occasion chefs were cooking prawns in garlic; fillet steak and the Sushi bar was stunning. Oh and for the "weight watchers" there was a chocolate buffet to tuck in to... and all this before dinner! Needless to say I never eat any of it because I find it hard to drink champagne and talk, take photos and balance on my stilettos and hold my handbag all at the same time. However, many tucked in and made up for those who didn't.

One of the highlights towards the end of a world cruise on Cunard (and may be other lines) is the County Fair charity event that raises money for worthy causes supported by Cunard. Passenger donate their cast-off clothes and other "collectables" and "inspired" purchases they made along the way but find they really shouldn't have bothered.

Paintings done by passengers in the art class also find their way in to the County Fair, and on Queen Elizabeth many were quickly snapped up because fellow travellers thought they had artistic merit. Other crafts were also on sale.

The Country Fair on Queen Elizabeth's 2014 world cruise raised US$8000. Not to be sniffed at!

Back to the broken glass in the door in the terminal in Palma I mentioned earlier.

One of MR MM's contacts who hails from Penryn, in Cornwall, and was doing the full world, knew all about it. The man from Penryn volunteered the information to MR MM. It went like this: One of the passengers on the Cornish resident's dinner table (they were early sitting and seated at the prestigious table reserved for The Captain on formal nights) hailed from somewhere in the Midlands in England.

He was always, allegedly, first to eat and left long before the others at the table had finished their meals.

They thought this odd but shrugged it off. Then a night before the liner reached Palma he didn't appear for dinner. The rest of the table weren't that bothered but then discovered their "table mate" was under cabin "arrest" with a guard posted outside his accommodation.

Why? Apparently the ship's security officers had been watching his "activities" for some time and realised he was "stealing".

They decided to pounce in EU territorial waters. And what did they find? According to the man from Penryn: expensive watches and rings from the shops on board Queen Elizabeth along with over 1,000 tea bags (he must be a teaholic!), sachets of sugar, numerous salt and pepper pots, dozens of tubs of honey and lots of cereal boxes from the Lido restaurant.

Once docked in Palma six Spanish police officers arrived on board to take him into custody, apparently. It was during his being escorted off the ship that he allegedly kicked out at the glass panelled door and shattered one pane in the lower part. The impact on the toughened glass was at raised foot height. Who would believe such a thing could happen on a liner like Queen Elizabeth?

Just to be clear, this man didn't dine with the Captain at the Captain's Table. The Captain is only there during second sittings on formal evenings NOT at first sitting.

Even then the Captain deputes other officers to host his table in the Britannia Restaurant on many of the formal evenings.

In Mayorca, Mallorca Majorca. There was Pedro the fisherman

Hola Senorita, says he. Welcome to my little boat

I always wanted to see my man in the boat so I said Hola ,Olay!

Come we look for fishy together. Get in zee boat

"What in these shoes?" I think I'd rather miss the boat. Gracias.

I SAW THREE SHIPS COME SAILING INTO LISBON

Our final port of call on the 2014 world cruise on Queen Elizabeth was Lisbon. It was a "special" and indeed unique occasion. We were with the other two Cunard ships, Queen Victoria, and QM2 for a "first" - first time they had tied up alongside each other in any port.

All three queens met up the evening before and we sailed in to Lisbon in convoy.

The transit began around 6-30am - Queen Victoria led the way followed by Queen Elizabeth and bringing up the rear was Queen Mary 2.

A large welcome party including helicopters and planes circled. It must have been a magnificent sight from air and land.

A fire boat gave the flotilla a watery welcome and continued to do so until all three queens were alongside.

This was the first time all three ships had been in the same berth together. They'd been in the same port before but not at one berth. It was spectacular!

Lisbon was bathed in sunshine for this historic maritime occasion.

We had to delay going ashore because I had arranged to meet a friend who happens to be the Godmother (Madrina) to the liner Queen Elizabeth.

She's Denny Farmer and was doing the 2014 world cruise on the QM2 (our favourite ship) but "pulled rank" and got a day pass to come onto her ship - Queen Elizabeth.

During the voyage she emailed me to ask if we could meet on board? (Her late husband was chief engineer for years on the QE 2.) I said "yes" so we made no plans for the day in Lisbon.

By 10-0am I was at the gangway with the Captain's secretary waiting to meet Denny. The last time we'd met was the night before we all set sail in January. We treated Denny to dinner in Southampton. She's a lovely lady and we are very fond of her.

After our meet and greet I left Denny with the Captain's secretary and we went ashore for a few hours having arranged to meet up again at one o'clock in the Golden Lion pub on board.

The sun was really starting to crack the flags so after a quick change of clothes off the ship we went to "explore" the area beyond the quayside.

There was a large tent type construction on the quay set up for a welcome ceremony. As we left all the "big wigs" from the other two liners were arriving.

All three Captains from the three Queens and other top members of the ships' company all chatting and shaking hands.

I noticed Commodore Christopher Rynd, who was the skipper of Queen Victoria on this voyage, walking next to me and I said good morning to him.

His wife, Julie, was by his side and she turned round and said: "Good Morning Maggie!" Hee! I thought, once seen never forgotten! That's me!

We'd met both of them when he was the master of Queen Mary 2 on its 2012 world cruise and she was travelling with him.

MR MM and I went out of the terminal and set off walking with no plan of action. Rather like Christopher Columbus - not knowing where we were, where we were going or where we had been!

We'd thought of getting a taxi, or tram or HOHO bus but there were three other cruise ships in Lisbon on this day besides the Cunard Queens and the crowds were horrendous.

Everything was full, queues a mile long and passengers packed like sardines on the buses. We carried on walking, We did not get too far before I realised I had the wrong type of shoes to walk on the cobbled streets of Lisbon. I feared falling. Didn't want that to happen again so decided I would pop back on board and change the shoes.

I got back to the gate where we left the quayside; showed my cruise card to the guy dressed in a security uniform and carried on walking.

Instantly I was set up on from behind. Someone grabbed my arm (the one that cost me a year out of my life 12 months earlier after I'd had the fall).

Then my arm was pulled into an arm lock and he grabbed my upper arm so tight.

It turned out it was a security guy from a company called Grupo8. It was all very fast, and I was shocked and shouted to him to get off me. The guy said I was not to go inside and I said I am going to the ship. He then held on to me even more firmly so my reaction was to whack him with my free arm. Well, as a strong Yorkshire lass what else would I do?

Then I thumped the guy three times in his chest and shouted "let go of my arm".

The punches to his chest knocked him off balance and he stumbled and dropped his mobile phone (ha! ha! serves him right). He had to let go of me then and I walked away from him. This was a blatant assault. MR MM was ahead and turned round after hearing my shouts. He stood, mouth wide open in shock after seeing me punch the lights out of the so-called security buffoon. Anyhow, it shook me up and I felt all of a dither.

I was attacked very badly when I was a young women and it has left me feeling vulnerable so when threatened my gut reaction is to hit back fast and hard.

MR MM went back to find the bully but he had disappeared and some guys were locking the gate where the incident happened.

Once I had changed my shoes and composed myself we left the ship again and this time I met Terry (duckling party Terry, remember I've written about him?).

Terry, who hails from Castleford in Yorkshire but these days lives at Flamborough Head, told me he'd received the same treatment from the same security man. Terry did not hit him like I did though!

Two minutes later my spirits lifted when I spotted Oliver Lau, a maitre 'd on QM2, whom we first met on the old rust bucket QE2. We've known each other ten years and he always walks me to my table when I am on his ship.

So reunions all round. Many crew from the three Queens were hugging and air kissing as they had not seen each other for ages. It was a good sight to see.

We left the terminal for a second time and walked into the old town. It was very busy everywhere. People already going back on the ship after hearing tales of pickpockets at work. We were careful and I had the Pac Safe bag with me. We never had a problem.

We walked up the hill to the NATIONAL PANTHEON, CHURCH OF SANTA ENGRACIA.

The area around this beautiful building (no longer a Church) was not very pleasant. Hundreds of drop outs and people selling everything imaginable. It was like a huge down market car boot sale - mainly all Second Hand Rose stuff.

The Pantheon building was very impressive. We climbed to the terrace about half way up around 220 steps all uneven and no hand rails. Once up there we had stunning 360 degrees views over Lisbon and of the three Queens in port.

After gingerly navigating our way down again we wandered out into the crowded streets leaving the peace and tranquility behind. The peace of the place made me feel better after the security guy had man-handled me earlier in the day.

We had one hour left to look around before our rendezvous with Denny, the ship's godmother. We found a store for MR MM. where he purchased some local Vino.

Having to meet my friend messed up the day really but at times one has to do these things, so we did not get to see much of Lisbon.

This was made up though by a fantastic sail away party. Lots of pomp and ceremony. Music including, Anchor's Away, Rule Britannia, Land of Hope and Glory and such like and passengers all singing along waving flags, and cheering from one ship to the other.

494

Some Americans and Germans questioned this style of sailaway they said because the three Cunard queens were not British ships! I couldn't be bothered wasting time explaining.

I just said enjoy it as only Cunard can do sailaways with such pomp and style.

The QM2 had Captain Christopher Wells RNR in charge on the bridge, the Blue Ensign fluttered proudly in the gently breeze.

He'd been our first captain on the world voyage but left in San Francisco for some shore leave.

Queen Mary 2 held up the sailaway because four of her tour coaches got stuck in traffic and failed to make it back to the ship on schedule. So we all waited. About half a hour that's about all.

Once the tour passengers had been counted back in Queen Mary 2 slipped her lines followed by Queen Elizabeth and then Queen Victoria. There was a lot of whistle-blowing from the three bridges of the liners. It took over 90 minutes before we all cleared the April the 25th bridge. The sun was still shining on the Statue of Discoverers, and Christ the King looked well pleased as he looked down on us mere mortals. Later at around 8-30pm - maybe it was later - all three ships lined up in formation as they entered the open sea. Unfortunately, not many of us got to see this as we were all at dinner.

But the Captain never announced that was about to happen so no one knew to dash out. Yet another case of Captain Alistair Clark

495

keeping passengers in the dark like he'd done on several occasions during his time in charge on our world voyage. Passengers like to know if a ship is passing an important landmark, like the Rock of Gibraltar for instance. And to be fair Captain Clark in his midday broadcast did inform us of the time we would pass The Rock - only he got the time wrong by one hour! It wasn't the first time Captain Clark had been wrong - his weather forecasts were so often wide of the mark they were out of sight.

MR MM had for a long time dubbed Captain Clark the "Michael Fish of the ocean waves." (Fish was the BBC weather man who famously failed to predict a hurricane would hit the UK just hours before it did in 1987!). So when MR MM heard the time the captain said Queen Elizabeth would pass The Rock he ignored it and was out on deck over an hour and a half earlier.

Many other passengers missed seeing this famous landmark because they believed what they heard from the Master.

As Queen Elizabeth headed for her home port of Southampton on the final leg of her 2014 world voyage she was blessed. In the Bay of Biscay the sea was not as many perceive; it was fairly smooth. In fact more than 90 per cent of this world voyage was done in good weather. And hey, our packing for disembarkation was 99% done when we reached the Bay of Biscay, thank goodness but not without a few tantrums from MR MM.

We went to the final formal farewell dinner. Earlier we had witnessed one of the best shows on a Cunard liner - the crew talent show. Some of the best acts all cruise - and they don't get paid a king's ransom - just their normal salary whatever that may be.

Our final day on board was foggy outside but quite calm in the cabin as we entered the Western Approaches. The packing was done, the 19 pieces of luggage ready to be taken by stewards before midnight. All was well!

In Lisbon there was a man
He wanted to arrest me, he found me very arresting
Where you go? he says. To the ship, I answer
You no come in here, you go walk in Lisbon
"What in these shoes?" The're not made for walking!

BACK IN BLIGHTY ALL CRUISED OUT

The 2014 world cruise on Cunard Queen Elizabeth was now over after 118 days of circumnavigating the globe.

We arrived in Southampton at 5am. Queen Elizabeth was the first of the trio of Cunard liners to enter port followed by Queen Victoria and Queen Mary 2. QM2 is celebrating her tenth birthday so to mark the occasion Queen Elizabeth played "Happy Birthday to you" on the ships whistle! This was at 5-30am on the dot as QM2 headed for her berth. The whole of Southampton would have had an early wake-up call!

We were up and about as it was daylight and MR Movie maker was making a final recording of the arrival home after four months at sea.

Good news was we left with the same amount of luggage that we took on board even after all my shopping for shoes!

We had used up all the toiletries and soap powder etc we'd taken on board, and I had given many items of clothing away. So with just hand luggage left we dressed and went to the Britannia for breakfast.

We had a arranged to meet a couple of friends for the last supper, or breakfast.

That done and all farewells made we gathered in the upper Britannia restaurant for our priority disembarkation - Priority because we're diamond Cunard loyalty members. Newspapers and refreshments were laid on to ease the wait.

We gathered at 8-30am and had around one hour to wait because the docks were so busy handling passengers from five ships that were in port. We were off the ship by 9-30am.

We nabbed two porters. They helped MR MM find the 19 pieces of luggage in no time (by the way, there were many people with the same amount of luggage but the score went to the newlyweds whose nuptials we'd attended at sea back in February. They went on with 29 pieces of luggage and came off with 31! Well done MR and MRS newlyweds - Monika and Glenn.

Here are a few facts and figures from the Captain of Queen Elizabeth:

At 120 days it was the longest world voyage for many years (118 for those getting off in Southampton). The World Voyage ended in Hamburg.

Queen Elizabeth had sailed 37,4042 nautical miles; the longest transit was from Southampton to New York at distance of 3,156 nautical miles - and in the roughest seas.

The shortest distance between ports was from Abu Dhabi to Dubai just 80 nautical miles.

Queen Elizabeth had an average speed on the World Voyage in 2014 of 16.74 knots; the liner had visited 43 ports in 24 countries, sailed under six bridges, transited two canals (Panama and Suez), crossed three oceans (Pacific, Indian and Atlantic) and navigated 10 seas.

Getting around the world Queen Elizabeth needed the services of 92 different pilots.

40,000 pineapples were consumed and 40,000 tea bags (wonder if that includes the thousand the guy from the Midlands allegedly had in his suitcase?). Passengers had drunk 40,000 bottles of water.

The hottest day on the World Voyage was 33C in Abu Dhabi and the coldest was New York New York at just 2C.

So what was it like?:

In a word. GREAT!!!

We saw some amazing sights and met some nice people. We had eaten well and were looked after very well by Cunard. The staff are always good on most cruises but on a world cruise it must be more demanding for them at times. However, they never failed to be happy and helpful.

Would I do it again? Of course.

Were we ever bored? NO. There was always something going on around the ship and if we wanted to partake that was our decision.

The entertainment changed all the time, but we often saw acts that have been on other cruises because many "do the rounds".

We had some different style of acts on in Asia and Australia. Nearing Europe the same old comedians showed up with the same jokes. I was not alone in finding them boring.

The Cunard Royal Court Theatre singers and dancers were excellent, but they do the same routine each segment so halfway around the world we had seen them all twice. I found the dancing in the Queen's Room excellent. Many passengers were wonderful dancers. There were a few gentleman dance hosts for ladies without partners.

The Cunard big band and resident singer Paul Richie were just great as was the string Quartet who played daily around the ship. I enjoyed the classical concerts in an afternoon. The harpist and pianists on board were talented.

Cunard world cruises are good. The company realise people are with them for long spells so make life on board as comfortable as possible. However, sometimes a live announcement updating passengers on a passing sight would be appreciated and so would an announcement about passing an island, or about big fish swimming around the ship.

We had some good parties and a fantastic World Cruise dinner shore side in Dubai.

The entertainment there was amazing and the venue just breathtaking! We were seated at a table with the Hotel Manager, David Hamilton and his partner, Kelly.

They were great hosts - we had a marvelous table. We were treated like royalty and this again is something special to Cunard.

We also received a few very nice gifts at the end of each segment, which is a nice touch and they were all Cunard related such as Wedgwood Coffee mugs with the World Cruise dates on, a nice silk scarf with QE logos. Two logbooks, a good quality casual bag and hats. Plus MR MM got a nice tie to add to his collection. Not so colourful as his own but still very nice. We also had the usual crossing the line certificates and a map of where we had been around the world as mementos. We also were presented with a list of names of all those who'd done the full world voyage. We gave our cabin steward the mugs as a memento from us along with some other items and we made sure we wrote him a note to say they were a gift in case he was suspecting of taking them. We made sure he was covered. He also got an extra gratuity for taking care of us despite the ever decreasing space in the cabin.

Did I get fed up of the food?

No, the menu changed every few weeks and also there is a vast variety of different foods in the three dining venues on a Cunard world cruise cuisine for different nationalities who are sailing.

We dined in Britannia restaurant and we were happy with our food. I ordered many things not on the menu. I always try to be disciplined where food is concerned because it's easy to get tempted on a cruise, but I managed to stay within my weight comfort zone. Just gained a kilo but not bad considering we had been travelling for five months.

I tried to exercise daily and I ate from the healthy option menu and I had extra vegetables each evening instead of potatoes or rice. I find I eat less if I use the main dining room as the portions are controlled but I could, like Oliver Twist, ask for more!

Head waiter Shetty walked me to my table at dinner for the 112 nights we dined in the evening. Brilliant service!

We had 40 different nationalities on board and the mix of people made it all the more interesting.

We have seen wonderful palaces, beautiful buildings, magnificent Churches and Mosques, fabulous houses, hotels, lakes, rivers, paddy fields, beautiful beaches, flowers, birds, whales, fish, dolphins and the best of all the Great Barrier Reef from the air.

We have seen cultural things and been in more Temples than I can count. We went on the Bullet train in Japan, the Maglev in China; flown in a small plane, been up towers, walked miles, and swam in lagoons and the sea.

We have laughed till we cried in some places, and cried at the sadness of others. We know more about peoples and places than we did when we set off. We feel blessed. There is an amazing world out there and if you ever get the chance to go on a world cruise take it! Do it when you are young enough to enjoy it, while you are still fit and able to get about.

The average age was around 65, I would say on this year's cruise, however, there were many younger people who came on for different segments. Some older passengers were infirm; one was in a stretched wheel chair (bed like) but all seemed to enjoy the experience they had - hats off to them. Their stamina and get up and go was amazing!

To sum up. We had a great cruise with Cunard. The ship is lovely but there is always room for improvement. Small things.

The towels for instance. Some were getting threadbare and so stiff that you felt you'd had an exfoliation each day.

The resident reggae band from St Lucia called Nexus got boring after a while because they played all the same style of music.

They would do better playing more internationally known party numbers at the sail away parties.

The cruise entertainment staff needed better, more colourful, outfits to wear especially at sailaways - they look plain daft in thick tights, black skirts with navy blue polo shirts dancing on deck in the tropics.

I also think the cabins on a world cruise would be better without the sofa. There would be more space. Our sofa became a dumping ground. We never sat on it once. It would be better to have some extra drawers or another wardrobe for a long voyage.

MR MM has just one gripe (or observation). Why have the American owners of British cruise ships changed the English to American "English"? Ships have cabins not staterooms, and ships carry passengers not guests!

We were in an outside ocean view cabin and we had enough room. It was a fabulous cruise and I would do it every year if I was in a position to do so.

Keep Calm and keep cruising and don't forget the slogan:

"We do it because ...WE ARE CUNARD!"

I went on a cruise I met a man
He walked the decks and had a suntan
He said let me show you my sexton
Oh! I said is it a big one?
Wait and see and follow me
We have 12 decks to climb and the bridge to cross
It's dangerous stuff so hold on, don't get lost
No! In these shoes I can't do that
and also I don't know your name
Well, Just call me Jack. Captain Jack
Wow! In these shoes I'm following you. Let's go do it!
THE END.

Acknowledgements

Thanks to all members of cruise forums who encouraged me put my writings and ramblings into this book.
Many have become my friends through cruising.

www.solentrichardscruiseblog.com

www.cruise.co.uk

www.cruiseclubforum.com

www.facebook.com /we are cunard fanzine

www.facebook.com /cunard.com

www.cruisingmates.co.uk

www.crowsnestonline.co.uk

www.silvertravelforum.com

Printed in Great Britain
by Amazon.co.uk, Ltd.,
Marston Gate.